T0330199

Maintaining a Sustainable Work–Life Balance

NEW HORIZONS IN MANAGEMENT

Series Editor: Professor Sir Cary Cooper, *50th Anniversary Professor of Organizational Psychology and Health at Alliance Manchester Business School, University of Manchester, UK and President of the Chartered Institute of Personnel and Development and British Academy of Management*

This important series makes a significant contribution to the development of management thought. This field has expanded dramatically in recent years and the series provides an invaluable forum for the publication of high-quality work in management science, human resource management, organizational behaviour, marketing, management information systems, operations management, business ethics, strategic management and international management.

The main emphasis of the series is on the development and application of new original ideas. International in its approach, it will include some of the best theoretical and empirical work from both well-established researchers and the new generation of scholars.

For a full list of Edward Elgar published titles, including the titles in this series, visit our website at www.e-elgar.com.

Maintaining a Sustainable Work–Life Balance

An Interdisciplinary Path to a Better Future

Edited by

Peter Kruyen

Assistant Professor of Public Administration, Institute for Management Research, Radboud University, Nijmegen, the Netherlands

Stéfanie André

Assistant Professor of Public Administration, Institute for Management Research, Radboud University, Nijmegen, the Netherlands

Beatrice van der Heijden

Professor of Strategic HRM, Institute for Management Research, Radboud University, Nijmegen, the Netherlands; the Open University of the Netherlands, Heerlen, the Netherlands; Ghent University, Ghent, Belgium; Hubei University, Wuhan, China; and Kingston University, London, UK

Edward Elgar
PUBLISHING

Cheltenham, UK • Northampton, MA, USA

© Peter Kruyen, Stéfanie André, and Beatrice van der Heijden 2024

This is an open access work distributed under the Creative Commons Attribution-NonCommercial-NoDerivatives 4.0 International (https://creativecommons.org/licenses/by-nc-nd/4.0/) license.

Published by
Edward Elgar Publishing Limited
The Lypiatts
15 Lansdown Road
Cheltenham
Glos GL50 2JA
UK

Edward Elgar Publishing, Inc.
William Pratt House
9 Dewey Court
Northampton
Massachusetts 01060
USA

A catalogue record for this book
is available from the British Library

Library of Congress Control Number: 2024930579

This book is available electronically in the **Elgar**online
Business subject collection
http://dx.doi.org/10.4337/9781803922348

ISBN 978 1 80392 233 1 (cased)
ISBN 978 1 80392 234 8 (eBook)

Printed and bound in Great Britain by
TJ Books Limited, Padstow, Cornwall

Contents

Figures

Tables

Contributors

Jos Akkermans is Associate Professor at the Department of Management and Organization, Vrije Universiteit Amsterdam, the Netherlands. His research focuses mainly on career shocks, career sustainability, career success, and employability. He has a special interest in studying the careers of early-career and non-standard workers. Jos is Associate Editor for the *Journal of Vocational Behavior*. He is also a past division chair of the Academy of Management Careers Division. Jos's research has been published in journals such as *Annual Review of Organizational Psychology and Organizational Behavior*, *Journal of Vocational Behavior*, *Human Resource Management*, and *Applied Psychology*.

Tammy Allen is Distinguished University Professor of Psychology at the University of South Florida, USA. Her research focuses on topics related to work and family, organizational practices such as remote work, and employee career development. She has published over 190 peer-reviewed journal articles, books, and book chapters and her work has been cited over 48,000 times. She is a Fellow of the American Association for the Advancement of Science, the Academy of Management, the American Psychological Association, the Association for Psychological Science, and the Society for Industrial and Organizational Psychology.

Stéfanie André is a policy sociologist working as Assistant Professor of Public Administration at Radboud University, the Netherlands. Together with Peter Kruyen, she leads the Radboud WORKLIFE consortium, bringing together interdisciplinary research and teaching on work–life balance. She is also part of the COGIS-NL research team that examined the consequences of COVID-19 on gender inequality in the Netherlands. Her research focuses on the (un)intended consequences of family and housing policy. Currently, she works with a Dutch NWO Veni Talent Grant (2022–2026) on the project 'Fathers combining work and care' on how organizational and national structures influence fathers' work–care attitudes and work–care behaviors.

Roseriet Beijers is Associate Professor at the Behavioural Science Institute, Radboud University, the Netherlands. She is also affiliated with the Radboud University Medical Center (Donders Institute) and the Radboud Baby and Child Research Center. Roseriet's main expertise lies in parental (work-related) stress during preconception, prenatal and postpartum phases, and its consequences for early human development and unraveling the underlying biological mechanisms. Since February 2023, Roseriet has been Head of Quality at the Dutch company Pro Parents, an organization that has built the first health-tech platform to help build parent-friendly workplaces.

Inge Bleijenbergh is Professor in Action Research at Radboud University, the Netherlands. She focuses on the field of equality, diversity, and inclusion. She wrote her PhD on the work–life dimension of European social rights, and uses participatory methods, such as focus groups and group model building, to involve organizational members in analyzing and addressing complex problems. She has published widely on subjects such as organizational change, gender inequality and diversity, work–life balance, change agents, and participatory action research. She is a co-editor of *The Oxford Handbook of Diversity in Organizations* and has written several textbooks on qualitative research methods.

Cécile Boot is Professor in Societal Participation and Health at Amsterdam University Medical Center, the Netherlands. Her research focuses on healthy working and how groups of workers living with vulnerabilities (e.g., chronic disease, informal caregiving tasks) can be supported at work. She particularly enjoys interdisciplinary collaboration. She is also Endowed Professor in Organization and Quality of Work in Elderly Care at Radboud University, the Netherlands, an adjunct scientist at the Institute for Work and Health in Toronto, Canada, a board member of the Research Center for Insurance Medicine in Amsterdam, and Program Leader in Societal Participation and Health at the Amsterdam Public Health Research Institute.

Michael Coker is Assistant Professor at the Department of Communication, Boise State University, Idaho, USA. His research interests relate to the intersections between organizational communication and communication technology, including understudied experiences in physical and virtual spaces, intersections between work and life, and emotions as organizing features across personal and professional contexts. You can find his work published in *Management Communication Quarterly*, *Computers in Human Behavior*, and *Communication Studies*.

Jessica de Bloom is a work and organizational psychologist and professor at the University of Groningen, the Netherlands. She has led and is currently co-leading several research projects financed by major national funding agencies and companies (e.g., Academy of Finland, Finnish Work Environment Fund, Swiss National Science Foundation), and has gained work experience inside and outside academia in five different countries. Her research focuses on vanishing boundaries between work and non-work as an aspect of today's rapidly changing working conditions and the impact of these changes on employee well-being and performance.

Melanie de Ruiter is Associate Professor of Work and Organizational Psychology at the Center for Strategy, Organization and Leadership at Nyenrode Business Universiteit, the Netherlands, where she is also Head of the PhD program. Her research topics are psychological contracts, employee motivation, stress and well-being, and leadership. Her research has been published in the *International Journal of HRM*, *Journal of Applied Behavioral Science*, and *Management Communication Quarterly*. She is Associate Editor of *Human Resource Development Quarterly* and serves on the editorial review boards of the *Journal of Applied Behavioral Science* and *Journal of Managerial Psychology*.

Ans De Vos is Professor at the University of Antwerp and Associate Dean of Education at Antwerp Management School, Belgium. She is the holder of the SD Worx chair 'Next Generation Work: Creating Sustainable Careers' and chair of the Partnership for Lifelong Learning in Flanders. Her main research areas are sustainable careers, career management, career inaction, and employability. Her work has been published in academic journals including the *Academy of Management Review*, *Journal of Vocational Behavior*, and *Academy of Management Annals*.

Laura den Dulk is Professor of Public Administration in Employment, Organization and Work–Life Issues at the Department of Public Administration and Sociology, Erasmus University Rotterdam, the Netherlands. Her main area of expertise is cross-national research on the work–life interface within the workplace. A central question in her work is how we can organize work that is both beneficial for the organization and the work–life balance and well-being of different types of workers, and the role of public policies therein.

Caroline Essers is Associate Professor of Entrepreneurship and Leadership at the Department of Business Administration, Institute for Management Research, Radboud University, the Netherlands. Her research centers on identity construction among diverse minority entrepreneurs and their inclusion/ exclusion. She focuses on the intersections of gender, ethnicity, religion, and generation, as well as class. She specializes in the narrative approach. Her work has been widely published in journals such as *Organization Studies*, *Journal of Management*, and *Organization*.

Leire Gartzia is Professor of Organizational Behavior at Deusto Business School, Spain. She holds degrees in psychology and anthropology from the University of the Basque Country and a PhD in organizational psychology from the same university. In 2012, she completed a postdoctoral fellowship at Northwestern University, Illinois, USA, and has been involved in several projects concerning change management at various business schools, taking a critical gender perspective. She combines research with activities in the business world, advising employees and managers on organizational behavior and gender equality and advising on work–life balance public policy through projects funded by the Basque government.

Emily Godager is Lecturer at Marquette University, Wisconsin, USA. Her research interests relate to organizational communication, including the intersections of work and life, organizational socialization, training and development, and communication consulting. Her research has been published in *Management Communication Quarterly* and *Communication Studies*.

Marc Grau-Grau is Associate Professor of Social and Family Policies, Vice-Dean of the Faculty of Education Sciences, and Coordinator of the Joaquim Molins Figueras Childcare and Family Policies Chair at the International University of Catalonia, Spain. Marc has also been a research fellow at the Women and Public Policy Program at Harvard Kennedy School. His research interests include work–family balance and fatherhood, childhood and childcare, family policies, and education and family relationships. He is the co-editor of four books and his research has appeared in academic journals such as *Organization*, *Journal of Family Issues*, and *Journal of Business Research*. Marc has a PhD in social policy from the University of Edinburgh, a master's degree in political and social sciences from the University Pompeu Fabra, and a degree in business administration from ESADE Business School.

Ron Hameleers is a specialist in elderly care medicine, a lawyer in labor and health law, and an organizational consultant. He specializes in education and research at the interface between health and law, and between health care and well-being. He is a member of the educational team for Wellbeing and Vitality, Faculty of Medical Sciences, Radboud University, the Netherlands.

Mark Heemskerk is Professor of Pension Law at Radboud University, the Netherlands. His research and teaching focus on employment-related pensions. He has a special interest in changes in the Dutch pension system, solidarity between generations, age discrimination, property rights in pensions, and employee participation in pensions. He has written several books and numerous articles on pension law. Mark has been combining pension law with pension practice since 2002. He is Attorney-Partner at Heldlaw and Deputy Judge at the appeal court of 's-Hertogenbosch, the Netherlands. He is a sought-after speaker and lecturer and a member of several journal editorial boards.

Philipp Kerksieck is a postdoctoral researcher at the Public and Organizational

Health Division, Center of Salutogenesis, Epidemiology, Biostatistics and Prevention Institute, University of Zurich, Switzerland. He is interested in crafting as a means of adjusting the boundaries between work and non-work and the balance of these two life domains. He leads a research project on crafting funded by the Swiss National Science Foundation and the Dutch Research Council.

Shelena Keulemans is Assistant Professor of Public Management at Radboud University, the Netherlands. Specializing in frontline workers, she takes an interdisciplinary approach which combines insights from public administration, psychology, and organizational science to understand the social processes within bureaucracies that shape the psychological disposition of civil servants, and their approach to citizens, decision making, and well-being. Her work has won multiple awards. Shelena is an academic fellow of the UNC School of Government's 'Local Government Workplaces Initiative', Chair of the Netherlands Institute of Governance's research colloquium 'Street-Level Bureaucracy of the 21st Century', and Editorial Secretary of the Dutch public administration journal *Bestuurskunde*.

Sanna Konsti holds a master's in economics and works as a MEANWELL project researcher at the Department of Psychology, University of Jyväskylä, Finland. Her PhD research focuses on how managers and leaders can make work more meaningful for their staff and individual employees. She also has her own company providing coaching to individuals, teams, and organizations.

Ellen Ernst Kossek is the Basil S. Turner Distinguished Professor at Purdue University's Mitchell E. Daniels Jr. School of Business, Indiana, USA. She holds a PhD from Yale University, an MBA from the University of Michigan, and a BA from Mount Holyoke College. She served as the first elected president of the Work-Family Researchers Network and is a fellow of the Academy of Management, the American Psychological Association, and the Society of Industrial Organizational Psychology. Ellen has won many awards for her research, teaching, and service to advancing gender and work–life understanding. Her current research examines initiatives designed to advance work–life equality and improve flexibility, work–family/life policies, and leadership interventions.

Gerbert Kraaykamp is Professor of Empirical Sociology at the Department of Sociology/ICS, Radboud University, the Netherlands. His research interests include educational inequality, health inequality, and family socialization. He has published widely in international journals on these subjects.

Peter Kruyen is Assistant Professor in Public Administration, Radboud University, the Netherlands. He investigates public servants' behavior, psychological characteristics, and competencies, and how their performance, well-being, and health are affected by human resource management. He develops scales and software to solve data problems, including DearScholar, a smartphone app for longitudinal diary research. Together with Stéfanie André, he leads the Radboud WORKLIFE consortium, bringing together inter-disciplinary research and teaching on work–life balance. Furthermore, he is a board member of the International Research Society for Public Management (IRPSM) and one of the permanent chairs of the 'HRM Special Interest Group' of the IRSPM.

Miika Kujanpää is a postdoctoral researcher at the School of Business, University of South-Eastern Norway. His research integrates perspectives from work psychology and leisure sciences to examine employees' crafting efforts, recovery, motivation, and psychological need satisfaction on and off the job. He is currently leading a work package in a large research project on work motivation funded by the Research Council of Norway.

Chang-Qin Lu is Research Professor at the School of Psychological and Cognitive Sciences, Peking University, China. He received his PhD in indus-trial and organizational psychology from the Institute of Psychology, Chinese Academy of Sciences. His research focuses broadly on job insecurity, work stress, technostress, self-efficacy, and the spillover and crossover effects of work–family conflict/balance. His work has been published in the *Journal of Applied Psychology*, *Personnel Psychology*, and *Journal of Organizational Behavior*, among others. Chang-Qin is also Associate Editor of *Applied Psychology: An International Review*.

Anne Mäkikangas holds a PhD in psychology and is Director of the Work Research Centre and Professor of Work Research at Tampere University, Finland. She is an expert in research into work stress and well-being at work from various perspectives, including job crafting. In recent years she has focused on studying new working arrangements (e.g., multilocational work). She has published over 120 scientific publications on these topics.

Sanna Markkula works as a MEANWELL project researcher at the Department of Psychology, University of Jyväskylä, Finland. She carries out intervention research on work well-being issues. She is interested in the mechanisms of change in these interventions and has focused particularly on mindfulness, acceptance, and value-based mechanisms. She has also partici-pated in developing both individual and organizational interventions targeting phenomena such as burnout and work meaningfulness. In addition, she has her own company providing consulting and coaching services for individuals, teams, and organizations.

Saija Mauno is Professor in Work and Organizational Psychology at Tampere University, Finland and Senior Lecturer at the Department of Psychology, University of Jyväskylä, Finland. In the field of occupational health psychology, she has led several projects relating to job stressors, stress buffers, well-being, work motivation, and job performance. She is leading a project on work intensification and its effects on employees' well-being and motivation. Saija has published in journals such as *Work and Stress*, *Journal of Vocational Behavior*, *European Journal of Work and Organizational Psychology*, and *Journal of Career Assessment*.

Samantha Metselaar is a PhD candidate at the Department of Public Administration and Sociology, Erasmus University Rotterdam, the Netherlands. Her research includes teleworking and its impact on work–life balance, satisfaction, and performance. She also focuses on leadership and boundary management in the context of teleworking.

Gabriele Morandin is Professor of Organizational Behavior and Dean of the School of Economics and Management, University of Bologna, Italy. He is also Associate Dean for Faculty and Research at Bologna Business School and a member of the International Network on Technology, Work, and Family at the Université du Québec in Montreal. Gabriele studies leadership and how it is connected with work and non-work domains.

Ariane Ollier-Malaterre is the Canada Research Chair in Digital Regulation at Work and in Life and Director of the International Network on Technology, Work and Family at the University of Quebec in Montreal, Canada. Her research examines work and life across different national contexts, with a focus on the regulation of digital technologies. She has published *Living with Digital Surveillance in China: Citizens' Narratives on Technology, Privacy, and Governance* (2023) and over 70 peer-reviewed articles and chapters in top-tier academic management, sociology, and information systems journals.

Sabrina Pellerin is a PhD candidate and member of the International Network on Technology, Work, and Family at the University of Quebec in Montreal, Canada. Her research focuses on the risk factors associated with the psychological health of first-line managers, particularly the various challenges of a supervisory role. Her master's thesis focused on the psychological mechanisms underlying the effects of rewards on psychological health. Sabrina is also a research assistant on psychological health, hybrid work, and workplace surveillance projects. She cherishes the idea of teaching human resources management while carrying out beneficial research projects for the workplace and its workers.

Pascale Peters is Professor in Strategic Human Resource Management at

Nyenrode Business Universiteit, the Netherlands, and Visiting Professor at Inland University of Applied Sciences, Norway. She is a member of the editorial board of *Tijdschrift voor Arbeidsvraagstukken* and also participates in *Holland Management Review*. Her research specialisms include sustainable human resources management, work–life balance and telework, new ways of working, and hybrid working. She has published on these themes in international and national journals and books, including *Human Relations*, *International Journal of HRM*, and *Gedrag & Organisatie*. She also edited the book *Virtual Management and the New Normal* (2023).

Gary Peterson was Professor and Clinical Training Director in the academic program Counseling and Psychological Services in Education, College of Education, Florida State University, USA. He is now Professor Emeritus and Senior Research Associate at the Center for the Study of Technology in Counseling and Career Development at the Florida State University Career Center. His research interests are cognition and personality assessment, and he contributes to theory, research, and assessments regarding how individuals can become better career problem solvers and decision makers.

Palina Prysmakova is Associate Professor at Florida Atlantic University, USA. Her professional interests include public and non-profit human resources and finance, public service motivation, international comparatives, development, and learning. Her research has been supported by grants such as the European Union Center of Excellence and Open Society Foundation.

Johanna Rantanen is Senior Lecturer at the Department of Psychology, University of Jyväskylä, Finland. Her research publications cover the themes of work–life balance and reconciliation as well as adult development, personality, and individuals' well-being over the life course. She leads the research project 'MEANWELL Meaningful Work as a Source of Well-Being in Organizations' (#210129, Finnish Work Environment Fund), which focuses on developing a research-based action model for work communities to promote meaningful work, occupational well-being, and organizational functionality. In addition, she has her own company providing supervision and counseling to individual employees and teams.

Chantal Remery is a sociologist by training and is Assistant Professor at the Utrecht University School of Economics, the Netherlands. Her major research interests include (international comparative) studies in the field of gender and employment, covering issues such as the reconciliation of work and private life, flexibility, and the position of women in (family) businesses. She has co-authored several reports for the European Commission and published in the *Journal of European Social Policy*, *International Small Business Journal*, and *PlosOne*, among others. Since 2020, she has participated in the COVID-19

Gender (In)equality Survey Netherlands, which studies the impact of the pandemic on gender equality.

Sarah Riforgiate is Associate Professor at the Department of Communication, University of Wisconsin-Milwaukee, USA. Her research focuses on the intersection between organizational and interpersonal communication, particularly regarding public paid work and private life, in order to increase our understanding of and develop practical solutions for improving interactions. Research projects include communication pertaining to work–life concerns, emotions in organizations, conflict negotiation, organizational leadership, and policy communication. Her work has been published in a variety of journals, including *Communication Monographs*, *Sustainability*, *Management and Communication Quarterly*, and *Journal of Family Communication*.

Ashkan Rostami is a PhD candidate in management at John Molson School of Business, Concordia University, Canada, and a member of the International Network on Technology, Work, and Family at the University of Quebec in Montreal. Ashkan has a background in engineering and holds an MBA. One of his main research interests is the employee–organization relationship. His master's research applied data-mining methods to predict employee turnover. His PhD research examines changes in work environments and arrangements through the lens of organizational justice. He also studies human–technology interactions and their effects on employees' lives.

Marcello Russo is Professor of Organizational Behavior at the University of Bologna, Italy and Global MBA Director at Bologna Business School, Italy. He was Visiting Scholar at Kedge Business School in France and at Teachers College at Columbia University, New York. He is an expert on work–life balance, with a particular focus on the individual strategies and organizational factors that can help individuals accomplish their ideal model of work–life balance. He has published in leading scholarly journals, including *Harvard Business Review*, *MIT Sloan Management Review*, *Journal of Management*, and *Academy of Management Annals*.

Pablo Sanabria-Pulido is Associate Professor at Florida Atlantic University, USA. He studies and teaches on the design, formulation, and implementation of public policies and the managerial challenges that public-service organizations and public officials face, aiming to disentangle how to make public organizations work better, particularly at the national and local levels.

Hans Schilderman is Professor in Religion and Care and chairs the Department of Empirical Practical Study of Religion at the Faculty of Philosophy, Theology and Religious Studies, Radboud University, the Netherlands. He engages in conceptual and empirical research regarding the existential and religious significance of quality of life in various spiritual care contexts. Hans was formerly president of the International Society of Empirical Research in Theology. He publishes on a wide variety of themes, including professional issues in spiritual care, exploring meaning in youth and old age, moral distress, and ritual performance.

Inyoung Shin is Lecturer at the Department of Computer Science, Yale University, Connecticut, USA. She is conducting research on the social implications of information and communication technology. Her research has been published in various academic journals, including *Information, Communication & Society*, *Social Science Computer Review*, and *Management Communication Quarterly*.

Jessica Sowa is Professor at the Joseph R. Biden Jr. School of Public Policy and Administration, University of Delaware, USA. She is a co-author of *Human Resource Essentials for Public Service: People, Process, Performance* (2022) and *Organizational Behavior: Real Research for Public and Nonprofit Managers* (2018) and co-editor of *The Nonprofit Human Resources Handbook* (2017) and *Serving in Silence: The Untold Stories of Essential Public Servants* (1994). She served as editor-in-chief of the *Review of Public Personnel Administration* until December 2023 and is currently co-editor-in-chief of *Perspectives on Public Management and Governance*.

Yidong Tao is Assistant Professor in Entrepreneurship and Innovation at the Department of Strategic Management and Organizations, International Business School Suzhou, Xi'an Jiaotong-Liverpool University, China. She was trained as a social psychologist and management scholar. Her main research interests concern the identity constructions of entrepreneurs, why individuals decide to become entrepreneurs, how they set up a business, how they experience cultural or social values, and how they use these values strategically as sources to (re)construct an entrepreneurial identity. Her other research interests include professional identity, career development, and cross-cultural management.

Marjolein van de Pol is Professor in Student Well-Being at Radboud University, the Netherlands. She is also Program Director for Medicine, an educational developer, and a practicing family physician. Her research focuses on shared decision making and student well-being. She is Founder of the Educational Team for Wellbeing and Vitality at the Faculty of Medical Sciences of Radboud University.

Beatrice van der Heijden is Professor of Strategic HRM at the Institute for Management Research, Radboud University, the Netherlands, and also Head of the Department Strategic HRM. In 2019, she was appointed as a member of the Academy of Europe, and in 2022 she was also appointed to the Royal Holland Society of Sciences and Humanities. She has been a Knight in the Order of the Lion of the Netherlands since 2021. Her main research areas are sustainable careers, employability, and aging at work. She is Associate Editor for the *European Journal of Work* and *Organizational Psychology* and Co-Editor for the *German Journal of Human Resource Management*.

Joëlle van der Meer is Assistant Professor at the Department of Public Administration and Sociology Erasmus University Rotterdam, the Netherlands. She conducts research on the changing requirements of civil servants in terms of their role perceptions. She also focuses on new ways of working and their effects on well-being, work–life balance, and performance.

Koen van Eijck is Professor in Cultural Lifestyles and Education Program Director at the Department of Arts and Culture Studies, Erasmus School of History, Culture and Communication, Erasmus University Rotterdam, the Netherlands. His research focuses on trends and inequality in patterns of taste and cultural participation, arts education, and the perception and appreciation of art, especially music and visual art.

Marloes van Engen is Associate Professor in Transformation Management at the Institute for Management Research, Strategic HRM, Radboud University, the Netherlands. Her teaching and research interests lie in understanding diversity and equality in organizations, fostering inclusive leadership and inclusive workplaces, and sustainability in combining work and private life. She is a member of the Radboud Work–Life Consortium and the Gender and Power in Management and Politics hotspot. Marloes is passionate about promoting responsible change by co-creating research with stakeholders in organizations. She invites students to take part in projects and helps them to explore their individual strengths.

Karen van Hedel is a postdoctoral researcher at Utrecht University, the Netherlands. Her research interests include gender in relation to health, chiefly from a work–life perspective. She is currently involved in the European Research Council Consolidator project CAPABLE, a large cross-national study on gender inequalities in work–life balance from a capability perspective. Karen investigates how work–life balance influences (mental) health and well-being in the Netherlands and (cross-nationally) in Europe, and how it is affected by economic insecurity and strategies for combining work with care.

Ellen Verbakel is Professor of General and Theoretical Sociology at the Department of Sociology, Radboud University, the Netherlands. She is a family sociologist with an interest in partner relations, work–family interplay, and well-being. Much of her research focuses on informal care. She studies the consequences of providing informal care for work outcomes and the well-being of informal carers. She has collected unique retrospective data on informal caregiving careers and was involved in the 'INequality in Care' project on how various care systems are associated with inequalities in care and well-being in later life.

Brenda Vermeeren is Associate Professor at the Department of Public Administration and Sociology, Erasmus University Rotterdam, the Netherlands. She is Vice-Dean of Education at Erasmus School of Social and Behavioral Sciences, a general board member of the Dutch Association for Public Administration, and an editorial board member of the Dutch journal *Tijdschrift voor HRM*. Her research interests include the relationship between human resources management and public performance and the role of line managers and employees in this relationship.

Klaske Veth is Professor of Applied Sciences Leadership and Sustainable Employment at the Hanze University of Applied Sciences, the Netherlands. She is responsible for new leadership in organizations and human resources strategy and leadership at the Academic Business School AOG School of Management. Within her professorship, she focuses on the research lines Well -being@Work and Leadership and Inclusive Entrepreneurship. She obtained her PhD at Radboud University in Nijmegen and was nominated for best dissertation at the International HRM conference. She has worked in various (management) human resources positions and sectors.

Mark Visser is Assistant Professor at the Department of Sociology, Radboud University, the Netherlands. His major research interests include older workers and retirement, social inequality, voting behavior, and the welfare state. He studies these subjects from a life-course and cross-national perspective and has published on them widely. In 2020, he obtained a major grant from Instituut Gak as principal investigator in a project entitled 'Understanding Old-Age Inequality: The Impact of Work, Family and Health Trajectories on Post-Retirement Economic, Social and Psychological Well-Being across Europe'.

Mara A. Yerkes is Professor of Comparative Social Policy at Utrecht University, the Netherlands, and Research Associate at the Center for Social Development in Africa, University of Johannesburg, South Africa. Her research centers on comparative social policy (including national and local welfare state policy and industrial relations), social inequalities (in relation to work, care, communities, and families, in particular relating to gender, generations, and sexual orientation) and the interplay between them. She is Principal Investigator of the European Research Council project CAPABLE, a comparative study on gender inequalities in work–life balance in eight European countries.

Foreword

Han van Krieken

In May 2023, on the occasion of the centennial of Radboud University, Michael Sandal was awarded an honorary doctorate. In his address to the academic community, he argued that the dignity of work is no longer valued highly enough in Western democracies, and that as a result the value of work and the respect it brings to individuals as members of a society is on the decline. The academic world may seem to have been less affected by this decline in the respect and recognition that work can bring. However, it seems to me that the importance of work as an integral part of a person's identity is losing its significance in academia, too. This makes an interesting contrast with the world of the arts or professional sports, for instance, where people are generally very passionate about their identity as professionals. The concept of *work–life balance* exemplifies this observation. It places work outside of life – as if *life* has to be something that happens when one is not working (and vice versa). Yet for many, and not only for craftsmen, work is central to their status and self-esteem. And what is more, especially in a secularized environment, it is the search for meaning that lies at the heart of the conversation around work–life balance.

Every person's life includes different roles: family member, worker, consumer, and member of different groups. It can be a challenge to reconcile these different roles, especially now that the number of social groups that we belong to has grown larger, not least because so many people are part of various online social networks. In other words, *fear of missing out* has become the most common cause of psychological distress.

Does work equal suffering, as so many protesters in France seem to believe? Is the goal of a 25-hour working week a worthy one? How do we reconcile the various aspects of our lives, including work, family, hobbies, leisure activities, social media, and so on? This book is a timely contribution on the important set of issues that are usually described as *work–life balance*. It includes contributions from researchers in various disciplines – essential in order to examine such a broad subject. And it certainly is a broad subject. Many individuals struggle to achieve the 'perfect balance', a struggle that involves high workloads and the challenge of achieving so many goals when there are only 24 hours in a day. No wonder ever more of us are ending up burnt out (no matter how we define that).

Every human being is different and I welcome the diversity of individual experience that this book explores. There are differences between individuals, but also changes within the same individual. Inevitably, people evolve during their lifetime: there may be periods when work and career take center-stage, and other times when family takes up most of our attention, or a specific leisure activity, or contributing to society as volunteer, or self-reflection. It is this variety that can make fitting in both life *and* work so challenging. It requires personal leadership and managers who are sensitive to colleagues who might be struggling.

I very much hope that this book will find a broad readership, partly because it provides some solutions, but even more because it contains some valuable reflections on the role that work plays in the meaningful lives that we all aspire to live. That role is bound to change over the course of an individual lifetime, to vary for every individual, and to be affected by the circumstances of both life as a whole and the work that often makes up a substantial part of that life.

Nijmegen, September 2023

Han van Krieken
Rector Magnificus, Radboud University

Preface

Peter Kruyen, Stéfanié André, and Beatrice van der Heijden

OUR JOURNEY

Our joint journey started in 2010, about 14 years ago, when Peter and Stéfanie met at Tilburg University. Peter was then halfway through his PhD research, and Stéfanie was about to start hers. Unfortunately, they lost contact when Peter moved to Radboud University in 2012 after completing his dissertation, but five years later, in 2017, Stéfanie ran into Peter on his way to the railway station. To their surprise, they were both heading for Radboud University, where Stéfanie had also recently been offered a job. After some chit-chat, the conversation turned to potential joint research projects and, eventually, they began working together on a few small projects on family policy for public servants. But the really big one came in 2019, when Stéfanie suggested writing a joint grant proposal for an interdisciplinary consortium on 'work–life challenges' at Radboud University. That proposal not only laid the foundations for this book, but also resulted in a deep friendship.

Peter and Beatrice met in 2013, when Peter was invited to speak at the European Association of Work and Organizational Psychology Conference, of which Beatrice is a very loyal attendee. Since then, they have been 'critical friends' to one another, teaming up for various research projects. Along with 21 other scholars from Radboud University, Beatrice became one of the founding members of the WORKLIFE Consortium. After joining the consortium, Beatrice and Stéfanie also became friends through working together on various research projects. In the process of writing this book, all three of us have experienced our ups and downs – at work, at home, and with respect to our work–life balance. We are very grateful to each other for the support, mutual understanding, appreciation, and honesty that we can show each other.

THE WORKLIFE CONSORTIUM

In the spring of 2019, the Executive Board of Radboud University issued a call for proposals for interdisciplinary consortia to promote sustained interdisciplinary research across the departments, institutes, and faculties of Radboud University. For Stéfanie and Peter, the process of bringing scientists together was a fantastic experience, giving the opportunity to exchange ideas with over two dozen scholars who were passionate about the challenges of work–life balance *and* study–life balance. So many stimulating ideas were shared by colleagues from the Faculty of Management Sciences (Public Administration, Business Administration, Research Methods, and Strategic HRM), the Faculty of Social Sciences (Sociology, Work and Organizational Psychology), the Faculty of Law (Pension Law, Social Law), Medical Sciences (Physiology, Psychiatry), the Faculty of Science (Institute for Science and Society), and the Radboud Teachers Academy. In fact, we started to feel a bit like Getafix, the village druid from the Asterix books (or Panoramix to French readers). We would like to express our sincere gratitude to Daniela Patru, our previous grant advisor, for helping us to mix our magic potion which, in the end, was granted funding by the Executive Board in early 2020.

Just after we hired Marjolein Missler in March 2020 as a research officer to start working on the ideas for our consortium, COVID-19 hit, derailing our plans completely. Not only were we unable to hold any meetings, but we were also (ironically) being distracted by all kinds of new challenges around work–life balance, ranging from additional teaching work and extra work to keep our research projects going to the need to homeschool our kids, the absence of social activities, and the challenge of developing new coping strategies to deal with the newly blurred boundary between work and non-work hours in our new home offices. At the same time, we had the opportunity to work with Janna Besamusca, Chantal Remery, Mara Yerkes, and Roos van der Zwan in our jointly founded COVID-19 Gender (In)equality Survey Netherlands project (COGIS-NL project).

In the summer of 2020, we made a tacit decision to focus on the two main ambitions that we had formulated in the proposal for our consortium: (1) to submit a major collaborative grant proposal for the Dutch National Research Agenda (*Nationale Wetenschapsagenda*, NWA); and (2) to write this book: an interdisciplinary book on work–life balance research. Even though the NWA proposal was not funded in the end, we are extremely proud that we managed to meet the deadlines for both applications. Furthermore, working with so many societal partners for the NWA enabled us to build up a great network for small-scale research projects. These included research on the work–life balance of teachers with the Rotterdam Association for Catholic Education, research on the careers of police officers in the Dutch National Police and Dutch Police Unions, and with the national government, research on work–life balance among civil servants. We would like to thank all our partners for their cooperation on these projects and for their interest in promoting healthy, happy, and productive careers for their employees. We also thank the Executive Board of Radboud University for giving us the opportunity to build the consortium, and to meet, collaborate with, and learn from so many bright researchers.

HOW TO WRITE AN INTERDISCIPLINARY BOOK ON WORK–LIFE BALANCE?

We would like to say a few words about how this editorial volume came about. In spring 2020, Peter and Stéfanie invited fellow consortium members to collaborate on our book proposal. In addition to Peter and Stéfanie, Beatrice, Marjolein, Inge Bleijenbergh, Hester Paanakker, and Shelena Keulemans all enthusiastically volunteered to take part. At several meetings in 2020 and 2021, we crafted the proposal for this book together. Even though they did not end up joining the editorial team, we are extremely grateful to these bright, talented colleagues for their initial thoughts and their work on the proposal. This book could not have been written without their support.

After our book proposal had been accepted by Edward Elgar in the autumn of 2021, we set to work 'recruiting' potential authors for the book. First we asked members of our consortium, and later extended our call to national and international experts, expanding the interdisciplinary scope of the book to include philosophers, leisure researchers, economists, gender scholars, and so on, *and* ensuring that the book would include stories from various continents. In total, 56 scholars from across the world – working in a whole range of disciplines, and at various stages in their academic careers – agreed to contribute.

In the first half of 2022, we received all the abstracts. In August 2022, the first versions of the full chapters came in and went through a thorough process of peer feedback in the autumn of 2022. In January 2023, we (the editors) provided a second round of feedback and there was additional feedback for some chapters in the spring of 2023. We would like to warmly thank Toby Adams, who conducted a systematic language check in the summer of 2023. In the autumn of 2023, after a long session on the sequencing of the chapters, we finished work on the core content of the book. We also want to thank our editorial support team at Edward Elgar for their continued support and trust in us, and for their enthusiasm for our book.

THE AUTHORS

Our largest gratitude is directed towards our authors. Working on this book with all these talented, friendly, and inspiring scholars has been a real privilege. We are very appreciative that they all stuck to the proposed outline for the book and met all our deadlines so punctually, and – more importantly – we have learned so much from their contributions, regarding themes and perspectives, theories, and methods that help us to understand work–life challenges better and to improve work–life balance. We wish to thank all the authors once again for their trust in us and for their willingness to contribute to this book. It has been a fantastic journey.

Last but not least, we have had a chance to be part of the lives of the authors for a while, sharing in their joys and trying to provide some support through difficult times. Some contributors have got married and had babies; others have lost loved ones, suddenly had to provide informal care, been involved in a serious accident, gone through work–life conflicts of their own, or been ill with COVID-19. This book has shown us that we are not only researching life, but also living our own research.

Nijmegen, September 2023

Peter Kruyen, Stéfanié André, and Beatrice van der Heijden

PART I

Setting the stage

1. Introduction to *Maintaining a Sustainable Work–Life Balance*

Peter Kruyen, Stéfanie André, and Beatrice van der Heijden

ON THE IMPORTANCE OF WORK–LIFE BALANCE (RESEARCH)

Maintaining a sustainable work–life balance – defined as the optimal allocation of time and focus between work and family or leisure activities (cf. Greenhaus et al., 2003; Guest, 2002) – has been labeled by scholars and practitioners as one of the greatest challenges of the twenty-first century. The Organisation for Economic Co-operation and Development (OECD, 2023) monitors work–life balance in its participant states, for example, and in 2019 the European Union issued the Work–Life Balance Directive to improve the work–life balance of its citizens (EU, 2019). In the field of care, long the domain of women, the EU's Gender Action Plan (European Commission, 2021) now actively promotes work–care equality between men and women, not only with respect to childcare but also other types of care, such as informal care.

Unsurprisingly, there has also been an increase in scientific research on the issue, and in September 2023 the term 'work–life balance' yielded over 650,000 hits on Google Scholar. Kelliher and colleagues (2019), in their exemplary overview of the field, provide an appealing outline of the evolution of academic work on the relationship between 'work' and 'life'. They indicate that interest in the domain started to grow after the Second World War (Roberts, 2007), when an increasing number of women entered employment outside the home (e.g., Gattrell et al., 2013). From the 1970s onwards, the focus expanded to include dual-career couples (e.g., Gilbert & Rachlin, 1987). By the turn of the twenty-first century, the scholarly domain of work–life balance had become more multi-disciplinary (e.g., Perry-Jenkins et al., 2000).

Importantly, up until now, scholarly research into work–life balance has largely adopted a limited conceptualization of domains of both 'work' and 'life', and consequently has not done justice to recent developments in working arrangements, employment relationships, and life worlds (Kelliher et al., 2019). In particular, Kelliher et al. (2019) posit that the extant literature on work–life balance has only partially considered both 'work' and 'life'; this builds on earlier critiques advanced by De Janasz et al. (2013), Eikhof et al. (2007), and Ozbilgin et al. (2011). Indeed, the dominance of an overly simplistic view of 'life' as comprising caring for dependent children, and a traditional view of 'work' that is based on the model of full-time, permanent employment with one employer, implies that existing work–life research still has a lot of ground to cover (Kelliher et al., 2019).

In this book, we respond to this call by extending our scope to new forms of care such as the provision of informal care, that is providing care to relatives, friends, or others without a formal contractual agreement. Furthermore, we combine research on different life stages, such as parenting young children and retirement. In line with Kelliher et al. (2019) and a number of policy organizations – such as the Chartered Institute of Personnel and Development, European Union, International Labour Organization, and OECD – we make the case for a more holistic and up-to-date understanding of work–life balance and argue that there is an urgent need to focus on both working arrangements *and* life events.

Because of the interdisciplinary character of the issue of work–life balance, there remains considerable uncertainty around cause and effect. This pertains to: (1) individual workers; (2) the organizations they work for; and (3) society at large. Explanations and effects are to be found at various levels of analysis, and these are the focus of different disciplines: there are psychological factors (e.g., employees' needs for certain forms of flexibility); there are work, team, and organizational arrangements (e.g., human resource management practices, work–life policies); occupational characteristics (e.g., professional norms); sociological factors (e.g., family background, cultural norms, and values); and government policies (e.g., flexibilization of labor markets, regulations, social services, and welfare arrangements) (cf. De Vos et al., 2020).

Researchers from different disciplines hold different pieces of the puzzle, and because all these different levels of analysis interact and intersect, our knowledge regarding work–life balance cannot be advanced without collaboration between those in different disciplines. In this book, therefore, we adopt an interdisciplinary approach to understand the whys and wherefores of a sustainable work–life balance that allows people to be happy, healthy, and productive (Van der Heijden, 2005).

Unfortunately, despite the key role of interdisciplinary collaboration in advancing our understanding of work–life challenges, interaction between researchers from different disciplines remains a challenge in itself. After all, most academic publications have a disciplinary focus, and this is problematic given the interdisciplinary, multi-level nature of work–life balance challenges. We understand the concept of 'multi-disciplinarity' as drawing on knowledge from different disciplines while staying within the boundaries of each; 'inter-disciplinarity', on the other hand, analyzes and harmonizes the connections between disciplines and, where necessary, synthesizes new links to form a coherent whole.

This book provides insights into how to start closing the knowledge gap that we have outlined by bringing together scholars from a broad array of disciplines. We aim to provide the reader a sound understanding of the meaning, causes, and consequences of a sustainable work–life balance throughout the various phases of life, as well as the instruments that can help to achieve and maintain a sustainable work–life balance at the level of individuals, families, organizations, and societies.

STRUCTURE OF THIS BOOK

There are many ways in which an edited volume such as this can be structured. We considered organizing the book along disciplinary lines, or according to levels of analysis, life stages, and recurring themes. Structuring the book along disciplinary lines would have been a less useful approach, however, because many of our contributors cannot be categorized easily into a single discipline. Indeed, this is one of the reasons we asked them for their contributions! We also asked the scholars to, where possible, form teams that spanned multiple disciplines and to combine the insights from those disciplines in their contributions. A second approach that we considered was to structure the book according to the different levels of analysis: individual, organization, and country, for example. However, the multi-level nature of work–life balance and the multi-level nature of many of the contributions made this an unattractive alternative, too. In the end, we opted for a structure based on life stages and recurring themes. Consequently, the book consists of six parts.

Part I (Setting the stage) contains chapters that encourage readers to reflect on the concept of work–life balance by analyzing the implied trade-off between 'work' and 'life', problematizing the 'life' aspect of the concept, showing how different categories of people have different perspectives on work–life balance, and exploring the connection between perceived work–life conflicts and work performance. Part II (Workplace support) focuses on the organizational side of work–life balance. It provides evidence of factors that can affect an individual's work–life balance, such as leadership support and coworker support. In Part III (Digitalization and homeworking), we focus on how digitalization has changed experiences of work–life balance, in both a positive and a negative sense. For example, we explore the new phenomenon of workers who feel they have to be constantly available for work, and we consider the flexibility that homeworking can provide but also the additional flexibility that it requires from workers. Part IV (Working parents) focuses on working mothers and fathers, how they seek to balance 'work' and 'life', and how organizations can foster a better work–life balance for these groups. Part V (Work–life balance and retirement) explores how retirees, too, can maintain a sustainable work–life balance even after they stop working. The chapters of Part VI (Individual strategies for fostering work–life balance) provide practical advice and a diagnostic instrument, encouraging employees to 'recraft' the way they work and alter their sensemaking perspective to maintain and enhance their work–life balance.

The interdisciplinary focus of this book has not only resulted in a wide variety of themes covered, as the description above illustrates, but also gives a flavor of the broad range of approaches that are being applied to improve our understanding of work–life balance and related needs and challenges. Some chapters use empirical data to explore and analyze elements of work–life balance, while others take a reflective stance towards the literature. In some contributions, a large-scale quantitative approach is adopted, while others analyze qualitative data from a small group of respondents. Some chapters opt for a positivistic framework to explain effects, while other chapters apply a critical lens to uncover and understand hidden mechanisms. We are proud that our book contains chapters that focus on the private sector, the public sector, or span both, and address the particularities of different sectors, which tend to be overlooked in other books.

Last but not least, this book was written during and after the COVID-19 pandemic: six chapters use data collected during the pandemic, and we specifically asked authors to reflect on the effect of the pandemic and on the relevance of their findings to the post-COVID-19 era.

ON FUTURE RESEARCH

Inspired by the chapters of this book and by our discussions with members of the WORK-LIFE consortium, we would like to present three ideas for future research.

Firstly, there is the question of to what extent a sustainable work–life balance should be a *right* for all workers or simply a *privilege* for certain groups of workers – middle-aged knowledge workers, in particular. In this book, we focus on factors that affect the work–life balance of specific categories of workers, including women, fathers, workers with a migrant background, and older workers. However, certain groups of workers, such as blue-collar workers, 'gig workers', and those without a permanent employment contract, have received little attention in this book. The same is true of workers outside the global North. This is unfortunate, because these types of workers have little specific leverage to negotiate work–life packages and fewer financial resources to pay for flexible work arrangements (Kruyen & Sowa, 2023; Teo, 2016; Warren, 2021). Future work on these topics is advised for as well.

A second observation that we would make is that employees have different perspectives on what constitutes a good work–life balance *and* they differ in the degree to which they regard an imbalance between work and life as problematic. This raises the question of which factors affect the subjective experience of work–life balance. The Conservation of Resources Theory (Hobfoll, 1989) suggests that work tasks require individual resources that need to be replenished through non-work-related activities to avoid mental and physical problems. Yet there are also workers to whom this rule of thumb seems scarcely to apply. Do employees who prefer to spend most, if not all, of their time on work-related activities have particular personality traits? Do they apply specific coping strategies, engage in extremely enjoyable tasks, or enjoy particular conditions at home or at work which make them feel especially comfortable in one of the two? More research on these topics is needed.

Lastly, and building on the point just outlined, we call for a whole-life approach that focuses on the domains of both work and private life (Van der Heijden et al., 2020) and for systemic research into the (long-term) effect of a poor work–life balance. We advocate a multi-stakeholder approach (i.e., workers, employers, colleagues, relatives, friends, representatives from the institutional context, and so on; De Vos et al., 2020). Of course, we can always speculate about the possible detrimental effects of too much (or too little) focus on work for individuals, organizations, families, and societies. However, empirical, longitudinal research is needed to draw firmer conclusions regarding those effects and to produce advice on how to achieve a sustainable work–life balance over time.

OUR AUDIENCE

Naturally, we hope that this book finds a wide audience. We have worked hard to make our book not only comprehensive but also comprehensible for scholars in different fields (with the aid of a peer-review process whereby authors from other disciplines provided feedback on the draft contributions submitted) as well as for practitioners. In other words, this book is not only intended to help students and scholars to understand the work–life balance from different perspectives and using various methodologies, but it can also help organizations to improve their practices when it comes to fostering their employees' happiness, health, and productivity (Van der Heijden, 2005). In addition to the chapters in Part VI which are explicitly oriented towards improving work–life balance, in every chapter, the authors reflect on the lessons that researchers and practitioners can learn from their contribution.

REFERENCES

De Janasz, S., Forret, M., Haack, D., & Jonsen, K. (2013). Family status and work attitudes: An investigation in a professional services firm. *British Journal of Management, 24*(2), 191–210.

De Vos, A., Van der Heijden, B. I. J. M., & Akkermans, J. (2020). Sustainable careers: Towards a conceptual model. *Journal of Vocational Behavior, 103196.*

Eikhof, D. R., Warhurst, C., & Haunschild, A. (2007). What work? What life? What balance? *Employment Relations, 29*(4), 325–333.

EU (2019). Directive (EU) 2019/1158 of the European Parliament and of the Council of 20 June 2019 on work–life balance for parents and carers and repealing Council Directive 2010/18/EU. Retrieved from: https://eur-lex.europa.eu/legal-content/EN/TXT/?uri=celex%3A32019L1158.

European Commission (2021). Towards a gender-equal world. Retrieved from: https://ec.europa.eu/international-partnerships/system/files/factsheet-draft-gender-action-plan-v08.pdf.

Gattrell, C. J., Burnett, S. B., Cooper, C. L., & Sparrow, P. (2013). Work–life balance and parenthood: A comparative review of definitions, equity and enrichment. *International Journal of Management Reviews, 15*(3), 300–316.

Gilbert, L. A., & Rachlin, V. (1987). Mental health and psychological functioning of dual-career families. *The Counseling Psychologist, 15*(1), 7–49.

Greenhaus, J. H., Collins, K. M., & Shaw, J. D. (2003). The relation between work–family balance and quality of life. *Journal of Vocational Behavior, 63*(3), 510–531.

Guest, D. E. (2002). Perspectives on the study of work–life balance. *Social Science Information, 41*(2), 255–279.

Hobfoll, S. E. (1989). Conservation of resources: A new attempt at conceptualizing stress. *American Psychologist, 44*(3), 513–524.

Kelliher, C., Richardson, J., & Boiarintseva, G. (2019). All of work? All of life? Reconceptualising work–life balance for the 21st century. *Human Resource Management Journal, 29*(2), 97–112.

Kruyen, P. M., & Sowa, J. E. (2023). Essential but ignored: Including blue-collar government workers into human resource management research. *Public Personnel Management,* 00910260231187540.

OECD (2023). Work life balance. Retrieved from: www.oecdbetterlifeindex.org/topics/work-life-balance/.

Ozbilgin, M. T., Beauregard, T. A., Tatli, A., & Bell, M. P. (2011). Work-life, diversity and intersectionality: A critical review and research agenda. *International Journal of Human Resource Management, 13*(2), 177–198.

Perry-Jenkins, M., Repetti, R. L., & Crouter, A. C. (2000). Work and family in the 1990s. *Journal of Marriage and Family, 62*(4), 981–998.

Roberts, K. (2007). Work–life balance: The sources of the contemporary problem and the probable outcomes: A review and interpretation of the evidence. *Employee Relations, 29*(4), 334–351.

Teo, Y. (2016). Not everyone has 'maids': Class differentials in the elusive quest for work–life balance. *Gender, Place & Culture, 23*(8), 1164–1178.

Van der Heijden, B. I. J. M. (2005). *'No one has ever promised you a rose garden': On shared responsibility and employability enhancing strategies throughout careers.* Heerlen: Open University of the Netherlands and Assen: Van Gorcum.

Van der Heijden, B. I. J. M., De Vos, A., Akkermans, J., Spurk, D., Semeijn, J., Van der Velde, M., & Fugate, M. (2020). Editorial special issue: Sustainable careers across the lifespan: Moving the field forward. *Journal of Vocational Behavior*, 103344.

Warren, T. (2021). Work–life balance and gig work: 'Where are we now' and 'where to next' with the work–life balance agenda? *Journal of Industrial Relations*, *63*(4), 522–545.

2. Questioning the balance of work and life: some philosophical observations

Hans Schilderman

INTRODUCTION

What do philosophy and theology have to contribute to a discussion of work–life balance? As intellectual disciplines, they may fall short when accounting for the many nuanced observations from social-scientific research because they tend to draw straight lines and offer sweeping statements. However, their insights may also be helpful when it comes to questioning assumptions and seeing the bigger picture. This chapter attempts to do just that by questioning the central concept of 'work–life balance' and offering some observations from three philosophers.

In the academic literature on the work–life interface, various phenomena have been reported, most of which can be grouped into categories such as flexible work arrangements, gender differences, and balancing policies and practices. As varied as these themes are, so is the huge number of competing theories that each provide empirical support, which makes it difficult to identify the correct view (Bello & Garba Ibrahim, 2020; Khateeb, 2021; Mathew & Natarajan, 2014). In recent years, in particular, the number of publications in this scholarly domain has increased significantly, indicating that the concept of work–life interface has gained traction in academia (Barik & Pandey, 2017; Rashmi & Kataria, 2021). But even as the literature on this topic burgeons, it is important to note that some critical observations have already been made regarding the assumptions that underlie the ongoing research into the work–life interface, such as the notion that the study of the work–life interface is gender-neutral, that work–life balance is based on personal choice and responsibility, or that it is free from cultural bias (Lewis et al., 2007). In addition, several authors maintain that a values-free conception of the work–life interface is impossible. Both conceptions of work and life differ in eastern and western parts of the world, and not only due to different economic circumstances but also because of divergence in the cultural value of family and work (Chandra, 2012). Still, other authors maintain that the idea of the personal balancing of work and life through 'quick fixes' is a myth, since it disregards the powerful economic forces that drive market economies (Gambles et al., 2008). There may be other blind spots as well. For a long time, then, work–life interference has primarily been considered as a conflicting role set which links 'work' with stress and connects 'life' with recreation, thereby suggesting that achieving a balance will require careful supervision or even clinical intervention. This emphasis on the stress side of the work–life balance overlooks the fact that tensions at work are not solely negative and that the role sets of work and family life may display a positive dynamic as well (Singh, 2013). Another blind spot concerns the almost complete absence of moral and spiritual considerations in the literature on the work–life interface. Employees are usually assumed to be self-interested individuals who seek to maximize personal benefit by following the instrumental incentives that the workplace offers. However, this fails to take account of the interplay between intrinsic, extrinsic, and transitive motivations, in which moral and spiritual concerns act as sources of inspiration and motivation that transcend formal job requirements.

In taking stock of these remarks, we must ask whether it is right to conceive of 'work' and 'life' as opposing concepts of more or less equal weight, as the metaphor of the balance suggests. Indeed, should we regard this balance as a zero-sum game, where one comes at the direct expense of the other? And if so, who would be able to alter the balance in this pair of scales? These philosophical questions get to the heart of the assumptions that frame the work–life interface. I will therefore elaborate on the perspectives of three philosophers, who would have been critical of the notion of the work–life interface as a balance. Even though they never addressed the work–life interface in explicitly social scientific terms, they may offer insights with which we can reformulate the subject at hand. With this in mind, I will draw on the work of Hannah Arendt, who redefines the private and public aspects of work through her view of action; Alfred Schütz, who demonstrates that the life-world is a requirement for both work and life; and Jürgen Habermas, who explores and criticizes the instrumentalization of both work and daily life by economic systems. In considering their observations, it will become clear that the metaphor of the balance is actually a misleading one which wrongfoots us, and that the concept of meaning is the notion that actually underlies the work–life interface.

ACTION

In her study of the 'human condition', Hannah Arendt was critical of the idea that the private sphere, understood as a life that is dedicated to mere inner thought with its emphasis on ultimate and universal ideas ('*vita contemplativa*'), might outrank the public sphere of practical life, in which ideas have to be negotiated in a socially plural environment ('*vita activa*'). The discrepancy between the private sphere and public sphere, and the priority of the former over the latter, had gained significance in Aristotelian thought, Roman law, and Christian belief, but it downplayed the political significance of activity (Vaddiraju, 2020). Arendt described this active life as being characterized by labor, work, and action: three forms of human activity that characterize mankind's ability to create and maintain institutions that allow us to work together to try to determine our destiny (Arendt, 2018). When we apply Arendt's distinction to the bipolar interface of work–life, it is reordered as one in which both 'work' and 'life' are practices that comprise at least three aspects. '*Labor*' refers to all activities that we engage in to fulfill our need for daily sustenance and primary biological needs. It refers to everything that we need to do in order to survive. To that extent, one is never free but in a certain sense 'enslaved' to satisfying these necessities. '*Work*' refers to reproducing ourselves through practices that transcend our own lives, including science, religion, and art. While in labor we are bound to what nature has to offer, in work we can create something new and transform nature. The extent to which we are free, however, remains bound to the inevitable instruments of achievement. Finally, '*action*' refers to self-disclosure: whenever one is actively engaged, one turns into a political agent with certain publicly expressed preferences and convictions. Through action, we demonstrate who we are: unique individuals in a world that is marked by a plurality of needs, motives, and goals. By acting, we appeal to a shared understanding of who we are as a collective. According to Arendt, this principle of public expression liberates us from the bounds of necessity and instrumentality. It is here that freedom has political significance, as it both expresses our self in what we do and it also implies that others may agree or disagree with that. Arendt employed the word 'natality' here, understood as the revolutionary freedom to begin something new. This third aspect of activity – that which is *meaningful* (action) – is primordial over the other two aspects; i.e. that which is *necessary* (labor) and *useful* (work). In this respect, Arendt questioned the validity of the distinction between private and public spheres. What is meaningful does not coincide with the private sphere, because in modern times this domain of life has developed as the hidden or secret counterpart of the public realm – the domain in which we do not encounter others. It is nevertheless experienced as a propriety; a personal sphere of self-referral that allows us to participate in society (Moneir, 2014). Private and public domains interact in any political system, even though totalitarianism seeks to submit the private realm to the public realm through violence (Freund, 1966). However, in work as well as in our daily lives, we are political entities, striving for meaningful lives while dealing with economic necessities and shaping our environment into something new. There is no zero-sum game or balancing act between work and life; rather, the work–life interface comprises a prudent practice in which we align labor, work, and action simultaneously in both domains. We should therefore drop the concept of opposing or balancing work and life, with its connotations of public and private, and understand both work and life through the umbrella concept of what is meaningful in action within both these domains.

LIFE–WORLD

If indeed 'meaning in action' is a primordial denominator in the work–life interface, to what extent does that provide a criterion for aligning labor and work? For an answer to this question, we can turn to Alfred Schütz, the founding father of interpretative sociology. His idea of the life-world offers such a criterion (Schütz, 1960; Schütz & Luckmann, 2017). According to Schütz, the life-world is the world of unquestioned assumptions that we share and that allow us to live together in an uncomplicated way. Even though we hardly realize it, we are constantly reconstructing the meaning of other people's actions and adapting them to make sense of our social environment. This reconstruction not only allows us to organize our daily experiences coherently but also facilitates the intersubjective coordination of these experiences, even over generations. It thus offers an antidote against the objectivation of social life (Vargas, 2020). This assumptive reality that we place our trust in is expressed in meaning domains, or 'dwelling places for the mind'. Schütz labeled these as 'finite provinces of meaning', each of which has its own assumptions, demands, and constraints that are characterized by specific 'cognitive styles' (Santiago-Delefosse & Carral, 2015, pp. 1269–1270). For instance, there is the domain of what it means to be a father, a son, a husband, an employee, a soccer player, a churchgoer, and so on, each to be lived in according to its own set of social norms and institutional codes. Without these assumptive – and therefore meaningful – domains, we would know neither who we are nor how to interact with one another. These domains of meaning allow us to step out of active life, temporarily, but we snap back to everyday life ('*Alltag*') as soon as a relevant event requires our attention. This switching between domains of meaning and this paramount reality forges all these roles or experiences into the unity of a personality and allows us to function as a socially reliable agent. One important observation is that while acting in paramount reality, we depend on our ability to engage in these domains of meaning. A latent mode of meaning can thus be considered as a tacit condition for action. This short summary clarifies that 'work' and 'life' are far too abstract to be taken as concepts when alignment is required. The balance of work and life results from an alignment of action, labor, and work within domains of meaning that require a far more fine-grained analysis than the work–life interface or the notion of the 'balance' would suggest. A background of meaningful settings is necessary in order to live an ordinary life properly, and mental and social problems are likely to occur whenever this continuous immersion of agents into domains of meaning fails.

SYSTEM

From the philosopher Jürgen Habermas – who supported Schütz's concept of the life-world, describing it as necessary for self-understanding, social inter-action, and cultural reproduction (Habermas, 1981; Rasmussen, 1984) – we learn that mental and social problems do occur, and on a particularly large scale in the system-guided procedures of modern society. However, Habermas also noticed that modernization processes encroach upon the life-world, which leads to pathologies in personalities, loss of meaning ('*Sinnverlust*') in culture, and anomalies of the social order. According to Habermas, the processes of modernity have led to the drifting apart of material (economic) and sym-bolic (cultural) reproduction. Changes in the public sphere ('*Öffentlichkeit*') are increasingly divorced from processes of social belonging and have instead become the playground of the collective agencies of markets and the bureaucratic state that affects trust-based interactions in the life-world. Habermas labeled this systematic encroachment of institutional agencies on the life-world as 'systems'. Over the course of civilization, these systems have differentiated themselves from the life-world and increasingly act as independ-ent forces that colonize the life-world according to their own strategic calculi, which are fueled primarily by the ambitions of power and capital (Fairtlough, 1991). Traditional worldviews that were based on social recognition have been replaced by a liberal system ethics, which addresses agents merely as competing individuals or targets for marketing. While Habermas – like Schütz – understood the life-world as the natural setting of communication that allows us to socially coordinate our intentions in an environment of mutual trust, he regarded these institutions and organizations as self-propelling agencies, the strategies and instruments of which encroach on the life-world. The life-world has therefore come to be seriously affected by the type of self-serving rea-soning that is pursued so aggressively by commercial or state bureaucracies. Their strategies increasingly delimit the fiduciary function of the life-world. In Habermas' philosophy, new means of communicative action are necessary in order to identify, understand, and correct these dominant processes of instrumental and strategic rationality (Fleming, 2000). Habermas' alternative is a 'communicative rationality' aimed at transparency in its argumentation, clarity regarding its intentions and claims, and which is focused on participa-tion. Habermas argued for an understanding-oriented action that is guided by communicative rationality and is transparent in its claims of truth, morality, and authenticity. Communicative action can be considered as a defense of the life-world which brings it to the public sphere with the aim of critically discussing the instrumental and strategic rationality that aims to take over the life-world in the pursuit of power and profit (Baxter, 1987). While in the philosophy of Arendt the work–life interface should be located in a 'forum of actions' and for Schütz it corresponds to 'a shared world of common sense', in Habermas' theory it should be understood as 'public discourse' and, as such, representing a regulative force that corresponds to Arendt's initial concern (Benhabib, 1997). Thus, both 'work' and 'life' are increasingly affected by the system pressures that undermine the resources of meaning in the life-world. This again demonstrates that work and life are not opposing concepts, with work being regarded as instrumental and life as meaningful. Instead, both represent domains in a life-world that is increasingly under threat from loss of meaning.

CONCLUSION

In conclusion, according to the visions of the philosophers presented here, I would argue that meaning in action is a primordial denominator in the work–life interface; that life-worlds offer a criterion for the alignment of labor and work in the work–life interface; and that systems act as its main threat, which subsequently calls for the political significance of action. What can we infer from these philosophical observations? Let me conclude by briefly formulating a number of points for discussion. The first note is that the work–life interface does not represent a conceptually valid distinction in research when taken as a balance of opposing domains. A more fruitful approach would be to view work and life as dimensions in a continuum of action. Second, a blind spot when studying work and life interfaces is the notion of meaning which acts as its common denominator. Psychological studies in particular could benefit from unraveling the cognitive styles according to which the manifold ways in which work and life experiences interact, by considering the rapidly evolving literature on meaning. Third, the whole idea of balancing work and life is based on the assumption of an individual agent who is in control of her work conditions. This disregards the political nature of work as a colonizing influence driven by power and a market that is increasingly eating away at the resources of meaning in the life-world. More studies that adopt this perspective would be invaluable. In this sense, the work–life interface is seriously out of balance.

REFERENCES

Arendt, H. (2018). *The Human Condition*. University of Chicago Press.

Barik, P., & Pandey, B. (2017). Review of Literature on Work Life Balance Policies and Practices. *Asian Journal of Research in Business Economics and Management*, *7*(6), 15–36.

Baxter, H. (1987). System and Life-World in Habermas's 'Theory of Communicative Action'. *Theory and Society*, *16*(1), 39–86.

Bello, Z., & Garba Ibrahim, T. (2020). Review of Work–Life Balance Theories. *GATR Global Journal of Business Social Sciences Review*, *8*, 217–227.

Benhabib, S. (1997). The Embattled Public Sphere: Hannah Arendt, Juergen Habermas and Beyond. *Theoria*, *90*, 1.

Chandra, V. (2012). Work–life Balance: Eastern and Western Perspectives. *International Journal of Human Resource Management*, *23*(5), 1040–1056.

Fairtlough, G. H. (1991). Habermas' Concept of Life-World? *Systems Practice*, *4*(6), 547–563.

Fleming, T. (2000). Habermas on Civil Society, Life-World and System: Unearthing the Social in Transformation Theory. *Teachers College Record*, www.tcrecord.org/Content.asp?ContentID=10877.

Freund, J. (1966). L'essence du politique. *Les Etudes Philosophiques*, *21*(3), 410–411.

Gambles, R., Lewis, S., & Rapoport, R. (2008). *The Myth of Work–Life Balance: The Challenge of Our Time for Men, Women and Societies*. Wiley.

Habermas, J. (1981). *Theorie des kommunikativen Handelns*. Suhrkamp Verlag.

Khateeb, F. R. (2021). Work Life Balance: A Review of Theories, Definitions and Policies. *CrossCultural Management Journal*, *1*, 27–55.

Lewis, S., Gambles, R., & Rapoport, R. (2007). The Constraints of a 'Work–Life Balance' Approach: An International Perspective. *International Journal of Human Resource Management*, *18*(3), 360–373.

Mathew, R., & Natarajan, P. (2014). Work Life Balance: A Short Review of the Theoretical and Contemporary Concepts. *Continental Journal of Social Sciences*, *7*(1), 1–24.

Moneir, S. (2014). Public and Private in the Anthropology of Hannah Arendt. *Agathos: An International Review of the Humanities and Social Sciences*, *2*(2), 146–150.

Rashmi, K., & Kataria, A. (2021). Work–Life Balance: A Systematic Literature Review and Bibliometric Analysis. *International Journal of Sociology and Social Policy*. https://doi.org/10.1108/ijssp-06-2021-0145..

Rasmussen, D. M. (1984). Explorations of the Lebenswelt: Reflections on Schutz and Habermas. *Human Studies*, *7*(2), 127–132.

Santiago-Delefosse, M., & Carral, M. d. R. (2015). The Life-World and Its Multiple Realities: Alfred Schütz's Contribution to the Understanding of the Experience of Illness. *Psychology*, *6*(10), 1265–1276.

Schütz, A. (1960). *Der sinnhafte Aufbau der sozialen Welt: eine Einleitung in die verstehende Soziologie*. Springer-Verlag.

Schütz, A., & Luckmann, T. (2017). *Strukturen der lebenswelt*. Utb.

Singh, S. P. (2013). Work-Life Balance: A Literature Review. *Global Journal of Commerce and Management Perspective*, *2*(3), 84–91.

Vaddiraju, A. (2020). Hannah Arendt and Modernity. *Indian Journal of Political Science*, *80*(4), 543–550.

Vargas, G. M. (2020). Alfred Schutz's Life-World and Intersubjectivity. *Open Journal of Social Sciences*, *8*(12), 417–425.

3. Work hard, play hard: on the reciprocity of work conditions and leisure lifestyles

Koen van Eijck

INTRODUCTION

The term *work–life balance* suggests a potential conflict, or imbalance, between work and 'life'. Too much work would seem to imply too little 'life' – the latter term representing everything we do when we are not engaged in paid work. In this chapter, I will argue that the notion of 'balance' in this context of paid work versus leisure and unpaid work is more complex than a straightforward metaphor of communicating vessels suggests. Drawing on the work of Gary Becker and Juliet Schor, I will explore how we can conceive of both work and leisure as products of households that make more or less predictable decisions regarding how to use the time and money required by both areas of life. This approach will be complemented by sociological work on the achievement of social status through consumption and how this causes people to live lives that are busier and more consumption-focused than scholars envisioned around 50 years ago. By addressing the issue of work–life balance from a more historical and sociological angle, I hope to show how the choices people make in this area are always socially embedded. This chapter thus seeks to clarify that apparently irrational decisions can be explained in large part by a combination of labor market dynamics, people's notions of social hierarchy, and an awareness of the fact that we tend to evaluate our own quality of life by comparing it to that of others, often in materialist terms.

THE CO-PRODUCTION OF WORK AND LEISURE

According to economist Gary Becker, what work and leisure have in common is that time and money are the crucial resources on which the realization of each rests. In his seminal 1965 article 'A theory of the allocation of time', Becker argued that households can be conceived of as small enterprises that produce both work and leisure through the input of time and money. What we call work–life balance today must be understood as the result of economic decisions based on considering the direct and indirect costs of leisure, which are determined, in turn, by the amounts of time and money people have at their disposal. This can be expressed in Becker's formula: $\Sigma p_i x_i + \Sigma T_c w = V + Tw$.

$\Sigma p_i x_i$ represents the sum of all 'leisure commodities' produced (x_i) multiplied by the cost of each of those commodies (p_i), where leisure commodities refer not so much to goods that might be used for leisure but to the benefits or enjoyment that those commodities bring. Thus, $\Sigma p_i x_i$ are the direct costs of leisure. The indirect costs are the earnings forgone, which is the sum of the time spent on consumption (T_c) multiplied by the (forgone) hourly wage (w). The sum of these direct and indirect costs of leisure should not exceed the maximum wage that could be earned if all available time was spent on work (Tw) plus money that comes from sources other than paid work (V). Both Tw and $T_c w$ are notional sums of money, but they do play a role in decision-making when it comes to work–life balance.

Becker's work helps us make sense of what happens when hourly wages or working hours change. If people earn more, Tw grows, which increases the financial resources available to spend on leisure activities. But if we also take the indirect costs of leisure into account, we can see that free time ($T_c w$) also becomes more costly in the sense that an extra hour of work will bring in more money and so each extra hour of leisure will therefore cost more in foregone earnings. According to Becker, this shifts the balance of the different inputs that people employ to create leisure commodities, or leisure activities.

A few decades ago, social scientists envisioned the advent of a leisure society in which growing incomes and the automization of production processes would allow people to work fewer hours and still lead comfortable lives (e.g., Dumazedier, 1974; Keynes, 1972 [1932]; Veal, 2019). However, Becker argued that increasing wages would actually make each leisure hour more expensive, due to rising indirect costs. This would alter the optimal ratio of the investment of money versus time in the pursuit of leisure commodities, because an increase in disposable income implies that leisure time becomes more costly, as both Tw and $T_c w$ increase along with w. As a result, leisure would have to yield more pleasure through the input of more money or goods per unit of leisure time in order to compete with the benefits of working.

The economic logic of Becker which underlies the choice between work or leisure may explain why dreams of the 'leisure society of the future' have not materialized, even though the underlying processes of growing productivity and increasing wealth have occurred as anticipated. Also, the rise of post-materialism (Inglehart, 2008) is limited largely to political values, while private materialism is actually on the rise (Strenze, 2021). Strenze has operationalized private materialism as 'work values', seeing that workers increasingly value income and job security over aspects such as free time or opportunities for self-development. The rise in political – or public – post-materialism has not led to a widespread shift towards meaningful experiences rather than material consumption. Keynes (1972 [1932], p. 365) more or less foresaw this almost a century ago. In 'Economic possibilities for our grandchildren', he drew a distinction between absolute and relative needs, arguing that the 'Needs of the second class, those which satisfy the desire for superiority, may indeed be insatiable; for the higher the general level, the higher still are they'.

THE WORK-AND-SPEND CYCLE

Juliet Schor (1991) came up with the concept of the work-and-spend cycle to explain why working hours have not declined. The cycle has two main drivers. The first is the fact that it is more efficient for organizations that need to increase their output to have their current workers work longer hours than to hire new ones. This means that workers, even if they would prefer more leisure time, are far more likely to work longer hours or do overtime – which in effect equals less leisure time and more money. Second, while they may originally have hoped otherwise, consumerism and the desire to 'keep up with the Joneses' make people spend that extra money and they quickly grow used to the more opulent lifestyle that it affords them, making it harder to go back to living on less money. Consumer expectations rise with income, making consumers insatiable, as Keynes also argued (1972 [1932]). A few decades before Keynes, sociologist Thorstein Veblen (1970 [1899]) had already identified this insatiability and attributed it to a phenomenon he labeled 'invidious comparison'. People's social standing is based on positional goods, meaning that if everyone increases their level of material consumption by earning and spending more, 'keeping up' simply means moving up along with everybody else in what is essentially a rat race or, in Schor's terms, a work-and-spend cycle that is difficult to escape.

According to Schor, the work-and-spend cycle is so powerful because corporate interests enable higher levels of consumption among employees and both parties ultimately believe that they benefit from the situation. While Keynes' distinction between absolute or primary needs versus relative or secondary needs is highly contentious (e.g., Baudrillard, 1969), it is true that insatiable consumer 'needs' are, in part, responsible for the fact that our work–life balance has not shifted to a more leisurely mode. For Baudrillard (1970), the object of consumption is a sign object, which means that it functions according to the logics of difference and status. He believes Veblen understood this better than any other consumption scholar at that time, quoting him approvingly as saying:

> The end of acquisition is conveniently held to be the consumption of the goods accumulated ... but it is only in a sense far removed from its native meaning that consumption of goods can be said to afford the incentive from which accumulation proceeds ... Possession of wealth confers honors: it is an invidious distinction. (Veblen, cited in Baudrillard, 1969, p. 68)

Reflecting both people's tastes and resources, we can argue with Bourdieu (1984) that consumption is a weapon in the battle for social status. And since status is always defined relative to certain reference groups, it turns out that the amount of money that people with comparable working conditions manage to save is negatively affected by the size of the gap between their own financial status and that of their reference group more than by any other factor (Schor, 1998, pp. 76–77). Another indication of the huge role played by the pursuit of status is the finding, in the same analysis, that higher education levels also lead to reduced saving and higher spending. People with a higher level of education tend to be more status-oriented and thus more eager to keep up with the relatively affluent groups to which they (aspire to) belong. This makes them less likely to achieve a satisfying work–life balance than those with fewer material ambitions, since more of their time will be devoted to making money or working hard to enhance their chance of promotion. At the same time, however, we should not forget that the less well-educated are increasingly at risk of having to work long hours or hold multiple jobs just to make ends meet.

Education is the main route to occupational success these days, and the link between class or status on the one hand and leisure time on the other has changed dramatically. Veblen wrote about the very wealthy as a 'leisure class' of people who typically owed their status to inherited assets that were largely maintained by their subordinates. Today however, an abundance of leisure time is no longer associated with the upper classes. Instead, it makes more sense to 'accord a similar degree of prestige to the relatively long hours of work which are, in the contemporary developed economies, a characteristic of the best-placed individuals in the society. Busyness becomes a symbolic marker of status' (Sullivan & Gershuny, 2018, p. 25). Clearly, Veblen has been turned upside down. In our information society, material success is more often determined by one's education (embodied cultural capital) than by inherited economic capital. This cultural capital (e.g., knowledge and expertise) does not work *for* you like farm laborers did for Veblen's leisure class. Rather, high-status people need to engage in intellectual or creative work themselves as it relies on knowledge and skills that only they can convert into economic capital by engaging in work. The more rare or remarkable one's expertise is, the more demand there will be for it and hence the busier one will be.

CONSUMERISM LEGITIMATED BY NEW ASPIRATIONS

It is not just that today's biggest spenders are likely to be very busy, as explained by both Becker and Schor; we can see that the nature of what is considered *prestigious* consumption has changed, too. Now that education has become a more typical route to success than inheriting economic capital, consumption should not only reflect wealth, but also a sense of sophistication and a certain set of typically cosmopolitan, liberal values (DellaPosta et al., 2015). The lifestyles of today's elites should not suggest that life is all about making lots of money, as this does not sit well with the cultural capital and refined tastes that today's upper classes wish to emanate. This does not detract from the importance of consumption, but just changes the types of goods and motivations that are deemed appropriate to the consumer lifestyle that one wishes to emulate. In the words of David Brooks (2000, p. 49): 'In the 1950s the best kind of money to have was inherited money. Today in the Bobo establishment the best kind of money is incidental money. It's the kind of money you just happen to earn while you are pursuing your creative vision.'

Brooks introduced the term 'Bobo' as an abbreviation for bourgeois-bohemian; a historically unlikely combination of a level of material well-being traditionally associated with bourgeois conservatism with a bohemian inclination for creativity and individuality that fits well with the higher educational levels typically achieved by today's liberal upper-middle classes. While for scholars such as Bourdieu the economic and the cultural elites were two separate class fractions with opposing tastes and worldviews, Brooks' 'Bobos' manage to reconcile those competing values by creating 'a way of living that lets you be an affluent success and at the same time a free-spirit rebel' (Brooks, 2000, p. 42). They are the educated class that make plenty of money due to their higher education and turn their consumption habits into an expression of creativity combined with living comfortably. To make that work, the comforts they afford themselves are not overly ostentatious – not multiple luxury cars or giant flatscreen televisions, but rather expensive kitchen appliances that support their elaborate yet healthy cooking, professional hiking gear for their adventurous holidays in nature, or just expensive, sustainable, or exotic versions of everyday consumer goods to demonstrate their moral righteousness.

Even if today's elite consumers have less gaudy tastes than in Veblen's days, the invidious comparison is still very much out there. However, the logic of distinction necessitates the ongoing adaptation of consumption norms, which in today's information society tend towards increasing subtlety and attempts to reconcile consumerism with the moral and intellectual ideals of the liberal educated class. While Brooks shows how this reconciliation is possible and appealing to many, Currid-Halkett (2017) has further updated his insights by introducing the terms 'aspirational class', 'inconspicuous consumption', and 'conspicuous production'. She shows how the contemporary values of the educated – or aspirational – classes, such as sustainability, authenticity, and support for fairtrade practices, push them towards products that are vegan, organic, artisanal, locally and sustainably produced, or hand-made (for example). But their aspirations extend into the next generation as well, as they are also very likely to invest in a university education for their children, insurance, and so on. By coining the term 'inconspicuous consumption', Currid-Halkett (2017) indicates that the aspirational class does not flaunt flashy and expensive goods, but rather the 'right' (and typically more expensive) versions of the things that everybody consumes, such as coffee (fairtrade), beer (craft), children's clothing (organically produced fabrics), and make-up (no animal-testing). No conspicuous brand labels are involved; rather, the signals are subtle and only picked up by those familiar with such products. Often these products are valued for the sustainable or artisanal way in which they were *produced*, hence the term 'conspicuous production'. This type of consumption is perhaps no less materialist than the type that Veblen wrote about, but it definitely requires more thinking and stylistic nuance, which probably makes 'keeping up with the Joneses' more of a challenge than ever. Taking the moral high road in consumer society is very expensive. Spending power therefore remains important even in the latest, subtler variants of the status game which incorporate post-materialist values such as sustainability and fair trade. It is therefore hard to believe that the desire to earn more money, and the consequent need to work long hours rather than investing time in one's leisure aspirations, will diminish any time soon. The promised 'leisure society' remains elusive and, at least for the upper classes that have led the way towards what many have come to consider 'the good life', what we have instead is: work hard, play hard.

This does not seem to bode well for finding an agreeable work–life balance. Rather than being communicating vessels, in a sense work and leisure, including family life, are both putting people increasingly under pressure, particularly among the upper-middle classes On the one hand, one needs to work hard to be able to live the life that one aspires to. On the other hand, it is becoming increasingly important to spend the money earned on the 'right' objects, outfits, services, and tuition fees in order to keep up with one's reference group. There is a lot of pressure to 'do the right thing', especially among those who, in principle, could comfortably take a step back financially and enjoy a more relaxing work–life balance. The less well-educated will have a more practical, functional approach to consumption, but they are of course more likely to struggle to make ends meet, and this is not conducive to a comfortable work–life balance either. With income inequality rising and a shrinking middle class in most Western countries (Vaughan-Whitehead, 2016), we are likely to see the work–life balance remain under pressure at both ends of the socio-economic spectrum.

REFERENCES

Baudrillard, J. (1969). The ideological genesis of needs. In J.B. Schor & D. Holt (Eds), *The Consumer Society Reader* (pp. 57–80). New York: The New Press.

Baudrillard, J. (1970). *The Consumer Society: Myths and Structures*. London: Sage.

Becker, G.S. (1965). A theory of the allocation of time. *The Economic Journal*, 75(299), 493–517.

Bourdieu, P. (1984). *Distinction: A Social Critique of the Judgment of Taste*. London: Routledge.

Brooks, D. (2000). *Bobos in Paradise: The New Upper Class and How They Got There*. New York: Simon & Schuster.

Currid-Halkett, E. (2017). *The Sum of Small Things: A Theory of the Aspirational Class*. Princeton, NJ: Princeton University Press.

DellaPosta, D., Shi, Y., & Macy, M. (2015). Why do liberals drink lattes? *American Journal of Sociology*, 120(5), 1473–1511.

Dumazedier, J. (1974). *Sociology of Leisure*. Amsterdam: Elsevier.

Inglehart, R.F. (2008). Changing values among Western publics from 1970 to 2006. *West European Politics*, 31(1–2), 130–146.

Keynes, J.M. (1972 [1932]). Economic possibilities for our grandchildren. In *Essays in Persuasion* (pp. 358–373). New York: Harcourt, Brace & Company.

Schor, J.B. (1991). *The Overworked American: The Unexpected Decline of Leisure*. New York: Basic Books.

Schor, J. (1998). *The Overspent American: Upscaling, Downshifting, and the New Consumer*. New York: Basic Books.

Strenze, T. (2021). Value change in the Western world: The rise of materialism, post-materialism, or both? *International Review of Sociology*, 31(3), 536–553.

Sullivan, O., & Gershuny, J. (2018). Speed-up society? Evidence from the UK 2000 and 2015 time use diary survey. *Sociology*, 52(1), 20–38.

Vaughan-Whitehead, D. (2016). *Europe's Disappearing Middle Class? Evidence from the World of Work*. Cheltenham, UK and Northampton, MA, USA: Edward Elgar Publishing.

Veal, A.J. (2019). *Whatever Happened to the Leisure Society?* London: Routledge.

Veblen, T. (1970 [1899]). *The Theory of the Leisure Class*. London: Allen and Unwin.

4. Volunteering and work–life balance

Jessica Sowa

INTRODUCTION

For many people across the world, paid work – their jobs and their professional identities – can lead to many kinds of stress (Ganster & Rosen, 2013). Some of this stress may come from the tension between work and non-work responsibilities, such as families, partners, and outside commitments – work–family and/or work–life conflict (Byron, 2005; Skinner & Pocock, 2008). To reduce this conflict, scholars and practitioners have been advocating for an increased focus on work–life balance, which includes active engagement in both work and life roles (e.g., non-work roles), and reducing conflict between these different roles (Sirgy & Lee, 2018). There are many personal characteristics, techniques, and organizational practices that can act as antecedents to or influence work–life balance (Sirgy & Lee, 2018), including wellness and stress management techniques, human resource management practices, boundary management between different roles, and the cultivation of psychosocial resources. These are defined as "individual differences and social relationships that have beneficial effects on mental and physical health outcomes" (Taylor & Broffman, 2011, p. 1).

One psychosocial resource that can have a positive impact on work and life is volunteering (Güntert et al., 2022). Wilson (2000, p. 215) defines volunteering as "any activity in which time is given freely to benefit another person, group, or organization." Volunteering is differentiated from other forms of helping behavior, such as caring for a family member, in that no obligation is implied in volunteering. The time is given freely, and this may be done in formal or informal ways. The International Labour Organization (2022) compiles studies from across the world on volunteering, and annual volunteering rates are 33.4 percent in Australia, 23.3 percent in France, 28.6 percent in Germany, 12 percent in Italy, and 30 percent in the United States. In the United States, in the 2019 Current Population Survey, in particular the section on Civic Engagement and Volunteering Supplement, 77.9 million people reported volunteering for an estimated 5.8 billion hours, implying an economic value of 147 billion dollars (AmeriCorps, Office of Research & Evaluation, 2021).

Clearly, volunteering is a big part of people's lives, which leads us to the question of how volunteering relates to work–life balance. What are the benefits of volunteering and how does it contribute to work–life balance?

Drawing on research from non-profit studies, management, and psychology, this chapter explores volunteering as a resource for or antecedent to work–life balance, considering the benefits and risks of volunteering as a specific work–life balance strategy. While volunteering has many benefits for individual well-being that contribute to work–life balance, volunteering as a specific resource with which to address work–life balance requires attention to boundary setting, as it can become a third role that needs to be balanced alongside work and family responsibilities (Cruz & Meisenbach, 2018).

VOLUNTEERING: BENEFITS AND COSTS FOR WORK–LIFE BALANCE

Why would volunteering be a resource or strategy that could enhance work–life balance? Volunteering can be seen as a quality-of-life enhancement strategy (Morawski et al., 2022). While volunteering helps individuals look beyond themselves and their own needs, it also promotes positive prosocial feelings and is associated with numerous positive outcomes. Specifically, volunteering has been found to have many benefits for individuals, including self-reported health levels (Piliavin & Siegl, 2007) and psychological well-being (Heo et al., 2016). Volunteering helps people feel that they matter because they receive positive feelings from giving time to help others and seeing the benefit of that work. Volunteering has also been shown to reduce depression and improve self-esteem and sense of overall satisfaction with life (Musick & Wilson, 2003). In addition, volunteering creates a sense of belonging that connects individuals to their communities, thus reducing loneliness and the associated negative effects of isolation (Warburton, 2006). As a work–life balance strategy, volunteering can provide opportunities to recover from work stress or act as a buffer to that stress, and it can provide opportunities to develop or access additional personal resources such as social support, self-confidence, and self-efficacy that can help balance different work and life roles, hopefully achieving better balance (Güntert et al., 2022).

While not all volunteering leads to positive outcomes (one randomized control study by Whillans et al. (2016) found no impact of service-learning volunteering, volunteering experiences offered through an educational institution), there is a large body of knowledge that shows the positive impact that volunteering can have on individuals, their health, and overall well-being (Güntert et al., 2022). As such, volunteering is often recommended as a strategy for improving work–life balance. Work–life balance is enhanced when individuals have the personal resources to manage their stress in the workplace; when they can keep their work in perspective and are able to work healthily and happily (Brough et al., 2020). Therefore, since volunteering is an activity that promotes health and well-being in individuals, this health and well-being should help individuals to balance their work and life needs.

However, if an individual is thinking about volunteering as a life enrichment strategy, to improve the balance between paid employment and the rest of their life, it is important to reflect on what kinds of volunteering opportunities will serve the individual and foster the desired work–life balance (Güntert et al., 2022). What is involved in the volunteering (see Maki & Snyder, 2017) and how much time is involved? Is the volunteering a brief episodic commitment or does it require regular commitment over time (Cnaan et al., 2022)? A regular commitment could be required in a leadership role, such as serving on a non-profit board of directors or leading a church in a volunteer role. The same may be true of a service delivery role, such as a youth mentor or a volunteer firefighter (Henderson & Sowa, 2018).

While volunteering can be a way to improve work–life balance and have other positive outcomes, this depends on the type and intensity of volunteering. If volunteering creates additional stress or pressure on the individual, it is less effective as a strategy for maintaining or enhancing work–life balance. An initial consideration should be what individuals are looking to get out of the volunteering experience. Perhaps an individual feels like they are not achieving sufficient impact in their work and feel frustrated or stymied. In such cases, an individual may look for volunteering opportunities that allow them to bring their paid work experience to others for the public good (such as a lawyer or accountant giving their services pro bono to a non-profit organization). Volunteering may also offer people the opportunity to develop new skills, or to explore changes in their paid employment without having to leave their current job.

For some, volunteering may be an opportunity to do something completely different to what they do at work, thus creating a boundary between their roles in their paid work and their volunteer work. These volunteering experiences could involve activities that do not require them to use their professional skills – for example, a doctor who volunteers weekly at a food bank, unloading donations and stocking shelves. Such volunteering may be part of work–life balance pursuits, as they allow individuals to "unplug" from the stress of their work and also provide satisfaction because the activity contributes to a greater public or social good. Or these could be volunteer opportunities that allow one to connect with larger questions of meaning, such as volunteering for religious organizations. This is an avenue that many individuals pursue when seeking to find connections through volunteering (Isham et al., 2006). Some people volunteer to foster relationships with others, build a community, and connect with others. For those individuals, if they are volunteering to balance work with the rest of their life, they may look for volunteering opportunities that involve personal interaction, such as helping environmental clean-up activities, fundraising for a non-profit, or participating in races or other physical events to raise money for charities.

If we view volunteering as a work–life balance strategy, careful consideration must be given to volunteering opportunities that involve repeated interaction. Einolf and Yung (2008) define a super-volunteer as "someone who volunteers 10 or more hours per week and who contributes a qualitatively higher type of service, often in a leadership or skilled professional capacity" (p. 790). In their study, the majority of these volunteers are older and retired, but there are many volunteering roles, such as volunteer firefighters, emergency service workers, and youth mentors, that involve a commitment to training (one-off or repeated) and imply an obligation between the volunteer and the organization and individuals they are serving. These forms of commitment cannot be abandoned easily without real costs, and thus need to be considered carefully.

Adding a third role to the balance (between work and family) could be a complication rather than a work–life coping strategy for some (Cruz & Meisenback, 2018). For those who choose to be super-volunteers, these positions can almost begin to become part-time, unpaid jobs. While they may provide meaning, connection, and other beneficial outcomes, they need to be considered carefully if pursued as a work–life balance strategy as they could actually have an adverse effect.

CONCLUSION

As people look for strategies to strike a balance between the responsibilities of their paid employment and outside obligations, volunteering is a strategy that can offer benefits. Workplaces have begun to offer volunteering opportunities as part of work–life balance initiatives, but there are numerous opportunities for individuals to get involved in their communities to give themselves meaningful outlets outside of their work. While volunteering has many benefits, both for volunteers and those they help, it is important to reflect on what one wants to accomplish by volunteering as part of a work–life balance strategy and to choose opportunities accordingly. In addition, volunteers who regularly give significant time each week need to be attentive to the boundaries between their roles at work, at home, and in the volunteer organization, to ensure that they do not experience role conflict that would reduce the possible benefits of volunteering.

IMPLICATIONS FOR RESEARCH AND PRACTICE

Volunteering opportunities may be pursued by individuals in their personal lives, but many workplaces also offer volunteer opportunities, with research finding positive outcomes for individuals in their role as employees, and for the organization (Cao et al., 2021; Longenecker et al., 2013). Workplace volunteering programs are "formal and informal policies and practices that encourage and help employees to volunteer in community service activities" (Tschirhart, 2005, p. 16). Workplace volunteering programs can involve individual activities, teams, or ongoing projects (Tschirhart, 2005), such as an organization "adopting" a classroom at a local school and interacting with that classroom through volunteer work over the course of a year. Workplace volunteer programs can also involve giving employees a certain amount of time off for volunteering per year, with employees still being paid by the organization but allowed to engage in volunteering activities (Booth et al., 2009). While formal workplace volunteering programs may be one way to encourage this behavior, certain pitfalls can arise if the programs are not designed effectively (Rodell, 2021). Volunteering programs should not become an additional obligation placed on employees, and employees should not be made to feel they have to participate due to social pressure. For workplace volunteering programs to be an effective part of work–life balance initiatives, they should be truly voluntary, regardless of the positive impact for the organization. Understanding how much people volunteer through their workplace or their communities as a specific work–life balance practice would allow for scholars and practitioners to gather more data on the prevalence and efficacy of this strategy for the future.

REFERENCES

AmeriCorps, Office of Research and Evaluation. (2021). *Key findings from the 2019 Current Population Survey: Civic engagement and volunteering supplement*, by Laura Hanson Schlachter. Washington, DC: AmeriCorps.

Booth, J. E., Park, K. W., & Glomb, T. M. (2009). Employer-supported volunteering benefits: Gift exchange among employers, employees, and volunteer organizations. *Human Resource Management, 48*(2), 227–249.

Brough, P., Timms, C., Chan, X. W., Hawkes, A., & Rasmussen, L. (2020). Work–life balance: Definitions, causes, and consequences. In T. Theorell (ed.) *Handbook of socioeconomic determinants of occupational health: From macro-level to micro-level evidence* (pp. 473–487). Springer.

Byron, K. (2005). A meta-analytic review of work–family conflict and its antecedents. *Journal of Vocational Behavior, 67*(2), 169–198.

Cao, Y., Pil, F. K., & Lawson, B. (2021). Signaling and social influence: The impact of corporate volunteer programs. *Journal of Managerial Psychology, 36*(2), 183–196.

Cnaan, R. A., Meijs, L., Brudney, J. L., Hersberger-Langloh, S., Okada, A., & Abu-Rumman, S. (2022). You thought that this would be easy? Seeking an understanding of episodic volunteering. *VOLUNTAS: International Journal of Voluntary and Nonprofit Organizations*, *33*(3), 415–427.

Cruz, D., & Meisenbach, R. (2018). Expanding role boundary management theory: How volunteering highlights contextually shifting strategies and collapsing work–life role boundaries. *Human Relations*, *71*(2), 182–205.

Einolf, C. J., & Yung, C. (2018). Super-volunteers: Who are they and how do we get one? *Nonprofit and Voluntary Sector Quarterly*, *47*(4), 789–812.

Ganster, D. C., & Rosen, C. C. (2013). Work stress and employee health: A multidisciplinary review. *Journal of Management*, *39*(5), 1085–1122.

Güntert, S. T., Wehner, T., & Mieg, H. A. (2022). *Organizational, motivational, and cultural contexts of volunteering: The European view*. Springer Nature.

Heo, J., Chun, S., Lee, S., & Kim, J. (2016). Life satisfaction and psychological well-being of older adults with cancer experience: The role of optimism and volunteering. *International Journal of Aging and Human Development*, *83*(3), 274–289.

International Labour Organization. (2022). ILOSTAT, statistics on volunteer work. https://ilostat.ilo.org/topics/volunteer-work/#[Accessed 15 September 2022].

Isham, J., Kolodinsky, J., & Kimberly, G. (2006). The effects of volunteering for nonprofit organizations on social capital formation: Evidence from a statewide survey. *Nonprofit and Voluntary Sector Quarterly*, *35*(3), 367–383.

Longenecker, C. O., Beard, S., & Scazzero, J. A. (2013). What about the workers? The workforce benefits of corporate volunteer programs. *Development and Learning in Organizations: An International Journal*, *27*(1), 9–12.

Maki, A., & Snyder, M. (2017). Investigating similarities and differences between volunteer behaviors: Development of a volunteer interest typology. *Nonprofit and Voluntary Sector Quarterly*, *46*(1), 5–28.

Morawski, L., Okulicz-Kozaryn, A., & Strzelecka, M. (2022). Elderly volunteering in Europe: The relationship between volunteering and quality of life depends on volunteering rates. *VOLUNTAS: International Journal of Voluntary and Nonprofit Organizations*, *33*, 256–268.

Musick, M. A., & Wilson, J. (2003). Volunteering and depression: The role of psychological and social resources in different age groups. *Social Science & Medicine*, *56*(2), 259–269.

Piliavin, J. A., & Siegl, E. (2007). Health benefits of volunteering in the Wisconsin longitudinal study. *Journal of Health and Social Behavior*, *48*(4), 450–464.

Rodell, J. (2021). Volunteer programs that employees can get excited about. *Harvard Business Review*, January–February. https://hbr.org/2021/01/volunteer-programs-that-employees-can-get-excited-about [Accessed 15 September 2022].

Sirgy, M. J., & Lee, D. J. (2018). Work–life balance: An integrative review. *Applied Research in Quality of Life*, *13*, 229–254.

Skinner, N., & Pocock, B. (2008). Work–life conflict: Is work time or work overload more important? *Asia Pacific Journal of Human Resources*, *46*(3), 303–315.

Taylor, S. E., & Broffman, J. I. (2011). Psychosocial resources: Functions, origins, and links to mental and physical health. *Advances in Experimental Social Psychology*, 44, 1–57.

Tschirhart, M. (2005). Employee volunteer programs. In J. L. Brudney (ed.) *Emerging areas of volunteering*. ARNOVA Occasional Paper Series, 1(2).

Warburton, J. (2006). Volunteering in later life: Is it good for your health? *Voluntary Action*, *8*(2), 3–15.

Whillans, A. V., Seider, S. C., Chen, L., Dwyer, R. J., Novick, S., Gramigna, K. J., Mitchell, B. A., Savalei, V., Dickerson, S. S., & Dunn, E. W. (2016). Does volunteering improve well-being? *Comprehensive Results in Social Psychology*, *1*(1–3), 35–50.

Wilson, J. (2000). Volunteering. *Annual Review of Sociology*, *26*, 215–240.

5. The impact of life and career stages on workers' career sustainability

Beatrice van der Heijden, Ans De Vos, and Jos Akkermans

CONCEPTUALIZING SUSTAINABLE CAREERS

A career is defined as the sequence of work experiences that evolves over an individual's life course (Arthur et al., 1989). There are two central elements in this definition: "work" and "time." More recently, Van der Heijden and De Vos (2015, p. 7) have introduced the concept of *sustainable careers*, defined as "the sequence of an individual's different career experiences, reflected through a variety of patterns of continuity over time, crossing several social spaces, and characterized by individual agency, herewith providing meaning to the individual."

In this chapter, we explore the possible impact of life and career stages on workers' career sustainability and work–life balance by taking a whole-life perspective (Hirschi et al., 2020; Van der Heijden et al., 2020). This means considering the intersection of work and non-work roles and interaction with surrounding stakeholders, thereby incorporating the person into their working and private life. Borrowing from the conservation of resources theory (Hobfoll, 1989; Hobfoll et al., 2018) and self-determination theory (Deci et al., 2017; Ryan & Deci, 2000), we argue that in order to have a sustainable career, people need to interact with surrounding stakeholders to fulfill their psychological needs (i.e. autonomy, competence, and relatedness), in order to bring about resource gains that form a pattern in which job and home resources are associated with other resources (i.e. resource caravans; Westman et al., 2004).

In addition, from selection optimization and compensation theory (Baltes et al., 1999) and socio-emotional selectivity theory (Carstensen, 1995, 2006), we know that individuals' goals change over their life span. First, selection optimization and compensation theory (Baltes et al., 1999) states that people are inclined to maximize the gains and minimize the losses they experience over time by using various strategies. Analogously, socio-emotional selectivity theory (Carstensen, 1995, 2006) proposes that changes in the perception of time that are related to age result in changes in social goals or motives, thereby shifting the motive for social interaction from gaining resources (i.e. instrumental, such as a promotion at work) towards affective rewards (i.e. emotional, such as receiving a volunteer award) and strengthening one's identity. Our whole-life perspective enables us to better understand individual perceptions about sustainable (and unsustainable) life and career phases and their causes, in both one's working life and private life. We differentiate between three age groups when discussing the impact of individual and organizational determinants on one's happiness, health, and productivity, the core indicators of career sustainability (De Vos et al., 2020; Van der Heijden, 2005). We see these three indicators both as key to the worker's prosperity and as the building blocks for the welfare of relatives and peers, the employer, and society.

Based on the job demands-resources model (Bakker et al., 2023; Demerouti et al., 2001) (an occupational stress model which suggests that strain is a response to an imbalance between demands put on the individual and the resources that they have to cope with these demands), Demerouti et al. (2012) differentiate between job demands and resources on the one hand and home demands and resources on the other, and posit that these are to some extent determined by the life and career stages that people go through. We build on this theoretical framework to disentangle the challenges and opportunities in both one's working life and private life that may impact career sustainability and work–life balance. We will explain our line of reasoning more clearly by discussing some key examples of the challenges and opportunities often encountered by starters (20–34 years), middle-aged workers (35–49 years), and seniors (≥ 50 years old) (Van der Heijden, 2000).

At the same time, we want to stress that we view sustainable careers and work–life balance through a non-normative lens (Van der Heijden, 2005). This perspective means that perceptions about positive and negative experiences in one's working and private life are idiosyncratic to the person, and dynamic across their particular life and career stages (De Vos et al., 2020; Van der Heijden & De Vos, 2015). In other words, people may take very different views on what constitutes a sustainable career and an ideal work–life balance, and it is the individual's perceptions about the interplay between one's working life and private life that determine their happiness, health, and productivity (i.e. their career sustainability) and their work–life balance. These views can also change over time. In addition, people may react very differently to career shocks (i.e. disruptive and extraordinary events that are, at least to some degree, caused by factors outside the individual's control and that trigger a deliberate thought process concerning one's career; Akkermans et al., 2018), depending on their personality, career competencies, resilience, and agentic orientation, to mention but a few (De Vos et al., 2020).

In the next section, we will further illustrate our whole-life perspective on sustainable careers and work–life balance using real-life examples. Depending on a person's life and career stage, different actors and events can affect career sustainability and work–life balance, and generally life and career stages are defined by age. As such, aging, in both one's working life and private life, entails a multi-dimensional process that comprises changes in a person's psychological, physical, social, as well as societal functioning over time (Sterns & Doverspike, 1989). The exemplary conceptualization of age, including subjective measures, developed by Sterns and Doverspike (1989) helps us to better understand age-related changes over time as a result of factors such as health, career stage, and family status, and to identify the potential implications for career sustainability. Our non-normative approach to sustainable careers and work–life balance (Van der Heijden, 2005) helps to disentangle specific challenges and hindrances, and in some cases even the career shocks that starters, middle-aged, and seniors may have to deal with. It can also be used as a starting point for in-depth discussions between all the stakeholders involved.

DEMANDS AND RESOURCES AMONG STARTERS

Generally speaking, starters are subject to high job demands and high home demands, and often lack resources in both domains (Demerouti et al., 2012). They need to find a job and invest time in the socialization process in the organization they are employed by. They also need to invest considerable energy in developing their knowledge and skills. Indeed, Akkermans et al. (2013) provided empirical support for the importance of career competencies for starters with regard to their perception of their own employability.

Once employed, starters in the labor market see their earnings increase, have access to intra- and extra-organizational networks, and may benefit from social support as they become better acquainted with other members of their working team, both their direct supervisor and close colleagues, thereby enhancing their productivity. As regards one's private life, a stable and meaningful relationship with a partner is a home resource that can help starters to cope with career shocks, such as a situation in which an employment contract is not extended, thereby protecting their happiness and health. Simultaneously, if the employee has children, home demands will increase and remain high until the youngest child reaches school age. This may have an impact on productivity.

However, it is important to note that workers usually enjoy having children, which can add resources that contribute to one's happiness and health. Conversely, workers without children may experience impediments in career sustainability and work–life balance, such as greater difficulty managing the work–non-work boundary, because it is more likely that work responsibilities may intrude into their private time. At the same time, many in this group benefit from the fact that they have more freedom in choosing how to spend their time and they have fewer family responsibilities.

DEMANDS AND RESOURCES AMONG MIDDLE-AGED WORKERS

In the mid-life phase, workers are generally exposed to higher job demands and average home demands, and also have high resources in both the work and non-work domains (Demerouti et al., 2012). To reach the level of expert at work, people need to invest considerable time and effort in building up their competencies. At the same time, many of them have more flexibility and autonomy to shape their careers than starters. One might be inclined to conclude that the position of middle-aged workers is more favorable than that of starters or seniors in the labor market.

However, it is also important to note that in the event of a serious life event (i.e. career shock), such as needing to care for elderly or sick parents or bereavement, career sustainability and work–life balance may be jeopardized. Even in cases where individuals in the mid-career stage no longer have children of preschool or primary school age, they might still need careful consideration by their employer in order to combine work and non-work roles and achieve the required productivity at work while also maintaining their happiness and health.

At the same time, from the theories of selection optimization and compensation (Baltes et al., 1999) and socio-emotional selectivity (Carstensen, 1995, 2006), we know that people's goals change over their life span. To illustrate, for many middle-aged workers, non-work roles become more valuable over time, such as volunteer work, community activism, and church and family-focused activities. Changes in what is perceived as meaningful in mid-life, in this case built around an increased focus on generativity, imply that motivational factors need to be taken into account when understanding what makes people happy, healthy, and productive across their life span.

DEMANDS AND RESOURCES AMONG SENIORS

In late adulthood, people generally have average job and home demands and high job and home resources (Demerouti et al., 2012). According to the life-span theories of selection optimization and compensation (Baltes et al., 1999) and socio-emotional selectivity theory (Carstensen, 1995, 2006), because of selectivity in choosing their career steps or because of their greater ability to choose because of their seniority, older workers are more likely to have shaped careers with a better balance between demands and resources, which will probably help them safeguard their productivity. At the same time, they are also likely to be more emotionally mature, to have more wisdom, and to have developed more effective coping strategies in relation to both work and private life, which are likely to improve their happiness and health.

Moreover, people's goals tend to change across their life span due to a changing future time perspective (Lang & Carstensen, 2002), and this may make senior workers more concerned with preserving certain resources (e.g. protecting their current job) as they become less inclined to invest in new resources (e.g. creating new career opportunities). Similarly, seniors may want to spend more time with children or grandchildren, travelling or pursuing other leisure activities, and they may prioritize family and private life activities over work. In particular, senior workers tend to attach greater value to high-quality social-emotional interactions than to developing a large social network, and therefore will typically invest more in high-quality relationships.

Notwithstanding the wide variety among individuals, which increases with age because everybody takes a unique path through life, seniors often lack career development support from their supervisor due to age-related stereotyping (Van der Heijden, 2005). However, understanding what motivates these workers is vital in order to sustain their happiness, health, and productivity. In general, older workers want to do meaningful work but are also striving for a better balance between demands and resources, and expect a reduction in both job and family role responsibilities (Demerouti et al., 2001). If the latter is not forthcoming, or if a serious life event (such as losing a partner) or other career shock (such as a major restructuring that threatens their employment) occurs, they may experience a decrease in career sustainability, reflected in lower happiness, health, and productivity. A (temporary) decrease in career sustainability is quite conceivable for many seniors, as more of them have one or more elderly parent(s) who need care. Due to an increased life expectancy and later retirement ages, this situation is unlikely to change in the foreseeable future. Figure 5.1 summarizes the main resources and demands among starters, middle-aged, and seniors.

IMPLICATIONS FOR RESEARCH AND PRACTICES

The age at which people start raising a family varies considerably these days, if indeed they opt to do so at all. The same applies to the age when they focus on their career the most, when they experience serious challenges and impediments, or face career shocks. Managers and workers alike therefore need to approach age as multi-dimensional, with highly idiosyncratic events and outcomes for work and private life. This means taking account of mental and physical health, private life, occupational competencies, and attitudes regarding opportunities in workers' remaining time at work. The latter could lead to the provision of tailor-made job resources, such as well-thought-out

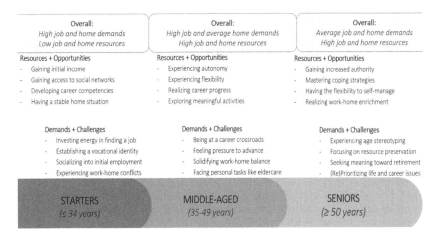

Overall:	Overall:	Overall:
High job and home demands	*High job and average home demands*	*Average job and home demands*
Low job and home resources	*High job and home resources*	*High job and home resources*

Resources + Opportunities
- Gaining initial income
- Gaining access to social networks
- Developing career competencies
- Having a stable home situation

Resources + Opportunities
- Experiencing autonomy
- Experiencing flexibility
- Realizing career progress
- Exploring meaningful activities

Resources + Opportunities
- Gaining increased authority
- Mastering coping strategies
- Having the flexibility to self-manage
- Realizing work-home enrichment

Demands + Challenges
- Investing energy in finding a job
- Establishing a vocational identity
- Socializing into initial employment
- Experiencing work-home conflicts

Demands + Challenges
- Being at a career crossroads
- Feeling pressure to advance
- Solidifying work-home balance
- Facing personal tasks like eldercare

Demands + Challenges
- Experiencing age stereotyping
- Focusing on resource preservation
- Seeking meaning toward retirement
- (Re)Prioritizing life and career issues

STARTERS
(≤ 34 years)

MIDDLE-AGED
(35-49 years)

SENIORS
(≥ 50 years)

Figure 5.1   *Overview of main resources and demands across career stages*

age-conscious human resource management practices (Veth et al., 2019) in the workplace, or to focused help by means of support systems in one's private life, being an important home resource.

The value of a given job or home resource – and even the saliency of the resource gain versus resource loss principles of conservation of resources theory – are likely to vary significantly over time and across different contexts (De Vos et al., 2020). In addition, over time, changes are likely to take place not only within the individual (see the age-related changes as portrayed in Sterns & Doverspike, 1989), but also within the broader context of the individual's career. Only when a systemic approach (Colakoglu et al., 2006) to sustainable careers is taken can we determine the influential factors that are associated with multiple stakeholders situated in the context of both work and private life and their evolution over time. By adopting a whole-life perspective, we argue that the different aspects of the ecosystem that surrounds an individual's career can be aligned and carefully balanced.

REFERENCES

Akkermans, J., Brenninkmeijer, V., Huibers, M., & Blonk, R. W. (2013). Competencies for the contemporary career: Development and preliminary validation of the career competencies questionnaire. *Journal of Career Development, 40*(3), 245–267.

Akkermans, J., Seibert, S. E., & Mol, S. T. (2018). Tales of the unexpected: Integrating career shocks in the contemporary career literature. *SA Journal of Industrial Psychology, 44*, e1503.

Arthur, M. B., Hall, D. T., & Lawrence, B. S. (1989). Generating new directions in career theory: The case for a transdisciplinary approach. In M. B. Arthur, D. T.

Hall & B. S. Lawrence (Eds), *Handbook of Career Theory* (pp. 7–25). Cambridge: Cambridge University Press.

Baltes, P. B., Staudinger, U. M., & Lindenberger, U. (1999). Lifespan psychology: Theory and application to intellectual functioning. *Annual Review of Psychology*, *50*(1), 471–507.

Carstensen, L. L. (1995). Evidence for a life-span theory of socioemotional selectivity. *Current Directions in Psychological Science*, *4*(5), 151–156.

Carstensen, L. L. (2006). The influence of a sense of time on human development. *Science*, *12*(5782), 1913–1915.

Colakoglu, S., Lepak, D. P., & Hong, Y. (2006). Measuring HRM effectiveness: Considering multiple stakeholders in a global context. *Human Resource Management Review*, *16*(2), 209–218.

De Vos, A., Van der Heijden, B. I. J. M., & Akkermans, J. (2020). Sustainable careers: Towards a conceptual model. *Journal of Vocational Behavior*, 103196.

Deci, E. L., Olafsen, A. H., & Ryan, R. M. (2017). Self-determination theory in work organizations: The state of a science. *Annual Review of Organizational Psychology and Organizational Behavior*, *4*, 19–43.

Demerouti, E., Bakker, A. B., Nachreiner, F., & Schaufeli, W. B. (2001). The job demands resources model of burnout. *Journal of Applied Psychology*, *86*(3), 499–512.

Demerouti, E., Peeters, M. C. W., & Van der Heijden, B. I. J. M. (2012). Work–family interface from a life and career stages' perspective: The role of demands and resources. *International Journal of Psychology*, *47*(4), 241–258.

Hirschi, A., Steiner, R., Burmeister, A., & Johnston, C. S. (2020). A whole-life perspective of sustainable careers: The nature and consequences of nonwork orientations. *Journal of Vocational Behavior*, *117*, 103319.

Hobfoll, S. E. (1989). Conservation of resources: A new attempt at conceptualizing stress. *American Psychologist*, *44*(3), 513–524.

Hobfoll, S. E., Halbesleben, J., Neveu, J. P., & Westman, M. (2018). Conservation of resources in the organizational context: The reality of resources and their consequences. *Annual Review of Organizational Psychology and Organizational Behavior*, *5*, 103–128.

Lang, F. R., & Carstensen, L. L. (2002). Time counts: Future time perspective, goals, and social relationships. *Psychology and Aging*, *17*(1), 125–139.

Ryan, R. M., & Deci, E. L. (2000). Self-determination theory and the facilitation of intrinsic motivation, social development, and well-being. *American Psychologist*, *55*(1), 68–78.

Sterns, H. L., & Doverspike, D. (1989). Aging and the retraining and learning process in organizations. In I. Goldstein & R. Katzel (Eds), *Training and Development in Work Organizations* (pp. 229–332). San Francisco, CA: Jossey-Bass.

Van der Heijden, B. I. J. M. (2000). The development and psychometric evaluation of a multi-dimensional measurement instrument of professional expertise. *High Ability Studies: The Journal of the European Council for High Ability*, *11*(1), 9–39.

Van der Heijden, B. I. J. M. (2005). *"No one has ever promised you a rose garden": On shared responsibility and employability enhancing strategies throughout careers*. Heerlen: Open University of the Netherlands and Assen: Van Gorcum.

Van der Heijden, B. I. J. M., & De Vos, A. (2015). Sustainable careers. In A. De Vos & B. I. J. M. Van der Heijden (Eds), *Handbook of Research on Sustainable Careers* (pp. 1–19). Cheltenham, UK and Northampton, MA, USA: Edward Elgar Publishing.

Van der Heijden, B. I. J. M., De Vos, A., Akkermans, J., Spurk, D., Semeijn, J., Van der Velde, M., & Fugate, M. (2020). Special issue: Sustainable careers across the lifespan: Moving the field forward. *Journal of Vocational Behavior*, 103344.

Veth, K. N., Korzilius, H. P., Van der Heijden, B. I. J. M., Emans, B. J., & De Lange, A. H. (2019). Understanding the contribution of HRM bundles for employee outcomes across the life-span. *Frontiers in Psychology*, *10*, 2518.

Westman, M., Hobfoll, S. E., Chen, S., Davidson, O. B., & Laski, S. (2004). Organizational stress through the lens of conservation of resources (COR) theory. In P. L. Perrewe & D. C. Ganster (Eds), *Interpersonal dynamics (research in occupational stress and well-being)* (Vol. 4, pp. 167–220). Bingley: Emerald Group Publishing.

6. The value of work–life balance: cross-country and cross-worker comparisons

Mara A. Yerkes and Karen van Hedel

INTRODUCTION

Work–life balance, or "the permeability and blurring of boundaries in the different spheres of life: work, family and leisure time for oneself" (Hobson, 2013: 2), is a well-studied topic (Casper et al., 2017; Crompton & Lyonette, 2006; Gregory et al., 2013; Hobson, 2013) that received increased interest following the onset of the COVID-19 pandemic (Hjálmsdóttir et al., 2021; Schieman et al., 2021; Yerkes et al., 2020). Even prior to the pandemic, the concept was highly debated (Gregory & Milner, 2009; Kelliher et al., 2019) given many conceptualizations of the term "balance" (Casper et al., 2017) and the assumption that work is central to an individual's life (Felstead et al., 2002; Kelliher et al., 2019). In many European societies, work–life balance is viewed as "the institutional and cultural times and spaces of work and non-work" (Felstead et al., 2002: 56). The term "balance" also implies that work and other activities outside work can and should be brought into equilibrium (Crompton & Lyonette, 2006), although other conceptualizations emphasize effectiveness, satisfaction, and fit (Casper et al., 2017). The empirical focus of many work–life balance studies is similarly diffuse. The psychological literature most often refers to satisfaction and effectiveness (Casper et al., 2017) but, overall, much research studies the extent to which individuals are able to balance work and care roles (see, e.g., Casper et al., 2017; Yerkes et al., 2020 for an overview) or degrees of conflict between work, family, and other roles (Greenhaus & Beutell, 1985).

A minority of the work–life balance literature suggests that individuals have reason to value a plurality of work–life activities, not just work but also activities such as care, volunteer work, education, and leisure (Hobson, 2013). Additionally, the value people place on work, care, or other activities differs across key social categories like gender and class, as does their ability to realize a valued fit between work and other activities (Yerkes & Warren, 2022). Psychological research suggests, moreover, that authenticity results from an alignment between people's values and the time, energy, and attention they can give to work or personal (and family) commitments (Wayne et al., 2019). Work–life fit, in turn, has been found to be an important indicator of subjective wellbeing (Riva et al., 2019). Given the importance of personal values for feelings of balance, authenticity, and wellbeing (Casper et al., 2017; Riva et al., 2019; Wayne et al., 2019), greater insights are needed across all social science disciplines to understand the nuanced ways in which individuals value work–life fit. We focus on what individuals value in how their work commitments fit with their personal and social commitments outside of work. We ask: *To what extent do we observe differences in the value of work–life fit across country contexts for various groups of workers?*

DATA AND METHODS

Data were taken from a cross-country survey using a multinational, multiregional, and multicultural contexts comparative method (Johnson et al., 2019) for the European Research Council-funded CAPABLE project in the Netherlands, Slovenia, Spain, and the United Kingdom (UK). Data were fielded in September 2021 and a booster sample collected in November and December in Slovenia and the UK to reach more lower-educated respondents. Data were based on a representative sample from eligible panel participants from Kantar Public, who fielded the survey via computer-assisted web interviews. All respondents received information about the study prior to participation and gave informed consent. The sample consisted of 4,161 respondents with response rates of 54 percent (the Netherlands), 66 percent (Slovenia), 48 percent (Spain), and 62 percent (UK). We excluded participants not in paid employment (N = 1,242). Our analytical sample consisted of 2,884 respondents (total missing for gender = 11, employment status = 7, work–life fit = 17).

Our analysis proceeded in three stages. First, we provided descriptive statistics on valued work–life fit, measured by one item: "I think it's important that my work commitments fit with my family and social commitments outside of work." Answer categories were a five-point Likert scale ranging from "strongly agree" to "strongly disagree," with responses reversed so that higher scores indicated greater agreement. We summed the percentages "strongly disagree," "disagree," and "neutral" due to low sample sizes. In the remaining analyses, average scores were used. Second, we ran independent sample t-tests to test differences across key groups of workers. We compared men to women (the category non-binary was too small for reporting), dependent workers to the self-employed (also including those working in a family business), part-time (<35 hours/week) to full-time workers (35+ hours), and different generations of workers (15–44 years versus 45–65 years). Third, we used one-way ANOVA and ANCOVA models with interactions (country * groups of workers) to test for differences across countries. We presented average marginal effects with Tukey post-hoc comparisons to help explain the ANCOVA results.

RESULTS

Significant cross-country variation is evident in the importance placed on work–life fit (see Table 6.1; note not all comparisons are significant). Across the four countries, approximately 91 percent of men and women agreed (47 percent) or strongly agreed (44 percent) that it is important for their work commitments to fit with family and social commitments outside of work. The remaining 9 percent either (strongly) disagreed or answered "neutral," with differences across countries. The percentage of men and women who place less importance on work–life fit (i.e., (strongly) disagree or neutral) was lowest in the Netherlands (5 percent) and highest in the UK (12 percent). Percentages of men and women agreeing are relatively similar across countries, although fewer UK respondents strongly agreed (39 percent) than in the Netherlands (47 percent) or Spain (46 percent).

We also find significant gender effects: women place greater value on work–life fit than men (see Table 6.2, mean difference: 0.12, p = 0.000). Compared to men, women are less likely to place little value on work–life fit (7 versus 11 percent, Table 6.1) and more likely to strongly value it (48 versus 40 percent). No gender difference is observed for those "agreeing" it is important that work commitments fit with family and other social commitments.

Across all countries, self-employed respondents place less value on work–life fit than dependent employees (see Table 6.2, mean difference: −0.13, p = 0.003). They are also more likely to place less importance on work–life fit (13 versus 8 percent) and less likely to strongly value work–life fit (38 versus 45 percent).

We see some differences between individuals working part time or full time (see Table 6.2, mean difference: −0.07, p = 0.008) and between generations (mean difference: 0.02, p = 0.480), but these differences are more nuanced than the variation across countries, gender, or employee type. Full-time workers and older workers are more likely to value work–life fit (49 and 50 percent agreed, respectively) than those working part time and younger workers (43 and 45 percent agreed, respectively). But part-time and younger workers are more likely to place a strong value on work–life fit, with 48 and 46 percent respectively strongly agreeing with the statement compared to their full-time and older counterparts (42 and 42 percent strongly agreed, respectively).

Table 6.1   Percentages/proportions value of work–life balance

	Places less value on work–life fit (strongly disagree/disagree/neutral)	Value work–life fit (agree)	Places more value on work–life fit (strongly agree)
All respondents	9	47	44
Country			
Netherlands	5	48	47
Slovenia	8	48	44
Spain	11	43	46
United Kingdom	12	50	39
Gender			
Women	7	46	48
Men	11	49	40
Employment status			
Dependent employees	8	47	45
Self-employed/working in family business	13	50	38
Work hours			
Part-time workers (<35)	8	43	48
Full-time workers (35+)	9	49	42
Generation			
Younger (15–44 years)	9	45	46
Older (45–65 years)	8	50	42

Note: For ease of interpretation, only group percentages are reported here. For a full table of group comparisons see Table 6A.1, and for levels of significance (Wald tests) and differences in proportions, see Table 6A.2 in the appendix to this chapter.

The importance placed on work–life fit also differs for workers across the different countries (see Table 6A.3 in the appendix to this chapter, ANOVA Model 1, $F(3, 2880) = 7.21$, $p = 0.000$). These country differences remain significant ($F(3, 2876) = 6.75$, $p = 0.000$) when controlling for the group characteristics analyzed here. Introducing interaction effects between country and worker characteristics (see Table 6A.3 in the appendix to this chapter), results are fairly similar for gender, employment status, and generation. These findings suggest that although workers differ in the value placed on work–life fit, the ways in which these groups differ is relatively similar across the four countries (i.e., the interactions between country and these worker characteristics were not statistically significant). The exception is the difference in the value of work–life fit between full-time and part-time workers (see Table 6A.3 in the

*Table 6.2   Mean differences on work–life fit between groups
(independent sample t-tests)*

	Mean (SD) / mean diff. (t-value, p-value)
Gender	
Women	4.40 (SD = 0.63)
Men	4.28 (SD = 0.69)
Difference	0.12 (t = 4.78, p = 0.000)
Employment status	
Self-employed/working in family business	4.23 (SD = 0.73)
Dependent employees	4.36 (SD = 0.66)
Difference	−0.13 (t = −3.03, p = 0.003)
Work hours	
Part time (<35)	4.39 (SD = 0.66)
Full time (35+)	4.32 (SD = 0.66)
Difference	−0.07 (t = −2.65, p = 0.008)
Generation	
Younger (15–44 years)	4.35 (SD = 0.69)
Older (45–65 years)	4.33 (SD = 0.63)
Difference	0.02 (t = 0.7057, p = 0.480)

appendix to this chapter; number of work hours: $F(1, 2864) = 4.30$, $p = 0.038$; country * number of work hours: $F(3, 2864) = 12.98$, $p = 0.000$). Average marginal effects with Tukey post-hoc comparisons (shown in Table 6.3) help elucidate these country differences. In the Netherlands, part-time workers and full-time workers value work–life fit similarly. However, we observe differences for the other three countries: compared to full-time workers, the value placed on work–life fit is higher among part-time workers in Slovenia (4.62 versus 4.31, p-value of difference = 0.000) and the UK (4.37 versus 4.19, p-value of difference = 0.022). In contrast, in Spain, the value placed on work–life fit is higher among full-time workers than part-time workers (4.39 versus 4.19, p-value of difference = 0.018).

DISCUSSION

This chapter aims to provide insights into the extent to which we observe differences in the value different groups of workers place on work–life fit across country contexts. Such insights can help to create more nuanced under-standings in current scholarly and policy work–life balance debates, where values remain understudied (e.g., Wayne et al., 2019). Clearly, most workers feel it is important that their work commitments fit with their family and

Table 6.3   *Average marginal effects of number of work hours by country*

Country	Part-time workers (<35 hours)	Full-time workers (35+ hours)	P-value Tukey's Honestly Significant Difference test of pairwise comparison by country
Netherlands	4.40 (4.32, 4.48)	4.44 (4.37, 4.51)	0.999
Slovenia	4.62 (4.49, 4.75)	4.31 (4.26, 4.36)	0.000
Spain	4.19 (4.08, 4.29)	4.39 (4.33, 4.44)	0.018
United Kingdom	4.37 (4.29, 4.45)	4.19 (4.13, 4.26)	0.022

Note: See Table 6A.4 in the appendix to this chapter for average marginal effects for the other groups.

social commitments outside of work. Yet our findings suggest important variation exists both within and across countries. Within countries, our findings confirm previous research that men and women can value different outcomes in reconciling work with other activities. Moreover, the outcomes of our analyses suggest important differences exist between dependent employees and the self-employed. These findings are in line with qualitative data for the Netherlands that suggest the self-employed do not always manage to use autonomy to their advantage, sometimes resulting in poorer work–life balance (Annink & den Dulk, 2012). Across countries, significant differences are also found, even after controlling for differences amongst groups of workers. For example, in the UK, fewer respondents strongly value having work–life fit compared to the other countries.

Although some variation is found within and across countries, our results generally point to consistent differences between groups of workers across countries in their valuing of work–life fit. The exception is the value of work–life fit emphasized by full-time and part-time workers. In the Netherlands, full-time workers and part-time workers value work–life fit in similar ways. In a country with the highest part-time work rates in Europe (OECD, 2023) such a finding is intriguing, as it is often assumed that part-time work is a strategy for reconciling work and care (Peters et al., 2009). Our finding is likely more reflective of the lower average weekly work hours in the Netherlands compared to the other countries, with less than 10 percent of workers working more than 40 hours a week (Statistics Netherlands, 2020). In the three other countries, however, significant differences are evident – with part-time workers valuing work–life fit more in the UK and Slovenia, and less so in Spain. More research into the work conditions of these workers would help to explain these nuanced cross-country differences. For example, the existence of a long-hours work culture in the UK (Burke & Cooper, 2008) might make full-time workers more resigned to having difficulties balancing work and life, leading them to place less value on work–life fit.

IMPLICATIONS FOR RESEARCH AND PRACTICE

For work–life balance scholars, our findings provide a foundation for examining nuanced differences in the value individuals place on combining work with other activities outside of work. Future research in this area could qualitatively consider the difference between agree and strongly agree in relation to the value of work–life fit or unpack further those respondents who are at the extreme ends of the scale (strongly agree, strongly disagree). Qualitative research from a sample of self-employed women in the Netherlands suggests, for example, that self-reflection on the reconciliation of work–life in relation to what one values can increase work–life balance satisfaction (Annink & den Dulk, 2012). As research interest in personal values grows, more in-depth research can continue to explore these differences across workers in their value of work–life fit and how this relates to feelings of balance, authenticity and wellbeing in workers' lives (Casper et al., 2017; Riva et al., 2019; Wayne et al., 2019). Moreover, future research could connect the work–life literature investigating differing value placed on work–life fit with social justice theorizing, to improve scientific understanding of how these differences create and perpetuate social inequalities. This literature shows, for example, that gendered differences in the outcomes valued by men and women at work (Yerkes et al., 2017) and at home (Thompson, 1991) are a key barrier to achieving greater gender equality. Improving our understanding of the extent to which differing groups of workers vary in the value they place on work commitments fitting with their personal and social commitments outside of work, which we do here, can highlight such inequality, leading to improved insights on how to counter these inequalities within organizations and societies. Policymakers in these countries can use these findings to consider how to improve the work–life balance of different groups of workers in society by understanding who places value on work–life fit and understanding whether current working conditions allow these employees to actually balance work–life in practice.

ACKNOWLEDGMENT

This work was supported by H2020 European Research Council grant number ERC CoG/771290.

REFERENCES

Annink, A., & den Dulk, L. (2012). Autonomy: The panacea for self-employed women's work–life balance? *Community, Work & Family, 15*(4), 383–402.

Burke, R. J. J., & Cooper, C. L. (2008). *Long Work Hours Culture: Causes, Consequences and Choices*. Emerald Group Publishing.

Casper, W. J., Vaziri, H., Wayne, J. H., DeHauw, S., & Greenhaus, J. (2017). The jingle-jangle of work–nonwork balance: A comprehensive and meta-analytic review of its meaning and measurement. *Journal of Applied Psychology, 103*(2), 182–214.

Crompton, R., & Lyonette, C. (2006). Work–life "balance" in Europe. *Acta Sociologica, 49*(4), 379–393.

Felstead, A., Jewson, N., Phizacklea, A., & Walters, S. (2002). Opportunities to work at home in the context of work–life balance. *Human Resource Management Journal, 12*(1), 54–76.

Greenhaus, J. H., & Beutell, N. J. (1985). Sources of conflict between work and family roles. *Academy of Management Review, 10*(1), 76–88.

Gregory, A., & Milner, S. (2009). Editorial: Work–life balance: A matter of choice? *Gender, Work & Organization, 16*(1), 1–13.

Gregory, A., Milner, S., & Windebank, J. (2013). Work–life balance in times of economic crisis and austerity. *International Journal of Sociology and Social Policy, 33*(9), 528–541.

Hjálmsdóttir, A., Bjarnadóttir, V. S., & Eðvarðs Sigurðssonar, M. (2021). "I have turned into a foreman here at home": Families and work–life balance in times of COVID-19 in a gender equality paradise. *Gender, Work & Organization, 28*(1), 268–283.

Hobson, B. (Ed.) (2013). *Work–Life Balance: The Agency and Capabilities Gap*. Oxford University Press.

Johnson, T. P., Pennel, B.-E., Stoop, I., & Dorer, B. (2019). The promise and challenge of 3MC research. In T. P. Johnson, B. E. Pennell, I. Stoop, & B. Dorer (Eds), *Advances in Comparative Survey Methods: Multinational, Multiregional and Multicultural Contexts (3MC)* (pp. 3–12). John Wiley & Sons.

Kelliher, C., Richardson, J., & Boiarintseva, G. (2019). All of work? All of life? Reconceptualising work–life balance for the 21st century. *Human Resource Management Journal, 29*(2), 97–112.

OECD. (2023). *Labour Force Statistics*. OECD Publishing.

Peters, P., den Dulk, L., & Lippe, T. van der. (2009). The effects of time-spatial flexibility and new working conditions on employees' work–life balance: The Dutch case. *Community, Work & Family, 12*(3), 279–297.

Riva, E., Lucchini, M., & Russo, M. (2019). Societal gender inequality as moderator of the relationship between work–life fit and subjective well-being: A multilevel analysis across European countries. *Social Indicators Research*, 143(2).

Schieman, S., Badawy, P. J., Milkie, M. A., & Bierman, A. (2021). Work–life conflict during the COVID-19 pandemic. *Socius, 7*, 1–19.

Statistics Netherlands. (2020). More than half of Dutch people work full-time. www.cbs.nl/en-gb/news/2020/08/more-than-half-of-dutch-people-work-full-time [Accessed August 1 2020].

Thompson, L. (1991). Family work. *Journal of Family Issues, 12*(2), 181–196.

Wayne, J. H., Matthews, R. A., Odle-Dusseau, H., & Casper, W. J. (2019). Fit of role involvement with values: Theoretical, conceptual, and psychometric development of work and family authenticity. *Journal of Vocational Behavior*, *115*(June), 103317.

Yerkes, M. A., & Warren, T. (2022). Living valued lives during the COVID-19 pandemic: Inequalities of gender and class. Work Family Researchers Network conference presentation.

Yerkes, M. A., Martin, B., Baxter, J., & Rose, J. (2017). An unsettled bargain? Mothers' perceptions of justice and fairness in paid work. *Journal of Sociology*, *53*(2), 476–491.

Yerkes, M. A., André, S., Remery, C., Salin, M., Hakovirta, M., & van Gerven, M. (2020). Unequal but balanced: Highly educated mothers' perceptions of work–life balance during the COVID-19 lockdown in Finland and the Netherlands *Journal of European Social Policy*, *32*(4), 376–392.

APPENDIX 6A

Table 6A.1   *Full table for groups of workers in the four countries*

N (percentage)	Netherlands	Slovenia	Spain	United Kingdom	Total (across all four countries)
All respondents					
Less value placed on WLF	36 (4.87)	57 (7.83)	78 (10.80)	82 (11.80)	253 (8.77)
Value of WLF	353 (47.77)	352 (48.35)	313 (43.21)	344 (49.50)	1,361 (47.19)
More value placed on WLF	350 (47.36)	319 (43.82)	332 (45.98)	269 (38.71)	1,270 (44.04)
By gender					
Women					
Less value placed on WLF	13 (3.25)	19 (5.51)	35 (9.75)	32 (8.91)	99 (6.77)
Value of WLF	175 (43.75)	158 (45.80)	147 (40.95)	188 (52.37)	668 (45.66)
More value placed on WLF	212 (53.00)	168 (48.70)	177 (49.30)	139 (38.72)	696 (47.57)
Men					
Less value placed on WLF	23 (6.78)	38 (9.92)	43 (11.85)	50 (14.88)	154 (10.84)
Value of WLF	178 (52.51)	194 (50.65)	165 (45.45)	156 (46.43)	693 (48.77)
More value placed on WLF	138 (40.71)	151 (39.43)	155 (42.70)	130 (38.69)	574 (40.39)
By employment status					
Dependent employees					
Less value placed on WLF	30 (4.44)	53 (8.05)	64 (9.85)	71 (11.43)	218 (8.37)
Value of WLF	324 (47.193)	315 (47.87)	280 (43.08)	303 (48.79)	1,222 (46.91)
More value placed on WLF	322 (47.63)	290 (44.07)	306 (47.08)	247 (39.77)	1,165 (44.72)
Self-employed working in family business					
Less value placed on WLF	6 (9.52)	4 (5.71)	14 (19.44)	11 (14.86)	35 (12.54)
Value of WLF	29 (46.03)	37 (52.86)	32 (44.44)	41 (55.41)	139 (49.82)
More value placed on WLF	28 (44.44)	29 (41.43)	26 (36.11)	22 (29.73)	105 (37.63)
By number of working hours					
Part-time workers					
Less value placed on WLF	16 (4.72)	3 (2.78)	29 (17.47)	25 (9.54)	73 (8.34)
Value of WLF	153 (45.13)	37 (34.26)	72 (43.37)	116 (44.27)	378 (43.20)
More value placed on WLF	170 (50.15)	68 (62.96)	65 (39.16)	121 (46.18)	424 (48.46)
Full-time workers					
Less value placed on WLF	20 (5.00)	54 (8.71)	49 (8.81)	57 (13.16)	180 (8.9\6)
Value of WLF	200 (50.00)	315 (50.81)	240 (43.17)	228 (52.66)	983 (48.93)

N (percentage)	Netherlands	Slovenia	Spain	United Kingdom	Total (across all four countries)
More value placed on WLF	180 (45.00)	251 (40.48)	267 (48.02)	148 (34.18)	846 (42.11)
By generation					
Younger generation (15–44 years old)					
Less value placed on WLF	11 (3.47)	42 (9.09)	53 (11.83)	46 (12.17)	152 (9.47)
Value of WLF	145 (45.74)	208 (45.02)	189 (42.19)	175 (46.30)	717 (44.67)
More value placed on WLF	161 (50.79)	212 (45.89)	206 (45.98)	157 (41.53)	736 (45.86)
Older generation (45–65 years old)					
Less value placed on WLF	25 (5.92)	15 (5.64)	25 (9.12)	36 (11.36)	101 (7.90)
Value of WLF	208 (49.29)	144 (54.14)	123 (44.89)	169 (53.31)	644 (50.35)
More value placed on WLF	189 (44.79)	107 (40.23)	126 (45.99)	112 (35.33)	534 (41.75)

Notes: Less value on work–life fit: strongly disagree, disagree, neutral; value work–life fit: agree; and strongly value work–life fit: strongly agree. WLF = work–life fit.

Table 6A.2   Results from Wald tests

All respondents

Less value placed on work–life fit	Netherlands	Slovenia	Spain	United Kingdom
Netherlands		F (1,2883) = 5.41 Prob > F = 0.020	F (1,2883) = 17.94 Prob > F = 0.000	F (1,2883) = 22.59 Prob > F = 0.000
Slovenia			F (1,2883) = 3.80 Prob > F = 0.051	F (1,2883) = 6.33 Prob > F = 0.012
Spain				F (1,2883) = 0.35 Prob > F = 0.554
United Kingdom				

Value of work–life fit	Netherlands	Slovenia	Spain	United Kingdom
Netherlands		F (1,2883) = 0.05 Prob > F = 0.823	F (1,2883) = 3.06 Prob > F = 0.080	F (1,2883) = 0.43 Prob > F = 0.513
Slovenia			F (1,2883) = 3.77 Prob > F = 0.049	F (1,2883) = 0.19 Prob > F = 0.666
Spain				F (1,2883) = 5.64 Prob > F = 0.018
United Kingdom				

More value placed on work–life fit	Netherlands	Slovenia	Spain	United Kingdom
Netherlands		F (1,2883) = 1.86 Prob > F = 0.173	F (1,2883) = 0.28 Prob > F = 0.598	F (1,2883) = 11.04 Prob > F = 0.001
Slovenia			F (1,2883) = 0.69 Prob > F = 0.407	F (1,2883) = 3.85 Prob > F = 0.050
Spain				F (1,2883) = 7.73 Prob > F = 0.006
United Kingdom				

By subgroup (for all four countries together)

	Men versus women	Employee versus self-employed	Part time versus full time	Younger versus older generation
Less value placed on work–life fit	F (1,2883) = 14.91 Prob > F = 0.000	F (1,2883) = 4.13 Prob > F = 0.042	F (1,2883) = 0.30 Prob > F = 0.586	F (1,2883) = 2.25 Prob > F = 0.134
Value of work–life fit	F (1,2883) = 2.80 Prob > F = 0.095	F (1,2883) = 0.85 Prob > F = 0.355	F (1,2883) = 8.11 Prob > F = 0.004	F (1,2883) = 9.23 Prob > F = 0.002
More value placed on work–life fit	F (1,2883) = 15.16 Prob > F = 0.000	F (1,2883) = 5.37 Prob > F = 0.021	F (1,2883) = 9.90 Prob > F = 0.002	F (1,2883) = 4.89 Prob > F = 0.027

Table 6A.3   Additional results from ANOVA and ANCOVA models

	Results
Model with only country	$F(3, 2880) = 7.21$, p = 0.000
Model 2 with country and key characteristics (no interaction terms)	$F(7, 2876) = 7.97$, p = 0.000
Country	$F(3, 2876) = 6.75$, p = 0.000
Gender	$F(1, 2876) = 16.26$, p = 0.000
Employment status	$F(1, 2876) = 9.25$, p = 0.002
Number of work hours	$F(1, 2876) = 2.84$, p = 0.092
Generation	$F(1, 2876) = 0.13$, p = 0.716
Model 3 with country and key characteristics (including interaction terms)	$F(19, 2864) = 5.47$, p = 0.000
Country	$F(3, 2864) = 7.20$, p = 0.000
Gender	$F(1, 2864) = 18.63$, p = 0.000
Country * gender	$F(3, 2864) = 1.32$, p = 0.265
Employment status	$F(1, 2864) = 10.05$, p = 0.002
Country * employment status	$F(3, 2864) = 0.59$, p = 0.624
Number of work hours	$F(1, 2864) = 4.30$, p = 0.038
Country * number of work hours	$F(3, 2864) = 12.98$, p = 0.000
Generation	$F(1, 2864) = 0.10$, p = 0.749
Country * generation	$F(3, 2864) = 0.67$, p = 0.568

Table 6A.4   Additional marginal effects for gender, employment status, and generation

By gender

Country	Women	Men	P-value Tukey HSD test of pairwise comparison within country
Netherlands	4.51 (4.44, 4.59)	4.34 (4.26, 4.41)	0.052
Slovenia	4.47 (4.39, 4.54)	4.34 (4.27, 4.41)	0.144
Spain	4.39 (4.32, 4.45)	4.27 (4.20, 4.34)	0.242
United Kingdom	4.26 (4.19, 4.33)	4.23 (4.16, 4.30)	0.999

By employment status

Country	Self-employed/working in family business	Dependent employees	P-value Tukey HSD test of pairwise comparison within country
Netherlands	4.37 (4.21, 4.54)	4.43 (4.38, 4.49)	0.997
Slovenia	4.31 (4.16, 4.47)	4.41 (4.36, 4.47)	0.937
Spain	4.17 (4.02, 4.32)	4.34 (4.29, 4.40)	0.396
UK	4.07 (3.92, 4.22)	4.27 (4.22, 4.32)	0.239

By generation

Country	Younger (15–44 years)	Older (45–65 years)	P-value Tukey HSD test of pairwise comparison within country
Netherlands	4.45 (4.38, 4.53)	4.39 (4.33, 4.46)	0.931
Slovenia	4.40 (4.34, 4.46)	4.41 (4.32, 4.49)	1.000
Spain	4.31 (4.25, 4.37)	4.35 (4.27, 4.43)	0.996
UK	4.26 (4.19, 4.32)	4.24 (4.27, 4.31)	1.000

PART II

Workplace support

7. Combining work and informal caregiving: workplace support to reduce work–care conflict

Ellen Verbakel and Cécile Boot

INTRODUCTION

The demand for informal care has increased rapidly in recent years. Informal caregiving is defined as unpaid care for a partner, relative, friend, or neighbor on a regular basis over a longer time period (Bom et al., 2018). It includes help with personal and nursing care, household tasks, coordinating care, assistance with healthcare visits, transportation, emotional support and/or administrative support (Candy et al., 2011). In Europe, one third of the total population provided informal care in 2014, on average (Verbakel et al., 2017). In 2019, about a quarter of the working population of the Netherlands combined paid work with informal caregiving tasks. About 20 percent of them provided care for over eight hours per week (de Boer et al., 2019). In the near term, even more workers are expected to be involved in informal caregiving due to the ageing population and increasing staff shortages in professional healthcare (Zigante, 2018).

The need to combine work and informal caregiving can give rise to work–care conflict (Greenhaus & Beutell, 1985) and, in turn, to sick leave or mental health issues such as stress and depression (Joling et al., 2018; Josten et al., 2022; Mikkola et al., 2022). From a societal perspective, this is undesirable because continued participation in both paid work and informal care are crucial. Previous studies have shown that workplace support, such as understanding from supervisors and colleagues, is associated with fewer depressive symptoms in working informal caregivers (Bijnsdorp et al., 2022; Broese van Groenou et al., 2015; Earle & Heymann, 2011).

The prevention of work–care conflicts is key to sustainable employability for the many workers who also have informal care responsibilities. An interdisciplinary approach is needed as work–care conflicts arise at the boundaries between work and home roles, and involve workers' health (occupational health), the work environment (human resource management) and the social context (sociology). This chapter examines how workplace support (i.e. flexibility and understanding at work) is associated with work–care conflict as a first step towards reducing work–care conflict and, in the longer term, undesirable health and productivity outcomes.

THEORY

Work–care conflicts imply that the roles of worker and carer cannot be performed optimally, particularly due to time constraints and the spill-over of strain caused by one role into the other (Greenhaus & Beutell, 1985). Workplace support, such as flexibility or understanding from supervisors or colleagues, may help working caregivers to combine both roles in a healthy and sustainable way. Flexibility at work is likely to alleviate time conflicts as it helps employees to gear their working hours to their care responsibilities. Understanding from supervisors and colleagues may help to reduce strain in the work role (Hammer et al., 2009). In particular, such forms of understanding can provide emotional support and may lead to certain tasks being reallocated and better acceptance of (temporarily) lower productivity levels due to the care role. This acceptance is likely to reduce feelings of guilt and stress in the caregiver. We therefore hypothesize that workplace support is negatively associated with work–care conflict.

We will study men and women separately because gender differences are likely in several respects. Gender roles predict that women are involved in informal caregiving more often than men (Haberkern, 2015; Josten et al., 2022). A meta-analysis has shown that women experience more stressors relating to informal care (Pinquart & Sörensen, 2006), which may exacerbate work–care conflict. The protective effects of support in the workplace have been shown to be greater among women than men (Earle & Heymann, 2011).

METHOD

We used retrospective data on informal caregivers collected within the Longitudinal Internet Studies of Social Sciences panel (LISS). The LISS panel is based on a representative sample of households in the Netherlands. In a dedicated module, "Retrospective informal care career" (Verbakel & CentERdata, 2021), fielded in March 2020, respondents reported on all episodes of providing informal care in their lives. We selected those informal care episodes on which the respondent provided detailed information (which was the case for a maximum of three randomly selected episodes per respondent) and during which the respondent was also in employment. After listwise exclusion of cases with missing values, our sample consisted of 3,746 episodes of 2,138 informal caregivers.

The dependent variable of work–care conflict was measured with the item "I found combining work and providing care to X stressful" (in which X was replaced by the name of the care recipient). Respondents answered on a five-point scale, ranging from completely disagree (1) to completely agree (5).

Workplace flexibility reflected the caregiver's assessment of the degree to which they could arrange work flexibly to combine informal care with work, the options being no flexibility, a little flexibility and considerable flexibility. Understanding from supervisors and direct colleagues was measured by asking whether the respondent's supervisor (or direct colleagues) showed understanding with regard to their caregiving to X. The response options were none, a little and considerable understanding, as well as "my supervisor [or direct colleagues] did not know I provided care" and "I had no supervisor [or direct colleagues]."

We estimated random intercept hierarchical models with episodes nested in carers, separately for men and women. The models were controlled for the caregiver's age, educational level, previous caregiving experience (in number of episodes), care intensity (average number of weekly hours), average number of different caregiving tasks and relationship with the care recipient (partner, parent, child, other family member, neighbor/friend/acquaintance).

RESULTS

Figure 7.1 shows that 14 percent of all men and 19 percent of all women in our sample reported finding the combination of work and informal caregiving stressful. Fifteen percent of men and 25 percent of women perceived no flexibility at work, whereas 48 percent of men and 38 percent of women perceived considerable flexibility. Considering working male and female carers with a supervisor only, we found that almost half of supervisors were aware of their employees' caregiving duties, and slightly more colleagues were. Twenty-nine percent of men and 26 percent of women reported considerable support from their supervisor, and 31 percent of men and 34 percent of women reported considerable support from their colleagues.

Considerable flexibility at work was significantly associated with lower scores on work–care conflict in both men and women, compared to no flexibility (Table 7.1). Considerable understanding from supervisors was significantly associated with lower scores on work–care conflict among women but not among men, whereas considerable understanding from colleagues was significantly related to lower work–care conflict among men but not women (both

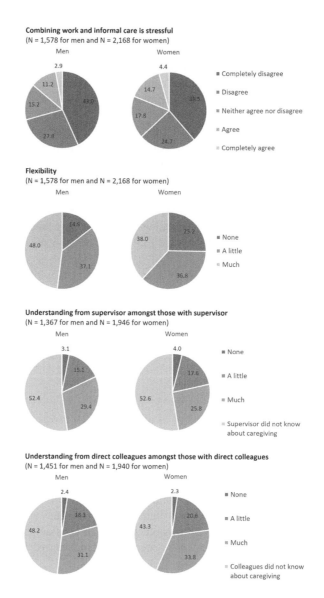

Figure 7.1   Work–care conflict, flexibility and understanding from supervisor and colleagues by sex, in proportions

compared to no understanding). Women who had not informed their supervisor or direct colleagues reported lower work–care conflict.

Table 7.1   *Relationship between workplace support and work–care conflict*

	Men		Women	
	b	se	b	se
Flexibility (ref = none)				
A little	0.01	0.08	−0.10	0.06
Considerable	−0.26**	0.09	−0.34***	0.07
Understanding from supervisor (ref = none)				
A little	0.07	0.20	−0.22	0.14
Considerable	−0.05	0.20	−0.36*	0.15
Supervisor not aware of caregiving	−0.38	0.20	−0.64**	0.15
No supervisor	−0.29	0.21	−0.53**	0.17
Understanding from direct colleagues (ref = none)				
A little	−0.30	0.21	−0.09	0.18
Considerable	−0.45*	0.22	−0.25	0.19
Colleagues not aware of caregiving	−0.35	0.22	−0.40**	0.19
No colleagues	−0.09	0.24	−0.25	0.21
Education level (ref = low)				
Medium	0.07	0.09	0.01	0.07
High	0.21*	0.08	0.21**	0.07
Average age during care episode	0.00	0.00	0.00	0.00
Number of previous care episodes	−0.03	0.02	−0.03	0.02
Care intensity (ref = low)				
Medium	0.38**	0.07	0.32**	0.06
High	0.67**	0.11	0.48**	0.09
Care tasks	0.12**	0.02	0.17**	0.02
Relationship to care recipient (ref = partner)				
Parent (including in-law and step)	−0.22**	0.08	−0.28**	0.09
Child	0.07	0.13	−0.04	0.12
Other family member	−0.25*	0.10	−0.56**	0.10
Neighbor, friend, acquaintance, colleague	−0.48**	0.10	−0.68**	0.10
Intercept	1.29**	0.25	1.88**	0.22
	est.	95% CI	est.	95% CI
Variance at caregiver level	0.64	0.58–0.71	0.60	0.54–0.66
Variance at episode level	0.79	0.74–0.83	0.84	0.81–0.88

Notes: Retrospective informal care careers (N = 1,578 episodes in 931 caregivers for men and N = 2,168 episodes in 1,207 caregivers for women). * $p < 0.05$; ** $p < 0.01$.

DISCUSSION

We tested the hypothesis that workplace support is negatively associated with work–care conflict among men and women. Our findings show that this hypothesis is confirmed for flexibility at work (among both men and women), for understanding from supervisors among women and understanding from colleagues among men.

Flexibility at work would appear to hold promise as a workplace resource to help working caregivers to reduce work–care conflict, particularly because both employers and employees gained so much experience with workplace flexibility during the COVID-19 pandemic. The availability of technical solutions to enable homeworking has increased considerably, for example. At the same time, we must be cautious as previous literature has shown that workplace flexibility, especially homeworking, tends to increase people's tendency to work overtime, which in turn may challenge work–life balance (Peters & van der Lippe, 2007).

Our finding that understanding from supervisors or direct colleagues was associated with less work–care conflict suggests that tools designed to enhance understanding in the workplace may be valuable. Obviously, an essential precondition for that understanding is that supervisors or colleagues are aware of the informal caregiving duties that their co-workers have. This was only the case in roughly half of the cases in our sample, however. Our models showed that women whose supervisor or direct colleagues did not know about their care role reported lower levels of work–care conflict. A clear selection effect seems to be at play here: those who do not experience any work–care conflict are less likely to feel the need to inform their employer about their care duties. However, disclosing one's care role at an early stage may be important in preventing work–care conflicts at a later stage of the care episode. Disclosure at work is not always easy, as the organizational culture may not be conducive to open and honest communication about this. Workers may also choose not to disclose because they prefer not to talk about their personal situation (e.g. a sick partner, child or parent) when they are at work, or because their work is a welcome distraction from worries at home. Supervisors can support their workers by making it easier for them to talk about such matters and coaching workers in their decisions on which information to share with their colleagues and when. Complete disclosure is not always necessary and staff often value advice on how to support their co-workers.

It must be acknowledged that we are not able to address causality issues on the basis of our data and therefore cannot claim that flexibility and workplace support lead to less work–care conflict. Experimental (or quasi-experimental) designs would be necessary for that. Nevertheless, potential selection issues in the realm of work and care probably do not alter the main message of our findings. First, if working caregivers with high work–care conflict selected themselves into care-friendly workplaces that offer more flexibility and understanding, then we would have observed a positive relationship between flexibility and understanding on the one hand and work–care conflict on the other. However, we found a negative relationship, which confirms the positive effect of workplace flexibility and support. This reverse causality would thus lead to an underestimation of the effects we found. Second, if workers in flexible and supportive workplaces are more likely to respond to the need for care in their social network because they feel that both roles can be combined without too much work–care conflict, we can still be positive about the role of workplace flexibility and support in addressing the growing need for labor market participation and informal care.

In conclusion, enhancing support at work by offering more flexibility and understanding may reduce work–care conflict and thereby improve the mental health of workers with informal care responsibilities. Both male and female caregivers in employment appear to benefit. Workplace arrangements and a supportive organizational culture can therefore provide a valuable tool in enabling the sustainable combination of work with informal care for the growing number of working caregivers.

REFERENCES

Bijnsdorp, F. M., van der Beek, A. J., Broese van Groenou, M. I., Proper, K. I., van den Heuvel, S. G., & Boot, C. R. (2022). Associations of combining paid work and family care with gender-specific differences in depressive symptoms among older workers and the role of work characteristics. *Scandinavian Journal of Work, Environment & Health*, 48(3), 190–199.

Bom, J., Bakx, P., Schut, E., & Van Doorslaer, E. (2018). Informal caregiving, a healthy decision? Determinants and health-related consequences of providing informal care. *Netspar Survey Paper*, 52, 1–38.

Broese van Groenou, M., Schakel, S., & Tolkacheva, N. (2015). Werk en mantelzorg. Een risico voor de psychische gezondheid? [Work and care: A risk to mental health?] *Tijdschrift voor Arbeidsvraagstukken*, 31(4), 393–410.

Candy, B., Jones, L., Drake, R., Leurent, B., & King, M. (2011). Interventions for supporting informal caregivers of patients in the terminal phase of a disease. *Cochrane Database Systematic Review*, 15(6), CD007617.

de Boer, A., Plaisier, I., & de Klerk, M. (2019). *Werk en Mantelzorg. Kwaliteit van leven en het gebruik van ondersteuning op werk*. [Work and informal care: Quality of life and the use of support at work]. The Hague: The Netherlands Institute for Social Research.

Earle, A., & Heymann, J. (2011). Protecting the health of employees caring for family members with special health care needs. *Social Science & Medicine*, 73(1), 68–78.

Greenhaus, J. H., & Beutell, N. J. (1985). Sources of conflict between work and family roles. *Academy of Management Review*, 10(1), 76–88.

Haberkern, K., Schmid, T., & Szydlik, M. (2015). Gender differences in intergenerational care in European welfare states. *Ageing & Society*, 35(2), 298–320.

Hammer, L. B., Kossek, E. E., Yragui, N. L., Bodner, T. E., & Hanson, G. C. (2009). Development and validation of a multidimensional measure of family supportive supervisor behaviors (FSSB). *Journal of Management*, 35(4), 837–856.

Joling, K. J., O'Dwyer, S. T., Hertogh, C. M., & van Hout, H. P. (2018). The occurrence and persistence of thoughts of suicide, self-harm and death in family caregivers of people with dementia: A longitudinal data analysis over 2 years. *International Journal of Geriatric Psychiatry*, 33(2), 263–270.

Josten, E., Verbakel, E., & de Boer, A. (2022). A longitudinal study on the consequences of the take-up of informal care on work hours, labour market exit and workplace absenteeism due to illness. *Ageing & Society*. DOI:10.1017/S0144686X22000204.

Mikkola, T. M., Mänty, M., Kautiainen, H., von Bonsdorff, M. B., Haanpää, M., Koponen, H., Kröger, T., & Eriksson, J. G. (2022). Work incapacity among family caregivers: A record linkage study. *Journal of Epidemiology Community Health*, 76(6), 580–585.

Peters, P., & van der Lippe, T. (2007). The time-pressure reducing potential of telehomeworking: The Dutch case. *International Journal of Human Resource Management*, 18(3), 430–447.

Pinquart, M., & Sörensen, S. (2006). Gender differences in caregiver stressors, social resources, and health: An updated meta-analysis. *Journals of Gerontology: Series B*, 61(1), 33–45.

Verbakel, E., & CentERdata (2021). *LISS panel: Retrospective informal care career: Main measurement*. DANS/KNAW database.

Verbakel, E., Tamlagsrønning, S., Winstone, L., Fjær, E. L., & Eikemo, T. A. (2017). Informal care in Europe: Findings from the European Social Survey (2014) special module on the social determinants of health. *European Journal of Public Health*, 27(suppl. 1), 90–95.

Zigante, V. (2018). *Informal care in Europe: Exploring formalisation, availability and quality*. Brussels: European Commission.

8. Leadership support and work–life balance

Laura den Dulk, Samantha Metselaar, Joëlle van der Meer, and Brenda Vermeeren

INTRODUCTION

Employees' perceptions of work–life balance are shaped by the organizational context, the policies that are in place, work practices, and culture. For this reason, leadership support is a crucial element in organizations and an important resource that helps employees to combine (paid) work and responsibilities in other life domains and avoid conflicting demands (e.g., Den Dulk et al., 2016). When considering leadership support, a distinction can be made between the support of senior managers (chief executive officers, directors, and board members) and direct supervisors. Senior managers are important actors in determining and designing the overall organizational and human resources strategy. They are in a position to develop and introduce work–life policies that aim to support work–life balance, such as leave and flexible work arrangements. Direct supervisors, meanwhile, affect the everyday experiences of employees by implementing those policies and attending to individual needs (Den Dulk et al., 2018). In this chapter, we focus on the leadership support of direct supervisors.

Direct supervisors can provide various types of work–life balance support. The emotional support offered by supervisors, such as expressing understanding for employees' work–life balance needs, has been identified as an important type of support (Abendroth & Den Dulk, 2011; Hammer et al., 2009). Later, Hammer et al. (2009, 2013) developed a multi-dimensional concept that measures family-supportive supervisor behavior (FSSB), which not only includes emotional support but also instrumental support (practical assistance such as pointing out the work–life options available), role-modeling behavior (showing how to combine work and family responsibilities), and creative work–family management (proactively redesigning work to help employees balance work and family life). Kossek et al. (2011) argued that providing this kind of specific support, rather than more general support, is actually more beneficial for employees' work–life balance. While general support involves expressing concern for the well-being of employees at work, specific support, such as FSSB, focuses on the work–life balance of employees and thus generates resources that help them combine work with their family and personal life (Kossek et al., 2011). Although it provides important insight, their meta-study only included studies up to 2010 and most of those were conducted in liberal, Anglo settings where formal policy support was limited. In a context with few or no policies on work–life balance, employees depend largely on the informal support of their supervisor when balancing work and family life (Den Dulk et al., 2016).

Conversely, in a context where formal work–life policies are in place and responsibilities and needs outside work are increasingly recognized and valued, supporting employees' work–life balance may become part of being a supportive supervisor (Den Dulk et al., 2016). To that end, scholars have introduced "servant leadership" as a concept to examine the relationship between leadership support and employees' work–life balance (Rofcanin et al., 2021; Tang et al., 2016; Zhang et al., 2012). Research on servant leadership suggests that by creating a work environment where employees feel empowered and their needs are recognized, valued, and supported, employees' lives beyond work may also be affected (Eva et al., 2019; Rofcanin et al., 2021). To explore the relevance of specific work–life balance leadership support (such as FSSB) versus a more general focus on the well-being of employees, we therefore examine the role of servant leadership. We use insights from sociology and public administration to take a contextualizing approach to work–life balance experiences and the role of servant leadership. In this chapter, we specifically explore whether FSSB and servant leadership are distinct constructs in the context of a Dutch public-sector organization. This organizational context is characterized by a substantial level of formal work–life policies and a supportive work–life culture. We address the following research question: How do support for work–life balance and servant leadership relate to the work–life balance experiences of public-sector employees in the Netherlands?

THEORETICAL BACKGROUND

Recent research suggests that servant leaders are more likely to support the work–life balance of employees (Rofcanin et al., 2021; Tang et al., 2016; Zhang et al., 2012). While other leadership styles tend to focus more on achieving goals set by the organization, servant leadership is characterized by an orientation towards the needs and interests of individual employees (Eva et al., 2019). A servant leader enables employees to make their own decisions based on their own needs and preferences, which in turn should lead to an increase in well-being, personal growth, and autonomy among employees

(Van Dierendonck, 2011). A servant leader is likely to focus on how employees want to organize their work and personal life and how they, as a leader, can support them in doing so. Servant leadership can thus be considered an important resource for the work–life balance of employees (Rofcanin et al., 2021). Another important dimension of servant leadership is empowering employees, which increases their job autonomy – i.e., the control over and responsibility for how, when, and where they do their job. Job autonomy is an important resource for achieving a good work–life balance because it gives employees the possibility to align their work and non-work responsibilities (Gajendran & Harrison, 2007). Based on this reasoning, we would expect servant leadership to have a direct and positive effect on work–life balance as well as an indirect effect via job autonomy.

Rofcanin et al. (2021) argued that servant leaders support the work–life balance of their employees by engaging in FSSB. As stated in the introduction, FSSB refers to specific behaviors on the part of supervisors to facilitate the work–life balance of employees. Work–life balance can be seen as an important need for employees, and by engaging in FSSB, servant leaders can address this need. In their study in two companies in Chile, Rofcanin et al. (2021) found a positive relationship between servant leadership and work–life balance via FSSB. However, the correlation between servant leadership and FSSB was high. Overall, we expect servant leadership to have a direct positive impact on work–life balance and indirectly via FSSB and autonomy as well.

DATA AND METHODS

Procedure and Participants

Data were collected at a Dutch government organization in summer 2022. The organization is characterized by generous work–life policies, such as partially paid parental leave and a supportive work–life culture. In addition, the data for this study relate to a post-COVID-19 situation, when employees were allowed to work partly from home and partly in the office (hybrid working) according to their own needs and preferences. In total, 2,668 employees across different departments were invited to participate. After cleaning the data, a sample of 671 employees (response rate = 25 percent) who completed the entire questionnaire remained. Of that sample, 56 percent are male and most are between 41 and 55 years old or older than 55. About one-third of respondents have childcare responsibilities for children living at home, and a similar proportion provide informal care.

Measures

Work–life balance was measured using the shortened three-item scale (Abendroth & Den Dulk, 2011) derived from the original five-item scale developed by Valcour (2007). An example item is: "How satisfied are you with your ability to meet the needs of your job and the needs of your personal or family life?" ($\alpha = 0.94$).

Autonomy was measured using three items derived from the Work Design Questionnaire (Morgeson & Humphrey, 2006, Dutch translation by Gorgievski et al., 2016). These items measure the decision-making autonomy of respondents. An example item is: "The job allows me to make a lot of decisions on my own" ($\alpha = 0.90$).

Family supportive supervisor behavior was measured using three items derived from the short FSSB scale developed by Hammer et al. (2013). An example item is: "My supervisor demonstrates effective behavior in juggling work and non-work activities" ($\alpha = 0.90$).

Servant leadership was measured using five items from the scale developed by Van Dierendonck and Nuijten (2011). We focused specifically on the empowerment dimension. An example item is: "My supervisor gives me the authority to take decisions which make work easier for me" ($\alpha = 0.92$). All scaled items used a Likert scale from 1 to 5.

As control variables, we included gender, age, and care responsibilities (yes/no). Age was measured using four categories (15–25, 26–40, 41–55, and older than 55 years old). With respect to care responsibilities, we distinguished between childcare responsibilities for children living at home and informal care. See Table 8.1 for descriptive statistics and correlations among variables.

Analysis

To explore whether FSSB and servant leadership are distinct constructs, we conducted an exploratory factor analysis (EFA). The EFA revealed that the items for FSSB and servant leadership loaded onto the same construct, both when the number of constructs was free and when we forced the items into two factors. Moreover, the results showed a relatively high correlation ($r = 0.710$) between these two forms of leadership support. We were thus unable to distinguish servant leadership and FSSB as two separate constructs in our study. We therefore had to exclude the relationship between servant leadership, FSSB, and work–life balance from our model. Instead, we built two different models. In the first model, we analyzed the impact of servant leadership on work–life balance via autonomy. In the second model, we analyzed whether FSSB has an impact on work–life balance (and controlled for autonomy).

Table 8.1   *Descriptive statistics and correlations among variables for work–life balance*

	Mean	SD	1	2	3	4	5	6	7	8
1. Work–life balance (1–5)	3.91	0.83	1	0.155**	0.160**	0.182**	0.096**	0.082*	−0.103*	−0.031
2. Autonomy (1–5)	3.99	0.72		1	0.173**	0.275**	−0.054	−0.052	0.045	−0.047
3. FSSB (1–5)	3.44	0.88			1	0.710**	0.018	−0.052	0.048	0.039
4. Servant leadership (1–5)	3.60	0.85				1	−0.018	−0.084*	0.056	0.005
5. Gender (0–1)	0.56	0.50					1	0.237**	−0.086*	−0.044
6. Age (1–4)	3.35	0.77						1	−0.325**	0.138**
7. Childcare (0–1)	0.36	0.48							1	−0.020
8. Informal care (0–1)	0.33	0.47								1

Notes: $*p < 0.05$; $**p < 0.01$.

We conducted structural equation modeling (AMOS), following a two-step approach (Anderson & Gerbing, 1988) distinguishing between the measurement model and the structural model. For the servant leadership (Model 1) as well as the FSSB (Model 2) analysis, fit measures of both the measurement model and the structural model were assessed. The measurement models concerned a confirmatory factor analysis and, in addition, we calculated the average variance extracted (AVE). The measurement model for Model 1 yielded a reasonable fit with values above 0.90 (Byrne, 2001), namely goodness of fit index (GFI) = 0.922, Tucker Lewis index (TLI) = 0.945, and comparative fit index (CFI) = 0.959. Unfortunately, at 0.094, the root mean square error of approximation (RMSEA) was slightly above the threshold of 0.08. The measurement model for Model 2 indicated a good fit with values above 0.95 (GFI = 0.988, TLI = 0.996, and CFI = 0.997) and a RMSEA below 0.05 (= 0.029). The AVE was above the 0.5 threshold for all constructs (in both models), showing convergent validity. Moreover, the square root of the AVE did not exceed the correlation values between our constructs, showing discriminant validity, and all factor loadings were well above 0.5 (these outcomes are available upon request from the first author).

The structural model for Model 1 yielded a reasonable fit with GFI = 0.935, TLI = 0.941, CFI = 0.959, and RMSEA = 0.072. The structural model for Model 2 indicated a good fit with the data (GFI = 0.986, TLI = 0.995, CFI = 0.997, and RMSEA = 0.022).

RESULTS

Model 1: Servant Leadership, Autonomy, and Work–Life Balance

Our findings show that employees who perceive more servant leadership also report a better work–life balance ($\beta = 0.175$, $p < 0.001$). Furthermore, there is a positive relationship between servant leadership and autonomy ($\beta = 0.245$, $p < 0.001$) and between autonomy and work–life balance ($\beta = 0.102$, $p < 0.05$). Subsequently, we examined whether the relationship between servant leadership and work–life balance was mediated by autonomy. Results show that the relationship between servant leadership and work–life balance is indeed partially mediated by autonomy ($\beta = 0.024$, $p < 0.05$), implying that servant leaders have a direct as well as an indirect effect on the perceived work–life balance of their employees. With respect to our control variables, we found that employees with childcare responsibilities perceive a worse work–life balance ($\beta = -0.093$, $p < 0.05$).

Model 2: FSSB and Work–Life Balance

Our findings show that employees who perceive more FSSB report a better work–life balance ($\beta = 0.162$, $p < 0.001$). With respect to the impact of the control variables, our results indicate that autonomy is positively associated with work–life balance ($\beta = 0.120$, $p < 0.01$), so employees who perceive greater autonomy report a better work–life balance. In addition, employees with childcare responsibilities perceive a worse work–life balance ($\beta = -0.095$, $p < 0.05$).

DISCUSSION

In this chapter, we have contributed to the literature on leadership support for the work–life balance of employees by exploring the role of servant leadership and FSSB. We investigated whether these two types of leadership support are distinct concepts in an organizational context that is characterized by a high level of formal work–life policies and a supportive work–life culture. Our findings suggest that in such a context, FSSB appears to be part of servant leadership. This means that in the context of this study, FSSB and servant leadership cannot be viewed as distinct constructs. The impact of FSSB and servant leadership were therefore examined in separate models. Our findings indicate that both FSSB and servant leadership are positively related to work–life balance. We also found that increased job autonomy is a relevant mechanism through which servant leadership positively affects the work–life balance of employees.

Future research should investigate this further, however, since we did not include all dimensions of the two concepts in our measurement. In addition, we were unable to compare between contexts that provide diverging levels of organizational support. A contextual approach is needed when studying the relationship between leadership support and work–life balance in future endeavors, as we do not yet fully understand how organizational conditions shape this relationship. Previous studies that took perceived organizational support for employee well-being into account provide evidence that the impact of servant leadership is greater when there is lower perceived organizational support (Zhang et al., 2012). Moreover, the study by Rofcanin et al. (2021) in Chile showed that servant leaders are likely to compensate for a lack of organizational support by showing more FSSB. However, our findings indicate that servant leadership is also a relevant resource in this context, which is characterized by a high level of organizational work–life support. In such a context, the dimensions of FSSB can become part of being a supportive supervisor serving the needs of employees. These findings suggest that leadership support is influenced by the perceived level of organizational work–life support. Leadership support therefore both reflects and shapes existing cultural norms and values within organizations (Den Dulk et al., 2016). Few studies have yet investigated the role of servant leadership in relation to work–life balance, and so we would encourage future work to focus on both the role of context (work–life policies and organizational culture) and mediating mechanisms.

REFERENCES

Abendroth, A. K., & Den Dulk, L. (2011). Support for work–life balance in Europe: The impact of state, workplace and family support on work–life balance satisfaction. *Work, Employment and Society*, *25*(2), 234–256.

Anderson, J. C., & Gerbing, D. W. (1988). Structural equation modeling in practice: A review and recommended two-step approach. *Psychological Bulletin*, *103*(3), 411–423.

Byrne, B. M. (2001). *Structural equation modeling with AMOS: Basic concepts, applications and programming*. Lawrence Erlbaum Associates.

Den Dulk, L., Peper, B., Kanjuo Mrĉela, A., & Ignjatović, M. (2016). Supervisory support in Slovenian and Dutch organizations: A contextualizing approach. *Community, Work & Family*, *19*(2), 193–212.

Den Dulk, L., Yerkes, M. A., & Peper, B. (2018). Work–family policies within the workplace. In: G. B. Eydal & T. Rostgaard (eds) *Handbook of Family Policy* (pp. 139–151). Edward Elgar Publishing.

Eva, N., Robin, M., Sendjaya, S., Van Dierendonck, D., & Liden, R. C. (2019). Servant leadership: A systematic review and call for future research. *The Leadership Quarterly*, *30*(1), 111–132.

Gajendran, R. S., & Harrison, D. A. (2007). The good, the bad, and the unknown about telecommuting: Meta-analysis of psychological mediators an individual consequence. *Journal of Applied Psychology, 92*(6), 1524–1541.

Gorgievski, M., Peeters, P., Rietzschel, E. F., & Bipp, T. (2016). Reliability and validity of the Dutch translation of the Work Design Questionnaire. *Gedrag & Organisatie, 29*(3), 273–301.

Hammer, L. B., Kossek, E. E., Yragui, N. L., Bodner, T. E., & Hanson, G. C. (2009). Development and validation of a multidimensional measure of family supportive supervisor behaviors (FSSB). *Journal of Management, 35*(4), 837–856.

Hammer, L. B., Kossek, E. E., Bodner, T., & Crain, T. (2013). Measurement development and validation of the family supportive behavior short-form (FSSB-SF). *Journal of Occupational Health Psychology, 18*(3), 285–296.

Kossek, E. E., Pichler, S., Bodner, T., & Hammer, L. B. (2011). Workplace social support and work–family conflict: A meta-analysis clarifying the influence of general and work–family-specific supervisor and organizational support. *Personnel Psychology, 64*(2), 289–289.

Morgeson, F. P., & Humphrey, S. E. (2006). The Work Design Questionnaire (WDQ): Developing and validating a comprehensive measure for assessing job design and nature of work. *Journal of Applied Psychology, 91*(6), 1321–1339.

Rofcanin, Y., Heras, M. L., Bosch, M. J., Berber, A., Mughal, F., & Ozturk, M. (2021). Servant leadership and family supportiveness: Looking into employees' work and family outcomes. *Journal of Business Research, 128*, 70–82.

Tang, G., Kwan, H. K., Zhang, D., & Zhu, Z. (2016). Work–family effects of servant leadership: The roles of emotional exhaustion and personal learning. *Journal of Business Ethics, 137*(2), 285–297.

Valcour, M. (2007). Work-based resources as moderators of the relationship between work hours and satisfaction with work–family balance. *Journal of Applied Psychology, 92*(6), 1512–1523.

Van Dierendonck, D. (2011). Servant leadership: A review and synthesis. *Journal of Management, 37*(4), 1228–1261.

Van Dierendonck, D., & Nuijten, I. (2011). The servant leadership survey: Development and validation of a multidimensional measure. *Journal of Business and Psychology, 26*(3), 249–267.

Zhang, H., Kwan, H. K., Everett, M., & Jian, Z. (2012). Servant leadership, organizational identification, and work-to-family enrichment: The moderating role of work climate for sharing family concerns. *Human Resource Management, 51*(5), 747–767.

9. Leadership, social support, and work–life balance of employees

Marloes van Engen and Leire Gartzia

INTRODUCTION

For most workers around the world, if not all, combining work responsibilities and providing care poses a daily challenge. Care can be understood in a broader sense, including caring for or supporting one's children, spouse, and elderly or care-dependent relatives and friends, as well as personal care (i.e., taking care of your mental and physical well-being) or caring for members of one's direct community such as neighbors or a wider community through volunteer work. Finally, care can also be provided at work to colleagues. The challenge of combining such care responsibilities with paid work represents a major problem for many working adults. In the European Union, one in three of the adult population aged 18–64 years has care responsibilities and a large proportion of them experience a significant level of work–life conflict (Remery & Schippers, 2019), which has various negative effects such as stress or reduced organizational commitment (Allen et al., 2020).

The difficulty of combining care and career has exacerbated during the COVID-19 pandemic (Hjálmsdóttir & Bjarnadóttir, 2020). In the aftermath of the pandemic, the worlds of work and care seem to have undergone important transformations. First, the pandemic fueled a trend that was already under way: the blurring of boundaries between work and home due to technological innovations (Kelliher & Richardson, 2012). Second, societies have increasingly been confronted with all kinds of global crises (energy, climate, political), which are affecting families and businesses around the world, and make families adrift. Third, aging populations in many countries, particularly in the Global North, pose a challenge for both the domains of work and care, as has become painfully clear since the slow reopening of societies after the COVID-19 pandemic. These countries are facing a growing labor shortage and increasing demands for caregiving due to their aging populations, as the imbalance between the working population and non-working population continues to grow. Data from the World Population Prospects of the United Nations reported that in 2018, for the first time in history, there were more people aged over 65 in the world than there were children aged under five. It is estimated that by 2050 one in four persons in Europe and Northern America could be aged 65 or older. Not only are people living longer, but they are also placing higher demands on health-care systems and informal care for the working population. This means that a smaller adult working population is having to do more in terms of both work and care, as well as facing the challenge of combining work with care. Coming up with ways to combine career and care sustainably is therefore an increasingly relevant social challenge.

For employers, and human resources managers in particular, this implies taking account of both the present and future well-being and performance of employees when organizing their work (Van Engen et al., 2012). For individuals, it implies making informed decisions around combining work and care and ensuring that their careers include being happy, healthy, and productive at work (Van der Heijden, 2005), as well as in their role as a parent, caregiver, neighbor, or citizen (Van Engen et al., 2012). These orientations are not always based on individual choices, however, and are also affected by individuals' perceptions of support in their environment (Byron, 2005; French et al., 2018; Gartzia et al., 2018).

In the following sections, we will review theory and research relating to combining career and care sustainably, with a particular focus on how others can influence people's experiences. First, however, we will explain the concepts of work–life conflict and work–life enrichment. Subsequently, we will describe how social support from both the personal domain (such as support from a spouse, friends, or family members) and the work domain (such as support from a supervisor and coworkers, and organizational culture, policies, and practices) enable workers to manage the boundaries between work and life domains, with a particular emphasis on the role of supervisors and coworkers. We will conclude this chapter by taking a closer look at how prevailing expectations regarding the roles of men and women in work and care affect people's choices and the policies and practices of organizations. Using social identity and gender role theories, we will set out the implicit social and psychological structures that underlie contemporary organizational principles and stand in the way of people combining career and care sustainably.

REDUCING WORK–LIFE CONFLICT AND PROMOTING WORK–LIFE ENRICHMENT

The majority of research that addresses the mutual effects of work and care has focused on work–life conflict, understanding the intersection between these two domains as "a form of inter-role conflict in which the role pressures from the work and family domains are mutually incompatible in some respect"

(Greenhaus & Beutell, 1985, p. 77; see also Michel et al., 2011). Research in this scholarly domain has demonstrated that this form of work–life conflict has harmful effects for individuals in terms of well-being and mental health (Burke & Greenglass, 1999) and for organizations (such as increased absenteeism and turnover intention).

More recently, research on the work–life interface has focused on creating more positive connections between work and private life by examining the benefits of multiple role involvement (Frone, 2003; Parasuraman & Greenhaus, 2002). Researchers have moved beyond the idea that demands in one domain directly affect functioning in the other domain. Based on work–life enrichment models, experiences in one role can also indirectly produce a positive effect in the other role in the form of increased energy or by generating resources that may enhance quality of life in the second role (Greenhaus & Powell, 2006).

Researchers have pointed out that work–life enrichment and an employee's abilities to combine career and care roles have a wide range of positive consequences. McNall et al. (2010) propose a typology of three specific categories of work–life enrichment consequences that include: (1) work-related outcomes such as increased job satisfaction, affective commitment, and reduced turn-over intention; (2) broader non-work-related outcomes such as greater life satisfaction and family satisfaction; and (3) health-related outcomes such as improved mental and physical health and ability to cope with stress (Hobfoll, 2002). Some of the mechanisms that have been suggested as explaining why involvement in multiple roles is beneficial center on the idea that multiple roles enable energy from one role to be used in another, the transfer of positive learnings, and the expansion of social networks (Greenhaus & Powell, 2006). For instance, based on Marks' (1977) expansionist approach and Greenhaus and Powell's (2006) work–life enrichment models, experiences in one role (e.g., care) may positively carry over to another role (e.g., career) in the form of increased energy and the generation of resources. This can enhance quality of life in the second role.

Consistent with conservation of resources theory (Hobfoll, 2002), earlier empirical work in this domain suggests that work–life enrichment operates through a "resource reservoir" (Hobfoll, 2002), so that participation in multiple roles can make people better equipped to solve problems in other domains and be less likely to suffer from the effects of stress. According to Greenhaus and Powell (2006), the resource reservoir that can be acquired from role experiences can include interpersonal skills and the ability to attend to another person's needs, as well as psychological and physical resources such as self-esteem. These resources are understood as enabling enrichment and improved performance in the other role through either the direct acquisition of skills or indirectly by generating positive emotions (such as experiencing positive emotions in one role domain that translate into positive emotions in the other).

In relation to the work-related outcomes of enrichment through non-work roles, research has shown that social exchange processes (Blau, 1964) can also be used to explain the positive effects of family on work enrichment, so that employees who perceive that somebody in their organization is helping them to deal with their personal life is more likely to feel supported and cared for, and this, in turn, results in more positive feelings about the job and the organization (Aryee et al., 2005; Wayne et al., 2007) along with better work outcomes such as increased job satisfaction, affective commitment, and lower turnover intention (McNall et al., 2010). Although the concept of work–life enrichment has attracted interest in recent years, the paths by which the two domains influence each other remain unclear (Beauregard & Henry, 2009). Moreover, although Greenhaus and Powell's (2006) model helps to explain the drivers of enrichment, current research provides only limited insight into the role that leadership and coworker support plays in the work–family interface.

THE ROLE OF SOCIAL SUPPORT

In recent decades, the role of social support in relation to the work–life interface has been the focus of numerous studies. In general, empirical research confirms that social support has beneficial consequences for general health outcomes, for example mental health (Xu et al., 2021), cardiovascular health (Heitman, 2006; Uchino et al., 2020), sleep quality (Xu et al., 2021), but also improving outcomes at the work–family interface (e.g., a reduction of work–life conflict; French et al., 2018; Kossek et al., 2011), work–life satisfaction, work-related burnout (Halbesleben, 2006), and parental burnout (Lin et al., 2022).

Social support can be defined as "psychological or material resources provided through social relationships that can mitigate strains" (French et al., 2018, p. 288). Social support can originate from both the work domain and the private life domain. The "domain specificity" hypothesis suggests that work support mitigates work-to-life conflict, while family support mitigates life-to-work conflict (Frone et al., 1997). Indeed, meta-analyses (Byron, 2005; French et al., 2018) have found partial support for the domain-specificity hypothesis, indicating that work support mitigates work-to-family conflict more strongly than family-to-work conflict, particularly in the case of organizational support (see below). However, both workplace and private life support mitigate work-to-family conflict. Some researchers suggest that the process by which support mitigates strain as support is that support acts as a "buffer" between stressors that stem from either the work domain or the private life domain and individual strain (buffer hypothesis). However, so far research has offered more support for the direct role of social support (main hypothesis) in reducing strain, meaning that support reduces work–life conflict directly.

In their seminal meta-analytic review of studies that examined the relationship between social support and work–life conflict, French et al. (2018) distinguish various kinds of support and operationalizations of support based on (1) the type of support or (2) the source of the support. They examine which kinds of support are more helpful in reducing work-to-family and family-to-work conflict and differentiate between four *types* of support: emotional; appraisal; informational; and instrumental. Emotional support refers to resources that target the receiver's feelings such as love, care, and trust. Appraisal targets the receiver's appraisal of strain – social support that acts as a psychological buffer to strain. Informational support refers to information, or advice on how to avoid strain. Instrumental support refers to tangible resources for individuals, such as time and money to invest in reducing strain. In their meta-analytic study comparing these four types of support, French et al. find that all types of support are helpful and that there is no difference between the four types of support and the effect on work-to-family and family-to-work conflict.

Sources of support refers to whether the support comes from the work domain (e.g., from a supervisor, coworker, or the organization) or the family domain (e.g., spouse, other family members). Furthermore, support can be defined more generally, such as supportive organizational perceptions, or more specifically, such as support from a supervisor or coworker. Importantly, all types of support reduce work–life conflict. Comparing the more general types of work domain support with more specific sources of support, French et al. (2018) find that general support from the organization is more helpful than supervisor or coworker support in reducing work-to-family conflict. Similarly, general support from the organization was more helpful than supervisor support in reducing family-to-work conflict, but did not differ in strength from coworker support. For family support, no differences were found between general and specific types of family support in the strength of reducing conflict between work and family and vice versa.

TOWARDS SUSTAINABILITY IN COMBINING CAREER AND CARE

There are several potential routes to overcoming the many challenges of combining career and care demands, including individual, family, organizational, and institutional dimensions. For instance, work–life conflict is influenced by workers' perceptions of an organization's work–family culture and by work conditions associated with the use of time such as the frequency of having to work overtime and the number of hours worked per week, the presence of shiftwork, and the flexibility of work schedules. Importantly, contextual variables can have an effect at macro-organizational levels (e.g., organizational structure, policies, and culture) and meso-organizational levels (e.g., unit goals, workload, and tasks; Gartzia, 2021b). The features of the organizational context therefore influence individuals' ability to combine career and care, and thus need to be addressed in order to bring about family-friendly practices and norms on a sustainable basis.

As we noted previously, research has shown that social exchange processes can explain the positive effects of support. For instance, employees who perceive that someone in their organizations is helping them to cope with the demands of their private life are more likely to feel supported and cared for, resulting in more positive feelings about the job and the organization, including better work outcomes such as increased job satisfaction, affective commitment, and reduced turnover intention (McNall et al., 2010). This is consistent with evidence that traditional working schedules, which are characterized by working long hours, do not lead to more effective work (e.g., Pencavel, 2015). Emotional support has been acknowledged as a particularly relevant feature in occupational stress and is particularly relevant for people experiencing stressful experiences to enhance employee performance (e.g., Patzelt et al., 2021).

Because supervisors are responsible for monitoring and regulating the performance of employees and making decisions about work conditions, their attitudes to work–life balance and the time that employees are expected to spend at work is important. Managers are in a key position to influence employees' work conditions and so managerial support in relation to work–life balance is critical (Gartzia et al., 2018). Indeed, in the leadership literature, there is agreement that supporting employees' personal and emotional needs (namely, supportive leadership behaviors; Kossek et al., 2011) is one of the most important functions of leadership. The notion of supportive leadership underscores the importance of managers' sensitivity to their employees' needs in various situations (Patzelt et al., 2021), including in the face of care and career constraints. Showing concern for individual needs, taking employees' preferences into account, and caring for and listening to employees are critical in organizations (Rafferty & Griffin, 2006).

Emotion-based support is a particularly relevant function that occurs when leaders express concern for employees and take account of their needs and preferences. This involves being sympathetic, caring, and listening. Since emotional support is a critical feature of leadership in order to help employees overcome negative and stressful experiences (e.g., Patzelt et al., 2021; Rajah et al., 2011), leaders' ability to provide emotional support to employees in relation to work–life balance is critical. When leaders display a supportive attitude, employees perceive their managers as respectful and sensitive to matters that are important to them (Paltzet et al., 2021). Extending these principles to balancing care and career, supportive leaders should be empathetic and understanding of employees' care needs, as well as their career needs, respectful and sensitive to their employees' care responsibilities, and supportive of employees' values and needs in their working life.

The majority of research on organizational work–life support has focused on supervisors and managers as sources of support, and researchers have only recently started to examine the role of coworkers. However, it can be argued that coworker support is particularly effective because the proximity of coworkers in the day-to-day work–life challenges that individuals face makes it much more likely that they can provide emotional and instrumental support (McMullan et al., 2018; Mesmer-Magnus et al., 2009). Indeed, coworker support has been shown to be related to reduced levels of work-to-life conflict and life-to-work conflict (French et al., 2018).

TOWARDS SUSTAINABLE SOLUTIONS FOR WORKERS WHO CARE AND CARERS WHO WORK

Demographic developments such as aging populations mean that working adults are finding it increasingly challenging to combine care responsibilities with paid work, leading to problems for many. In contemporary workplaces, then, managers and human resource practitioners' ability to develop an empathetic understanding of employees' experiences and individual needs should undoubtedly include their care responsibilities. Leaders can foster the uptake of work–life arrangements that reduce strain, they can channel coworker support and create a supportive and family-friendly climate within the organization, and they can act as role models, demonstrating effective work–family behaviors (Kossek et al., 2011). Given that managers are relevant role models for employees, revising how managerial values and practices can shape the actual uptake of family benefits is critical. This is especially important for male leaders, who often display stereotypically masculine traits that are contrary to communal values and care needs (Gartzia, 2021a; Gartzia & van Knippenberg, 2016; Gartzia et al., 2018). The growing challenge of creating more caring workplaces involves overcoming the mismatch between the traditional breadwinner model – which is derived from a domestic division of labor whereby employees (mainly men, who rely on the female partner to fulfill care responsibilities in the home) worked long hours – and today's dual-earner family models, in which both partners share these care responsibilities (Van Engen et al., 2012). Overcoming the outdated approach to work in which family and care demands are neglected is important not only from the perspective of individual and family development, but also from that of organizational approach. Based on the shown associations between work–life balance and organizational functioning, understanding and promoting the sustainable combination of care and career should be a priority in current workplace practices. We should also note that the traditional approach of long hours and breadwinner ideals is inefficient and does not translate into more effective work, based on evidence from economic research.

All in all, the implementation and sustainability of organizational policies that acknowledge the relevance of care and individual life require a profound transformation in organizational practices consistent with demands for gender equality. Research in this field (e.g., Gartzia, 2021b) suggests that the implementation of gender action, including work–life balance policies, requires coordinated action from policymakers, private firms, and employees, and work–life sustainability therefore involves policy and action that address these multilevel influences. Public policy and legislation can guide organizational principles and practice by providing norms regarding the relevance of work–life balance and procedures for how to implement them. Organizations, by contrast, can align care goals with their organizational strategy and shared values, and there is a particularly relevant role for managers and coworkers in supporting care needs. The institutional and organizational factors interrelate in complex ways through individual psychological resistance, identities, and motivation, and thus they should be addressed in an integrated manner. If we are to understand fully how to facilitate and improve the overarching practice of providing care that is imperative in today's societies, it is necessary to conduct a focused analysis of how the different layers of institutional forces, organizational practices, and decision-making by couples and individuals on how to combine work and life are intertwined.

REFERENCES

Allen, T. D., French, K. A., Dumani, S., & Shockley, K. M. (2020). A cross-national meta-analytic examination of predictors and outcomes associated with work–family conflict. *Journal of Applied Psychology, 105*(6), 539–576.

Aryee, S., Srinivas, E. S., & Tan, H. H. (2005). Rhythms of life: Antecedents and outcomes of work–family balance in employed parents. *Journal of Applied Psychology, 90*(1), 132–146.

Beauregard, T. A., & Henry, L. C. (2009). Making the link between work–life balance practices and organizational performance. *Human Resource Management Review, 19*(1), 9–22.

Blau, P. (1964). *Exchange and power in social life.* Wiley.

Burke, R. J., & Greenglass, E. R. (1999). Work–family conflict, spouse support, and nursing staff well-being during organizational restructuring. *Journal of Occupational Health Psychology, 4*(4), 327–336.

Byron, K. (2005). A meta-analytic review of work–family conflict and its antecedents. *Journal of Vocational Behavior, 67*(2), 169–198.

French, K. A., Dumani, S., Allen, T. D., & Shockley, K. M. (2018). A meta-analysis of work–family conflict and social support. *Psychological Bulletin, 144*(3), 284–314.

Frone, M. R. (2003). Work–family balance. In J. C. Quick & L. E. Tetrick (Eds), *Handbook of Occupational Health Psychology* (pp. 143–162). American Psychological Association.

Frone, M. R., Yardley, J. K., & Markel, K. S. (1997). Developing and testing an integrative model of the work–family interface. *Journal of Vocational Behavior, 50*(2), 145–167.

Gartzia, L. (2021a). Self and other reported workplace traits: A communal gap of men across occupations. *Journal of Applied Social Psychology.* https://doi.org/10.1111/jasp.12848.

Gartzia, L. (2021b). Gender equality in business action: A multi-agent change management approach. *Sustainability, 13*(11), 6209.

Gartzia, L., & van Knippenberg, D. (2016). Too masculine, too bad: Effects of communion on leaders' promotion of cooperation. *Group and Organization Management, 41*(4).

Gartzia, L., Sánchez-Vidal, M. E., & Cegarra, D. (2018). Male leaders with paternity leaves: Effects of work norms on effectiveness evaluations. *Journal of Work and Organizational Psychology, 27*(6), 793–808.

Greenhaus, J. H., & Beutell, N. J. (1985). Sources of conflict between work and family roles. *Academy of Management Review, 10*(1), 76–88.

Greenhaus, J. H., & Powell, G. N. (2006) When work and family are allies: A theory of work–family enrichment. *Academy of Management Review, 31*(1), 72–92.

Halbesleben, J. R. (2006). Sources of social support and burnout: A meta-analytic test of the conservation of resources model. *Journal of Applied Psychology, 91*(5), 1134–1145.

Heitman, L. K. (2006). The influence of social support on cardiovascular health in families. *Family and Community Health,* 131–142.

Hjálmsdóttir, A., & Bjarnadóttir, V. S. (2021). "I have turned into a foreman here at home": Families and work–life balance in times of COVID-19 in a gender equality paradise. *Gender, Work & Organization, 28*(1), 268–283.

Hobfoll, S. E. (2002). Social and psychological resources and adaptation. *Review of General Psychology, 6*(4), 307–324.

Kelliher, C., & Richardson, J. (2012). *New ways of organizing work, developments, perspectives and experiences.* Routledge.

Kossek, E. E., Pichler, S., Bodner, T., & Hammer, L. B. (2011). Workplace social support and work–family conflict: A meta-analysis clarifying the influence of general and work–family-specific supervisor and organizational support. *Personnel Psychology, 64*(2), 289–313.

Lin, G. X., Goldenberg, A., Arikan, G., Brytek-Matera, A., Czepczor-Bernat, K., Manrique-Millones, D., … & Gross, J. J. (2022). Reappraisal, social support, and parental burnout. *British Journal of Clinical Psychology, 61*(4), 1089–1102.

Marks, S. R. (1977). Multiple roles and role strain: Some notes on human energy, time and commitment. *American Sociological Review, 42,* 921–936.

McMullan, A. D., Lapierre, L. M., & Li, Y. (2018). A qualitative investigation of work–family-supportive coworker behaviors. *Journal of Vocational Behavior, 107,* 25–41.

McNall, L. A., Nicklin, J. M., & Masuda, A. D. (2010). A meta-analytic review of the consequences associated with work–family enrichment. *Journal of Business and Psychology, 25*(3), 381–396.

Mesmer-Magnus, J., & Viswesvaran, C. (2009). The role of the coworker in reducing work–family conflict: A review and directions for future research. *Pratiques Psychologiques, 15*(2), 213–224.

Michel, J. S., Kotrba, L. M., Mitchelson, J. K., Clark, M. A., & Baltes, B. B. (2011). Antecedents of work–family conflict: A meta-analytic review. *Journal of Organizational Behavior*, *32*(5), 689–725.

Parasuraman, S., & Greenhaus, J. H. (2002). Toward reducing some critical gaps in work–family research. *Human Resource Management Review*, *12*(3), 299–312.

Patzelt, H., Gartzia, L., Wolfe, M. T., & Shepherd, D. A. (2021). Managing negative emotions from entrepreneurial project failure: When and how does supportive leadership help employees? *Journal of Business Venturing*, *36*(5).

Pencavel, J. (2015). The productivity of working hours. *The Economic Journal*, *125*(589), 2052–2076.

Rafferty, A. E., & Griffin, M. A. (2006). Refining individualized consideration: Distinguishing developmental leadership and supportive leadership. *Journal of Occupational and Organizational Psychology*, *79*(1), 37–61.

Rajah, R., Song, Z., & Arvey, R. D. (2011). Emotionality and leadership: Taking stock of the past decade of research. *Leadership Quarterly*, *22*(6), 1107–1119.

Remery, C., & Schippers, J. (2019). Work–family conflict in the European Union: The impact of organizational and public facilities. *International Journal of Environmental Research and Public Health*, *16*(22), 4419.

Uchino, B. N., Cronan, S., Scott, E., Landvatter, J., & Papadakis, M. (2020). Social support and stress, depression, and cardiovascular disease. In P. D. Chantler & K. T. Larkin (eds) *Cardiovascular implications of stress and depression* (pp. 211–223). Academic Press.

Van der Heijden, B. I. J. M. (2005). *No one has ever promised you a rose garden: On shared responsibility and employability enhancing strategies throughout careers.* Open University of the Netherlands.

Van Engen, M. L., Vinkenburg, C. J., & Dikkers, J. S. (2012). Sustainability in combining career and care: Challenging normative beliefs about parenting. *Journal of Social Issues*, *68*(4), 645–664.

Wayne, J. H., Grzywacz, J. G., Carlson. D. S., & Kacmar, K. M. (2007). Work–family facilitation: A theoretical explanation and model of primary antecedents and consequences. *Human Resource Management Review*, *17*, 63–76.

Xu, R., Lin, Y., & Zhang, B. (2021). Relationship among sleep quality, depressed mood, and perceived social support in older adults: A longitudinal study. *Journal of Pacific Rim Psychology*, *15*. DOI: 18344909211052658.

10. Work–life balance in essential and non-essential occupations in the Netherlands

Stéfanie André and Chantal Remery

INTRODUCTION

A healthy and sustainable work–life balance implies the ability to combine work and caregiving without marginalizing either of these two aspects. In the Netherlands, the one-and-a-half-earner model is seen as an 'ideal' solution when it comes to combining work and care in households, with men mainly working full time and women working part time and taking on most household tasks (Plantenga, 2002; Yerkes, 2009). The Netherlands ranks fairly high in the National Work–Life Balance Index (Fernandez-Crehuet et al., 2016). This situation was put to the test, however, when the COVID-19 pandemic started and the Netherlands went into its first lockdown in March 2020. People were urged to work from home as much as possible and many households faced additional care tasks as schools and daycare facilities closed. As a result, working parents had to find a new balance between work and care tasks.

At the same time, early in the COVID-19 pandemic, some sectors, such as retail, transport, and public services like education and care, were categorized as 'essential' for the functioning of society. Workers in essential occupations often had to continue working on location, and sometimes for longer hours. More women were essential workers than men, due to their overrepresentation in education and care for instance (Queisser et al., 2020). This meant that women were more likely to be working outside the home. Given this 'new' and gendered group of workers and the challenges for work–life balance posed by the pandemic, our research question is: *What is the influence of essential worker status on the work–life balance of male and female workers in the Netherlands?*

In this chapter, we explore the impact of working in an essential occupation on perceived work–life balance and present the results of analyses on how easy men and women found it to combine their work with care tasks (e.g. childcare, informal care) in November 2020. At that point, there was not a full lockdown, but regulations to contain the pandemic were in force, such as wearing masks in public spaces.

We use a combined sociological and economic perspective to understand how governmental labeling may have influenced micro household behaviors and perceptions of work–life balance. We do this using bargaining theory, which is derived from sociological/psychological exchange theory (Blood & Wolfe, 1960), and economic specialization theory (Becker, 1981). In addition, we take work–life boundary management style into account (Kossek & Lautsch, 2012).

THEORY

To prevent the spread of the COVID-19 virus, many countries, including the Netherlands, put strict measures in place. During the first lockdown in the Netherlands, schools and daycare centers were closed, and even when these regulations were relaxed, certain strict rules remained in place for children (known as the 'runny nose rule'). As a result, many parents faced more care tasks (André et al., 2023) and, furthermore, most people with informal care tasks experienced the burden of having to combine working with informal care-giving tasks during COVID-19 (Raiber & Verbakel, 2021). These additional care tasks presumably had a negative impact on perceived work–life balance.

The exact impact likely differed between households and work characteristics. One factor that is particularly relevant was 'essential occupation status'. At the start of the COVID-19 pandemic, the government declared certain occupations to be essential for the functioning of society. These included f.e. jobs in education, care, logistics, and waste disposal. Given the importance and demanding character of essential occupations during the pandemic, we expected that working in these occupations would undermine perceived work–life balance, particularly in cases where both partners were working in an essential occupation. This leads to our first hypothesis.

Hypothesis 1   *Workers in dual-earner households where both partners worked in essential occupations had a worse work–life balance than workers in households where both partners worked in non-essential occupations.*

At the same time, the urgency of the situation forced many households to renegotiate the allocation of responsibilities. When studying the impact of working in an essential occupation on work–life balance, these renegotiations must be considered. Bargaining theory predicts that partners in the household will bargain over who will perform which household tasks (Blood & Wolfe, 1960). The partner that has more resources (education, income) will win this negotiation and focus on paid work, while the partner with fewer resources will focus on unpaid work. According to Becker (1981) this is rational, since specialization in either paid or unpaid work maximizes household utility. Although the theory can be seen as gender-neutral, the outcome is not, because women generally have fewer resources than their male partners.

We theorized that the label attributed to essential workers could be considered as a (new) resource that could be used in negotiating paid and unpaid work within the household. This would be the case particularly if one of the partners was designated an essential worker and the other was not. We expect that workers with essential worker designation would be in a stronger position to renegotiate the division of work and care than workers not in an essential occupation, and would therefore have more power to achieve a better work–life balance. Since more women worked in essential jobs than men, this resource could have resulted in a better work–life balance for women, because they renegotiated care tasks with their partner. This leads to our second hypothesis:

Hypothesis 2   *Workers in an essential occupation, whose partner worked in a non-essential occupation, will have a better work–life balance (in relative terms) than workers in households where both partners worked in a non-essential occupation. This relationship is expected to be stronger among women.*

Furthermore, homeworking, hybrid working and homeschooling became common during the pandemic. This brought work into the private sphere, and people's private lives into the work sphere. This blurring of boundaries could collide with people's boundary management strategy – i.e. their preference for integration or separation when it comes to managing work and family roles (Kossek & Lautsch, 2012). We theorized that those who prefer to separate their work life from their home life would have been more likely to experience a deterioration in work–life balance during the COVID-19 pandemic.

Hypothesis 3   *The work–life balance of workers with a separating boundary management strategy will be worse than workers with an integrating boundary management strategy.*

METHODS

We used the Dutch Longitudinal Internet Study for the Social Sciences panel, which has followed Dutch workers over time in the COVID and Gender (In) Equality Study Netherlands (CentERdata, 2022). We focused on the work–life balance of those in dual-earner households (N = 423). In the first wave only working parents with at least one minor co-resident child were included; from the second wave onwards, the sample was extended to working adults in the same age range, without co-resident minor children. Questionnaires were completed individually. The following questions were used with respect to work–life balance:

1. How easy or difficult was it for you to combine your paid work with your care responsibilities prior to the COVID-19 pandemic?
2. How easy or difficult has it been for you to combine your paid work with your care responsibilities since the general closure of schools and child-care centers? (Wave 1)
3. How easy or difficult is it for you to combine your paid work with your care responsibilities at present? (Waves 2–5)

The scores were coded to ensure that higher scores indicated a better work–life balance. For the regression analysis, we used Wave 4 (November 2020) because this included boundary management items. Our main explanatory variable was working in an occupation deemed 'essential' using four groups: (1) neither of the partners worked in an essential occupation; (2) only the respondent worked in an essential occupation; (3) only the partner worked in an essential occupation; and (4) both partners worked in an essential occupation. Boundary management was coded so that a higher score indicated a strategy more focused on separation than integration of work–family roles. We controlled for working hours, working from home, gender, age, and the age group of non-adult children living at home (no children was the reference). We conducted regression analyses for all respondents and, in order to study gender differences, for men and women separately.

RESULTS

Before discussing the results of the regression analyses, we will describe the average work–life balance of men and women in the different types of house-holds with combinations of essential occupation status between March 2020 and November 2021 (Figure 10.1). Combining work and care became more difficult in the first lockdown for all groups, especially when both partners worked in an essential occupation and therefore had to juggle working (outside the home) with care tasks. Although it was possible for essential workers to use daycare and emergency schooling if both parents worked in an essential occupation, most children in the Netherlands stayed at home during the first lockdown (88 percent). This could have been because parents were anxious about the new disease, their children had to be completely healthy (no 'runny

noses'), and all teaching took place online and not in person. It is interesting
to note that in November 2021, 18 months into the COVID-19 pandemic and
just before a new lockdown, households in which both partners worked in an
essential occupation were finding it particularly difficult to combine work
with care tasks, while among other groups the levels plateaued, with levels
comparable to those before COVID-19. One possible explanation is that work
pressure remained high and constant in sectors like healthcare and education.
Women experienced more difficulty combining work and care tasks than men,
particularly during the first months of the pandemic. These differences seem
small, however.

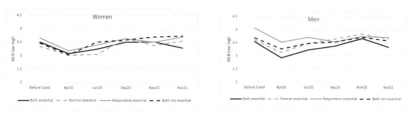

Note: N = 239 women and N = 184 men, respectively.

Figure 10.1   *Work–life balance of men and women in two-earner
household across time according to the household's essential
worker status*

The regression analysis in Model 1 of Table 10.1 shows that the different combinations of essential/non-essential occupation status did not affect work–life
balance. Respondents in households where both partners worked in an essential occupation did not find it any more difficult to combine work and care, and
Hypothesis 1 is therefore rejected. Moreover, boundary management strategy
had no effect on work–life balance either, so Hypothesis 3 is also rejected.
However, working at home had a positive impact on work–life balance. In
addition, men had a better work–life balance than women, on average. The
presence of children aged 12–18 years in the household appears to be relevant:
in those households, respondents reported a better work–life balance than
households without children. The analyses for men and women show that an
essential occupation had a different effect for men and women, but in a different
way to that hypothesized. Women who worked in a non-essential occupation
and whose partner worked in an essential occupation found it more difficult to
combine work and care than women with a partner in a non-essential occupation. As a result, Hypothesis 2 is also rejected. Remarkably, the explanatory
variables in our model are hardly relevant for men, as the variables included

Table 10.1   Regression analyses to explain perceived work–life balance

			Females		Males	
	b	SE	b	SE	b	SE
Essential occupation in household (none = ref)						
Both have essential occupation	−0.07	0.12	−0.01	0.16	−0.10	0.20
Respondent has essential occupation	−0.08	0.12	−0.17	0.15	0.15	0.24
Partner has essential occupation	−0.09	0.13	−0.45**	0.22	0.07	0.17
Boundary management	−0.00	0.04	−0.01	0.06	0.02	0.07
Working at home	0.24**	0.10	0.39***	0.13	0.14	0.15
Working hours per week (full time = ref)						
20–34 hours	0.08	0.12	0.05	0.15	−0.01	0.25
Less than 20 hours	−0.04	0.13	−0.06	0.17	−0.03	0.21
Working hours missing	−0.03	0.12	−0.17	0.17	0.09	0.19
Gender (men = 1)	0.22**	0.10				
Age	−0.00	0.01	−0.01	0.01	0.00	0.01
Age youngest child (no children = ref)	0.26***	0.09				
0–3	0.00	0.14	−0.06	0.19	0.02	0.21
4–11	0.24	0.11	0.31***	0.14	0.16	0.17
>12	0.60**	0.15	0.69***	0.19	0.49**	0.25
Constant	3.35***	0.36	3.63***	0.46	3.33***	0.60
R^2 adjusted	0.06		0.09		0.00	
N	423		239		184	

Notes: N = 423; * $p < 0.10$, ** $p < 0.05$, *** $p < 0.01$.

appear not to be significant with the exception of the presence of children aged 12–18 years. It appears that the work–life balance of men is impacted by factors other than those included in our analyses.

Based on these results, we cannot conclude that workers in essential occupations were better able to renegotiate care tasks and found it less difficult to combine work and care than those not working in an essential occupation.

DISCUSSION

Early on in the COVID-19 pandemic, certain occupations were labeled as essential for the continued functioning of society. This framing of essential occupations could, in theory, have given workers in those occupations more bargaining power at home to negotiate a better work–life balance. However, in this study we found no evidence of this effect. Work–life balance in November 2020 in the Netherlands was hardly impacted at all by working in an essential occupation. Men seem more positive regarding their work–life balance than women. Specifically, women who worked in a non-essential occupation and had a partner in an essential occupation experienced a worse work–life balance than women in households in which both partners had a non-essential occupation. These results suggest that occupational status did not act as a relative resource. In addition, boundary management strategy had no impact: workers with a separating boundary management strategy did not have a worse work–life balance than workers with an integrating boundary management strategy.

IMPLICATIONS FOR RESEARCH AND PRACTICE

It would be interesting to examine the effect of labeling certain occupations as essential (or more important) if future (economic) shocks hit the world. To better understand the relationship between 'essential' job status as a relative resource and work–life balance, future research could also include other countries where more women work full time. It is possible that changes are smaller in the Netherlands because most women work part time.

Looking forward, the question of whether governments can affect work–care balance within households remains unanswered – for example, when implementing policies that can positively affect work–life balance, such as introducing paternity leave or informal care leave. It is important that these types of leave not only help women combine work and care, but also encourage men to take on an increased share of care tasks in order to bring about more gender equality in work and care. Governments can signal that unpaid work is just as important for men as it is for women, and promote a discussion about alternative divisions of work and care.

REFERENCES

André, S., Remery, C., & Yerkes, M. A. (2023). Extending theoretical explanations for gendered divisions of care during the COVID-19 pandemic. Journal of Marriage and Family, 1–18. https://doi.org/10.1111/jomf.12950.
Becker, G. (1981). *A treatise on the family*. Harvard University Press.
Blood, R. O., & Wolfe, D. M. (1960). *Husbands and wives: The dynamics of family living*. Free Press Glencoe.
CentERdata. (2022). *LISS panel*. Tilburg University.
Fernandez-Crehuet, J. M., Gimenez-Nadal, J. I., & Reyes Recio, L. E. (2016). The National Work–Life Balance Index: The European case. *Social Indicators Research*, *128*, 341–359.

Kossek, E. E., & Lautsch, B. A. (2012). Work–family boundary management styles in organizations: A cross-level model. *Organizational Psychology Review, 2*(2), 152–171.

Plantenga, J. (2002). Combining work and care in the polder model: An assessment of the Dutch part-time strategy. *Critical Social Policy, 22*(1), 53–71.

Queisser, M., Adema, W., & Clarke, C. (2020). COVID-19, employment and women in OECD countries. CEPR VoxEu, April.

Raiber, K., & Verbakel, E. (2021). Are the gender gaps in informal caregiving intensity and burden closing due to the COVID-19 pandemic? Evidence from the Netherlands. *Gender, Work & Organization, 28*(5), 1926–1936.

Yerkes, M. A. (2009). Part-time work in the Dutch welfare state: The ideal combination of work and care? *Policy & Politics, 37*(4), 535–552.

11. The use of work–life arrangements in academia: a critical analysis of the potential to transform organizational norms

Inge Bleijenbergh

INTRODUCTION

A growing number of organizations provide work–life arrangements to enhance the work–life balance of their employees, such as the possibility of combining work with non-work responsibilities. These responsibilities include caring for dependent children, elderly parents, and loved ones (McDonald et al., 2006), which is the focus of this chapter. Work–life arrangements were introduced to ensure equal opportunities (Ely & Meyerson, 2000a) for people of all genders in the workplace, and particularly to enable women to compete on equal terms with men for positions, working conditions, and promotion. Enabling employees to fulfill care responsibilities more easily is supposed to create a more gender-equal workplace and a more equal division of work and care at home (Rehel, 2014).

But despite the claim that work–life arrangements contribute to gender equality, research shows that these instruments are often underutilized by the employees who are eligible for them (McDonald et al., 2006) and that the utilization of work–life arrangements is gendered. It has been shown that the uptake of work–life arrangements is informed by normative beliefs about traditional gender roles, which causes women to utilize leave and work part time more often than men (Van Engen et al., 2012). Scholars (Ely & Meyerson, 2000b; Lewis, 1997) have also criticized work–life arrangements for their limited potential to transform hegemonic masculine norms. These hegemonic norms relate to the 'ideal worker as always available and disengaged from family duties' (Toffoletti & Starr, 2016, p. 497), which implies that employees with caregiving tasks disrupt the gender order. This chapter addresses the question of whether and how work–life arrangements challenge gendered organizational norms and thereby contribute to transformational change towards gender equality. It focuses on work–life arrangements in academia, an example of a sector where hegemonic masculine norms regarding constant availability for work prevail but are also potentially contested (Thun, 2020; Van Engen et al., 2021). It contributes to the discussion in this book about the limitations of work–life instruments.

THEORY

This chapter contributes to the debate about transformational change in academia (Clavero & Galligan, 2021; Thun, 2020; Van den Brink & Benschop, 2012; Van Engen et al., 2021) by conceptualizing whether and how work–life arrangements contribute to transformational change towards gender equality. Work–life arrangements in academia include childcare facilities, paid and unpaid parental leave, other leave options, and flexible work arrangements (Tofolleti & Starr, 2016). Transformational change involves stakeholders in academia becoming aware of and critically examining and/or changing hegemonic norms (Knights & Richards, 2003). The aim is to change the way that work is defined, carried out, and evaluated (Ely & Meyerson, 2000a, 2000b). Mescher et al. (2010) showed that organizational norms concerning work–life balance are complex due to their ambiguous, differentiated, shared, and gendered nature.

Transformational change in organizational norms may occur when the hegemonic masculine norm of constant availability for paid work (Toffoletti & Starr, 2016) shifts towards the model of the 'integrated worker' (Bailyn & Harrington, 2004), whereby workers combine paid work with different aspects of unpaid or non-work, such as volunteer work, care (for children, elderly, significant others), political participation, personal development, leisure activities, and so on. Moving towards the 'integrated worker' norm contributes to gender equality, assuming that combining work and caregiving is equally accessible and accepted and has equal career consequences for men and women alike. We assume that the continuation of hegemonic masculine norms impedes organizational change towards gender equality in academia.

In order to challenge the status quo and change hegemonic norms, Poelmans (2012) argues that three steps must be taken: first, employees need to nominate the norms by explicitly discussing them; second, they need to be able to navigate norms by negotiating ways to achieve work–life balance; and third, they need to create new, more integrated norms. Indeed, Herschberg et al. (2014, p. 20) suggest that negotiation is a 'research space for studying incremental change in scientific organizational culture'. This chapter explores when and how work–life arrangements help academics to nominate, navigate, or create new norms (Poelmans, 2012). We explore this by means of a case study involving two research institutions at a university in the Netherlands.

METHODS

Our case study is a university in the Netherlands with about 24,500 students and 5,600 staff members. The university is committed to sustainable employability for its employees and aims to be a 'family-friendly organization'. As regards work-related services, the university website mentions flexible working arrangements, part-time work, leave opportunities, and childcare facilities. We selected two research institutes with different disciplinary backgrounds as subcases: an institute for management research and an institute for brain and cognition research. We held five focus groups with a total of 21 academics (10 women and 11 men) with young children (younger then 12 years old). Through snowball sampling, we identified and invited 60 colleagues with young children within the two research institutes, of which 21 took part in the focus groups. We created a safe and comfortable environment by separating the participants at each institute depending on whether they made use of work–life arrangements or not. At each institute, we conducted focus groups with academics with children. We split between academics working full time who had children and could therefore potentially have made use of flexible work arrangements (flexible hours and homeworking), and academics working part time (less than 36 hours) and/or who were taking parental leave. The participants included both Dutch and non-Dutch academics in heterosexual and homosexual relationships with one or two children whose ages ranged between six weeks and 11 years. Our sample consisted of 11 academics (six men and five women) working part time and 10 academics (five men and five women) working full time.

A semi-structured interview guide was used during the focus group sessions. This included questions about the participants' motivations for making use of work–life arrangements or not, how this subject was discussed with colleagues and management, and how the use of these arrangements was embedded in the culture of their organization and ways to transform this. In a series of inductive coding rounds (Corbin & Strauss, 2008), we identified tensions in the data regarding the boundaries between work and private life, and we considered what these tensions revealed about gendered organizational norms, and to what extent work–life arrangements reconfirmed hegemonic norms or supported the negotiation of new, more integrated norms both among colleagues collectively and in the minds of individual employees.

RESULTS

Our analysis shows that academics using work–life arrangements both reproduced organizational norms and contested them. A majority of participants reproduced the hegemonic organizational norm of constant availability in the sense that they considered working in academia as a 'calling' (Participant 4, man, management research, full time) that 'obviously' calls for working more than the number of working hours they were officially contracted for. Although participants stated that work was not always their main priority, they also supported the normative belief that work *should* be their main priority. For example, one participant from the Institute for Management Research referred to his willingness to be available for work on days off by making changes to his private commitments.

> In principle, we are quite flexible. So in principle we say 'no', but if it's possible to change something, and in many cases that is possible, we might schedule a meeting on my day off … So, yes, we change days to make sure that we can be flexible as well, and you don't always have to say that you're not available [for work] on that day. (Participant 7, man, management research, part time)

Hegemonic masculine norms are not only evident in prioritizing work commitments over private commitments, but also in perpetuating the idea that significant caregiving responsibilities impede one's career. Employees mentioned that taking parental leave would make them less likely to fit the image of the ideal worker. Participants from the Institute for Brain and Cognition referred to managers who had warned them not to get pregnant during their PhD or post-doc position because that would undermine their work performance.

> I remember what – it wasn't my direct supervisor but the big boss at the institute – said at that time, after I told my direct supervisor [that I was pregnant]. He said: 'Hmm, too bad, she does not have her priorities straight'. So afterwards, it was a little hard to go and talk about parental leave. (Participant 16, woman, brain and cognition, full time)

> But in my case they were not happy either. They actually told me when I started: 'You shouldn't get pregnant' and I thought 'Oh, I don't even have a boyfriend, so what are you talking about?' But yes, I did get pregnant, but they were just afraid that I wouldn't finish on time. (Participant 17, woman, brain and cognition, full time)

The participants in our focus groups negotiated their work–life balance both in the workplace and at home. At home, the partner was the main bargaining partner. The participants explained that the anticipated effect that making use of work–life arrangements would have on their careers played a role in the bargaining process at home, as did their own preferences for a more egalitarian division of caregiving tasks. Participants sometimes recounted how their personal preferences for an egalitarian division of tasks had been put on hold to prevent any loss of income or the expected adverse career consequences.

> I said to my girlfriend: 'I don't want to be the bread winner, we're going to do it together … At the moment, we're fairly balanced, but that has only been the case for the past year. Before that I always worked long hours, under protest so to say, but also because it was easier and I had to work longer hours because we had to make sure we had enough income. But with regard to care responsibilities, I would have liked to work fewer hours … Uh, you might wonder whether that would have been accepted … It certainly wouldn't have put me on the map. (Participant 1, man, management institute, part time)

The data showed that negotiations in different domains intertwine, and that the uptake of the work–life arrangements is dynamic over time. We focused on negotiations in the organizational domain, since these negotiations are directly related to the norms in the workplace that are the focus of organizational change towards gender equality in (academic) organizations.

The academics in our sample sometimes cited organizational norms which needed to change. Academics with young children mentioned non-hegemonic norms regarding the ideal worker by setting boundaries at work and trying to manage the expectations of others regarding availability. In doing this, they implicitly distanced themselves from the hegemonic masculine norm of constant availability for paid work. Non-hegemonic norms may become stand-ard if more colleagues adopt the norm of the 'integrated worker' (Bailyn & Harrington, 2004). For example, in the focus group made up of male academics working part time, several participants confirmed that they were distancing themselves from the ideal of being constantly available:

> I increasingly see my attitude as: 'Yes, I'll work as much as I can'. But I don't feel like working all night and I need to get my work done in the time available. I don't see myself being a workaholic for the next 30 years. This job might be like this, but not for me at least. That's where my attitude is heading. I think this is … yes … a good attitude, I guess. (Participant 8, man, management research, part time)
>
> That sounds healthy, yes. (Participant 9, man, management research, part time)
>
> Yes, I recognize that. (Participant 7, man, management research, part time)

Our analysis shows that male and female employees in academia working part time are setting stricter limits around working hours and opening up space for new organizational norms regarding work–life balance. The question is whether working part time allows more space to negotiate new organizational norms than working full time. Our analysis suggests that employees working full time also have room for negotiation, but derive this from their more senior position in the organization. For example, one participant from the Institute for Management Research has negotiated new norms around availability in the university building:

> Usually I say 'no', which makes me extremely unpopular with secretaries and others, uh … sometimes, but it has to be done. I'm not saying that it's set in stone but, uh … but if it's unimportant I just say no, sorry. So on Fridays I'm never usually here. That's clear. But again, if it's a collective thing like a meeting or a conference or a project meeting where there are ten people involved, then okay. But that's rare. Otherwise people just have to cope. I'm in no doubt that it helps that I have a fairly senior position … I'm under no illusion: they wouldn't be so flexible if I was an assistant professor. (Participant 4, man, management research, full time)

The potential for organizational change is embedded in the room that negotiations create to nominate hegemonic norms and create new norms that enable the roles of parent and ideal worker to be combined.

CONCLUSION

This research shows that academics who make use of work–life arrangements both reproduce hegemonic masculine norms and have space to negotiate new norms. Some of the employees that we spoke to had taken up work–life arrangements while also reproducing hegemonic norms about the ideal worker – for example, the idea that workers should be available for work outside office hours or that caregiving should not interfere with work. Participants also created new and more integrated norms about presence at work by insisting on taking one day a week off for caregiving responsibilities as a strict boundary. We also found that work–life balance is dynamic and changes during people's life cycle, with employees having more caregiving responsibilities when they have young children and dependent elderly relatives. Since the data were collected prior to the COVID-19 pandemic, we would suggest that norms regarding the need to be physically present in the university building may have become more relaxed, but that norms regarding online availability outside office hours may actually have increased.

Overall, we would suggest that work–life arrangements do not necessarily contribute to gender equality. Neither do work–life arrangements impede transformational change, since they provide organizational members with space to challenge organizational norms regarding the ideal worker and create new norms regarding physical presence in the workplace and limitations on working hours. The bargaining space that employees have is dynamic, depending on whether they have caregiving tasks, the resources they have gained in the workplace, and their career phase. The data suggest that hegemonic masculine norms regarding the need to work long hours persist, and that more measures than just work–life arrangements are needed to bring about transformational change towards gender equality. These measures might include building remuneration and rewards systems around the norm of the integrated worker, which may in turn necessitate a reconsideration of output norms and criteria. It may also be necessary to organize work schedules based on the assumption that all employees have caregiving responsibilities or other private commitments, and therefore avoid (online) meetings that begin early in the day or social events at the end of the working day, the evening, or weekend. Other measures relate to consistent and visible role modeling of organizational leadership regarding the importance of work–life balance, with leaders taking parental leave or working part time and adhering strictly to working hours.

ACKNOWLEDGMENT

With thanks to Joke Leenders for her role in data collection, data analysis, and the first draft of the results.

REFERENCES

Bailyn, L., & Harrington, M. (2004). Redesigning work for work–family integration. *Community, Work & Family*, 7(2), 197–208.

Clavero, S., & Galligan, Y. (2021). Delivering gender justice in academia through gender equality plans? Normative and practical challenges. *Gender, Work & Organization*, 28(3), 1115–1132.

Corbin, J., & Strauss, A. (2008). *Basics of qualitative research: Techniques and procedures for developing grounded theory* (3rd ed.). London: Sage.

Ely, R. J., & Meyerson, D. E. (2000a). Advancing gender equity in organizations. *Organization*, 7(4), 589–608.

Ely, R. J., & Meyerson, D. E. (2000b). Theories of gender in organizations: A new approach to organizational analysis and change. In B. M. Staw & R. I. Sutton (Eds), *Research in organizational behaviour* (Vol. 22, pp. 103–151). Amsterdam: JAI Elsevier Science.

Herschberg, C., Vinkenburg, C. J., Bleijenbergh, I. L., & Van Engen, M. L. (2014). Dare to care: Negotiating organizational norms on combining career and care in an engineering faculty. In D. Bilimoria & L. Lord (Eds), *Women in STEM careers: International perspectives on increasing workforce participation, advancement and leadership* (pp. 204–234). Cheltenham, UK and Northampton, MA, USA: Edward Elgar Publishing.

Knights, D., & Richards, W. (2003). Sex discrimination in UK academia. *Gender, Work & Organization*, 10(2), 213–238.

Lewis, S. (1997). Family friendly employment policies: A route to changing organizational culture or playing about at the margins? *Gender, Work and Organization*, 4(1), 13–23.

McDonald, P., Brown, K., & Bradley, L. (2006). Explanations for the provision–utilisation gap in work–life policy. *Women in Management Review*, 20(1), 37–66.

Mescher, S., Benschop, Y., & Doorewaard, H. (2010). Representations of work–life balance support. *Human Relations*, 63(1), 21–39.

Poelmans, S. (2012). The 'Triple-N' model: Changing normative beliefs about parenting and career success. *Journal of Social Issues*, 68(4), 838–847.

Rehel, E. M. (2014). When dads stay home too: Paternity leave, gender, and parenting. *Gender & Society*, 28(1), 110–132.

Thun, C. (2020). Excellent and gender equal? Academic motherhood and 'gender blindness' in Norwegian academia. *Gender, Work & Organization*, 27(2), 166–180.

Toffoletti, K., & Starr, K. (2016). Women academics and work–life balance: Gendered discourses of work and care. *Gender, Work & Organization*, 23(5), 489–504.

Van den Brink, M., & Benschop, Y. (2012). Slaying the seven-headed dragon: The quest for gender change in academia. *Gender, Work and Organization*, 19(1), 71–92.

Van Engen, M. L., Vinkenburg, C. J., & Dikkers, J. S. E. (2012). Sustainability in combining career and care: Challenging normative beliefs about parenting. *Journal of Social Issues*, 68(4), 645–664.

Van Engen, M. L., Bleijenbergh, I. L., & Beijer, S. E. (2021). Conforming, accommodation or resisting? How parents in academia negotiate their professional identity. *Studies in Higher Education*, 46(8), 1493–1505.

PART III

Digitalization and homeworking

12. Digital regulation in the service of sustainable work–life balance

Ariane Ollier-Malaterre, Tammy Allen, Ellen Ernst Kossek, Chang-Qin Lu, Gabriele Morandin, Sabrina Pellerin, Ashkan Rostami, and Marcello Russo

INTRODUCTION

Digital technologies are an increasingly salient part of people's lives, used every day to work, communicate, and access goods, services, and entertainment. The COVID-19 pandemic has increased people's reliance on technology, with 40 percent or more individuals across the globe working remotely or in a hybrid model (World Health Organization & International Labour Organization, 2021), 70 percent of employers intending to continue offering hybrid work in the coming years (Bloom, 2021), and a larger share of healthcare, education, and public services being provided online (Véliz, 2021).

So much of people's work lives, family lives, social lives, and leisure now unfold online, but what will this mean for our work–life balance over the long run? In this chapter, we focus on constant connectivity through mobile devices as a striking example of how technology both facilitates and undermines people's work–life balance. Because constant connectivity is a double-edged sword, we argue that the active regulation of digital technologies by (1) individuals, (2) organizations, and (3) policy makers and unions is the key to sustaining a healthy work–life balance.

The concept of constant connectivity means always being tethered to work and other obligations through our mobile and wearable devices, such as laptops, tablets, smartphones, and smart watches (Mazmanian et al., 2013; Wajcman & Rose, 2011). On the one hand, greater connectivity brings many benefits for work–life balance, allowing flexibility and choice as people combine work and life commitments. Workers in occupations and jobs that provide some degree of control over work–life boundaries (Kossek et al., 2012) may choose to work from home or to change their working hours to improve the way different parts of their lives fit together: this flexibility is likely to improve work–life balance, which is a subjective appraisal of how well a person is performing and feeling in the roles that matter most to them (Casper et al., 2018; Greenhaus & Allen, 2011).

On the other hand, constant connectivity can also erode the boundaries between work and private life (Ollier-Malaterre et al., 2019), exposing individuals to never-ending demands from work, family, and other domains (Olson-Buchanan et al., 2016), and leading to frequent distractions from whichever domain they are currently in (Russo et al., 2019) and a lack of detachment from work when they are engaged in other domains (Foucreault et al., 2016). Constant connectivity is also associated with technostress (Ma et al., 2021) – stress induced by the use of technology at work (Tarafdar et al., 2019), because it increases workload ("techno-overload") and spills over into life outside work ("techno-invasion"). We therefore call for the active regulation of connectivity at several levels.

Digital regulation – i.e., the actions that can be taken to better regulate the use of digital technologies and align them with our values and goals in life – is both an individual and a collective endeavor (Ollier-Malaterre, 2023). Our interdisciplinary approach, which combines insights from across management, sociology, and industrial-organizational psychology, analyzes the steps that can be taken at various levels by individuals, organizations, unions, and policy makers.

CONNECTIVITY REGULATION BY INDIVIDUALS

Individuals can activate agentic behaviors to improve their capacity to make connectivity decisions regarding "if, when and how much to connect" (Dery et al., 2014, p. 559). *Mindset* is important: people with a growth mindset (as opposed to a fixed mindset) – i.e., the belief that it is possible to enhance one's skills and capacities through training and effort – are more likely to engage in proactive behaviors (Dweck, 2006). Hence, the very first step to disconnecting is accepting the idea that *disconnecting is possible*. A recent study invited French and Italian students to disconnect from their smartphones for a full day (Russo et al., 2018). Most students reported that the initial fear of being excluded by their social network or missing important news was largely replaced by the happiness of being more present in their environment and discovering alternative ways of regulating their life and needs. They described a learning process, characterized by trial and error, and a reflection on what worked for them.

Such decisions do not happen in a vacuum, and constant connectivity is rooted in well-established *habits*. Neuroscience (e.g., Wood, 2019) suggests that habits should be gradually phased out rather than discontinued abruptly, and new habits can be imagined and then actualized. Positive emotions can accelerate the adoption process. In the long term, gradually reducing the use of smartphones is more durable and beneficial than complete abstinence (Brailovskaia et al., 2022). As such, there is no need to give up the use of mobile devices entirely. After all, they are now a major part of our lives and, in many cases, serve a very useful purpose. However, individuals benefit greatly from reflecting on when not using them would be beneficial. A useful strategy is to set *new positive goals* that reflect one's lifestyle, such as improving role performance, developing a personal digital philosophy, minimizing undesirable social behaviors, and protecting one's priorities in life (Russo et al., 2019).

Lastly, interpersonal relationships matter. Establishing common norms with coworkers (Nurmi & Hinds, 2020) and communicating frequently with one's supervisor about family demands (van Zoonen et al., 2020) mediates the relationship between the demand for connectivity and family and work outcomes (such as work–family conflict, job satisfaction, and organizational identification). Organizations therefore also have an important role to play in digital regulation, as we will discuss in the next section.

CONNECTIVITY REGULATION BY ORGANIZATIONS

To enable employees to regulate their connectivity better, some organizations have enacted "right to disconnect" practices. These include defining periods when emails cannot be sent (Mattern, 2020). However, these practices are only effective when they also address factors that stand in the way of an employee detaching – i.e., when work culture and norms also support disconnection (Pellerin et al., 2023). Some pioneering organizations have therefore worked to curtail expectations of employee availability by prohibiting the use of company mobile devices during holidays and monitoring work hours (Weber & Vargas Llave, 2021). Nonetheless, these practices may be less effective for employees who prefer to integrate work and nonwork.

Other approaches include more comprehensive interventions that aim to promote a more supportive work–life culture (Kossek et al., 2014) such as *Support-Transform-Achieve-Results* (STAR) (Kossek et al., 2014). STAR builds on research that recognizes that increasing employee perceptions of control over their working time and providing workplace support for nonwork roles are key resources in reducing work–family conflict (French et al., 2018). STAR includes training for supervisors that is designed to increase their nonwork and work supportive behaviors, identifying new work practices (e.g., making meetings optional) that give employees more control over their work schedules and connectivity, and the reorientation of work cultures toward results rather than "facetime" (Kelly et al., 2014; Kossek et al., 2017). Over 18 months, STAR helped to reduce voluntary turnover, presenteeism, and the use of healthcare (defined as emergency department episodes, outpatient visits including those specifically related to drug, alcohol, or mental health use, and days spent in the hospital, and excluding preventative healthcare use like wellness check-ups or vaccines), leading to an average organizational cost reduction of $1.68 for every $1.00 spent on STAR (Barbosa et al., 2015). Such an approach may be more effective than narrow interventions that focus only on connectivity, such as those that restrict email hours, because these may not be consistent with the job needs or lifestyle of all employees (Russell & Woods, 2020).

CONNECTIVITY REGULATION BY POLICY MAKERS AND UNIONS

Constant connectivity also represents a pervasive societal challenge that has attracted attention from policy makers in many countries (Pellerin et al., 2023). The question is, what can be done at the policy level to help workers switch off outside work hours without fearing negative repercussions from employers?

To address this issue, a growing number of countries are establishing a "right to disconnect," a legal provision that allows workers not to respond to work communications after work hours. The first such policy was adopted in France in 2017 (Von Bergen & Bressler, 2019). Although the right to disconnect provides a solid legal safeguard to address the challenges of increased connectivity, it also comes with some pitfalls that could compromise its effective application (Pellerin et al., 2023).

An important challenge is that the right to disconnect is not accompanied by clear obligations for employers (Pansu, 2018), and evidence shows that its interpretation on the ground leaves room for improvement (Hesselberth, 2018; Lerouge, 2020). As we have discussed, implicit barriers, such as expectations about availability and performance or prevailing organizational norms, may undermine effective implementation (Pellerin et al., 2023). Employers and unions therefore hold the key to the success of the right to disconnect. They can engage in active sensibilization and point out the benefits of disconnecting for mental health, work–life balance, and work performance. It may be up to unions to lead the way, however. Employers may only get on board when they perceive disconnecting as a resource that enables employees to detach from work psychologically and recharge, rather than a constraint that limits their authority (Lerouge, 2020).

A second important challenge is the social acceptability of such policies among workers. They would need to perceive the policy as relevant, accessible, and collectively accepted. Tailoring implementation to different occupations, organizational contexts, and individual preferences while remaining consistent with the principles of equality and inclusiveness could be the answer

(Pellerin et al., 2023). This is another area where the advocacy of labor unions is needed. In many occupations, the debate should also extend to workload (Lerouge, 2020; Pansu, 2018), since this is the core obstacle to disconnecting after work hours. The right to disconnect is a striking example of the role that policy makers could have in promoting the regulation of digital technologies with an eye to a sustainable work–life balance.

IMPLICATIONS FOR RESEARCH AND PRACTICE

In the previous sections, we have pointed out several concrete ways in which individuals, managers, and executives within workplaces, union leaders and representatives as well as policy makers can foster greater control over constant connectivity. We wish to emphasize that digital regulation is both an individual and a collective endeavor, and therefore it requires a multi-level and systemic (i.e., taking into account the entire social system in which they are embedded) approach. Even though it will help individuals to become aware that disconnecting is possible and that gradually changing their habits by setting positive goals is a way forward, these efforts will be undermined if they are not backed up by cultural changes within organizations that address work devotion schemas and availability expectations (Afota et al., 2022) and public policy that requires workers and organizations to challenge constant connectivity. The "digital contracts" promoted by one Italian association among local families, schools, and sports clubs regarding when and how children can use digital devices (www.pattidigitali.it) provide a promising way forward in this regard. "Patti digitali" takes families – too weak to withstand constant connectivity on their own – out of isolation and gives effect to the popular adage "It takes a village to raise a child."

Likewise, we encourage multi-level and interdisciplinary research designs into efforts to regulate constant connectivity in a systemic way. Such research may uncover the synergies between actions at different levels that effectively enable digital technologies to be regulated sustainably.

CONCLUSION

To summarize, technology can both enhance and undermine a sustainable work–life balance. Using constant connectivity to represent this complex reality, we have argued for the active regulation of digital technologies by individuals, organizations, unions, and policy makers to ensure that technology benefits work–life balance and well-being rather than undermining it.

REFERENCES

Afota, M. C., Provost Savard, Y., Ollier-Malaterre, A., & Léon, E. (2022). Work-from-home adjustment in the US and Europe: The role of psychological climate for face time and perceived availability expectations in the US and Europe. *International Journal of Human Resource Management.* https:// doi.org/ 10.1080/ 09585192.2022.2090269.

Barbosa, C., Bray, J. W., Dowd, W. N., Mills, M. J., Moen, P., Wipfli, B., ... & Kelly, E. L. (2015). Return on investment of a work–family intervention: Evidence from the work, family, and health network. *Journal of Occupational and Environment Medicine*, *57*(9), 943–951.

Bloom, N. (2021). Hybrid is the future of work. SIfEP Research. https://siepr.stanford .edu/publications/policy-brief/hybrid-future-work [Accessed February 7 2024].

Brailovskaia, J., Delveaux, J., John, J., Wicker, V., Noveski, A., Kim, S., Schillack, H., & Margraf, J. (2022). Finding the "sweet spot" of smartphone use: Reduction or abstinence to increase well-being and healthy lifestyle?! An experimental intervention study. *Journal of Experimental Psychology: Applied.* https://doi.org/ 10.1037/ xap0000430.

Casper, W. J., Vaziri, H., Wayne, J. H., DeHauw, S., & Greenhaus, J. (2018). The jingle-jangle of work–nonwork balance: A comprehensive and meta-analytic review of its meaning and measurement. *Journal of Applied Psychology*, *103*(2), 182–214.

Dery, K., Kolb, D., & MacCormick, J. (2014). Working with connective flow: How smartphone use is evolving in practice. *European Journal of Information Systems*, *23*(5), 558–570.

Dweck, C. S. (2006). *Mindset: The new psychology of success*. Random House.

Foucreault, A., Ollier-Malaterre, A., & Ménard, J. (2016). Organizational culture and work–life integration: A barrier to employees' respite? *International Journal of Human Resource Management*, 1–21.

French, K. A., Dumani, S., Allen, T. D., & Shockley, K. M. (2018). A meta-analysis of work–family conflict and social support. *Psychological Bulletin*, *144*(3), 284–314.

Greenhaus, J. H., & Allen, T. D. (2011). Work–family balance: A review and extension of the literature. In J. C. Quick & L. E. Tetrick (Eds), *Handbook of occupational health psychology*, 2nd Edition (pp. 165–183). American Psychological Association.

Hesselberth, P. (2018). Discourses on disconnectivity and the right to disconnect. *New Media & Society*, *20*(5), 1994–2010.

Kelly, E. L., Moen, P., Oakes, J. M., Fan, W., Okechukwu, C., Davis, K. D., Hammer, L. B., Kossek, E. E., King, R. B., Hanson, G. C., Mierzwa, F., & Casper, L. M. (2014). Changing work and work–family conflict: Evidence from the work, family, and health network. *American Sociological Review*, *79*(3), 485–516.

Kossek, E. E., Hammer, L. B., Kelly, E. L., & Moen, P. (2014). Designing work, family and health organizational change initiatives. *Organizational Dynamics*, *43*(1), 53–63.

Kossek, E. E., Ruderman, M. N., Braddy, P. W., & Hannum, K. M. (2012). Work–nonwork boundary management profiles: A person-centered approach. *Journal of Vocational Behavior*, *81*, 112–128.

Kossek, E., Wipfli, B., Thompson, R., Brockwood, K., & Work Family Health Network Writing Team. (2017). The Work, Family & Health Network intervention: Core elements and customization for diverse occupational health contexts. In F. Leong, D. Eggerth, D. Chang, M. Flynn, K. Ford, & R. Martinez (Eds), *Occupational health* disparities among racial and ethnic minorities: Improving the well-being of racial and ethnic minorities* (pp. 181–215). APA.

Lerouge, L. (2020). The right to disconnect from the workplace: Strengths and weaknesses of the French legal framework. In J. Carby-Hall & L. M. Méndez (Eds), *Labour law and the gig economy* (pp. 222–229). Routledge.

Ma, J., Ollier-Malaterre, A., & Lu, C. q. (2021). The impact of techno-stressors on work–life balance: The moderation of job self-efficacy and the mediation of emotional exhaustion. *Computers in Human Behavior, 122,* 106811.

Mattern, J. (2020). A classification of organizational interventions to enable detachment from work. *Proceedings of the 33rd Bled eConference.* https:// doi .org/ 10 .18690/978-961-286-362-3.8.

Mazmanian, M., Orlikowski, W. J., & Yates, J. (2013). The autonomy paradox: The implications of mobile email devices for knowledge professionals. *Organization Science, 24,* 1337–1357.

Nurmi, N., & Hinds, J. P. (2020). Work design for global professionals: Connectivity demands, connectivity behaviors, and their effects on psychological and behavioral outcomes. *Organization Studies, 41,* 1697–1724.

Ollier-Malaterre, A. (2023). Eroding boundaries and creeping control: "Digital regulation" as new normal work. In S. Bergum, P. Peters, and T. Vold (Eds), *Virtual management and the new normal: New perspectives on HRM and leadership since the COVID-19 pandemic* (pp. 313–332). Palgrave Macmillan.

Ollier-Malaterre, A., Jacobs, J. A., & Rothbard, N. P. (2019). Technology, work and family: Digital cultural capital and boundary management. *Annual Review of Sociology, 45,* 425–447.

Olson-Buchanan, J. B., Boswell, W. R., & Morgan, T. J. (2016). The role of technology in managing the work and nonwork interface. In T. D. Allen & L. E. Eby (Eds), *The Oxford handbook of work and family* (pp. 333–361). Oxford University Press.

Pansu, L. (2018). Evaluation of "right to disconnect" legislation and its impact on employee's productivity. *International Journal of Management and Applied Research, 5*(3), 99–119.

Pellerin, S., Ollier-Malaterre, A., Kossek, E. E., Afota, M. C., Cousineau, L., Lavoie, C. E., Leon, E., Beham, B., Morandin, G., Russo, M., Jaga, A., Ma, J., Lu C.-q., & Parent-Rocheleau, X. (2023). The right to disconnect. *Stanford Social Innovation Review.* https://ssir.org/articles/entry/the_right_to_disconnect [Accessed February 7 2024].

Russell, E., & Woods, S. A. (2020). Personality differences as predictors of action-goal relationships in work-email activity. *Computers in Human Behavior, 103,* 67–79.

Russo, M., Bergami, M., & Morandin, G. (2018). Surviving a day without smartphones. *MIT Sloan Management Review, 59*(2), 7–9.

Russo, M., Ollier-Malaterre, A., & Morandin, G. (2019). Breaking out from constant connectivity: Agentic regulation of smartphone use. *Computers in Human Behavior, 98,* 11–19.

Tarafdar, M., Cooper, C. L., & Stich, J. F. (2019). The technostress trifecta – techno eustress, techno distress and design: Theoretical directions and an agenda for research. *Information Systems Journal, 29*(1), 6–42.

van Zoonen, W., Sivunen A., & Rice, R. E. (2020). Boundary communication: How smartphone use after hours is associated with work–life conflict and organizational identification. *Journal of Applied Communication Research, 48,* 372–392.

Véliz, C. (2021). Privacy and digital ethics after the pandemic. *Nature Electronics, 4*(1), 10–11.

Von Bergen, C. W., & Bressler, M. S. (2019). Work, non-work boundaries and the right to disconnect. *Journal of Applied Business and Economics, 21*(2), 51–69.

Wajcman, J., & Rose, E. (2011). Constant connectivity: Rethinking interruptions at work. *Organization Studies, 32*(7), 941–961.

Weber, T., & Vargas Llave, O. (2021). Right to disconnect: Exploring company practices. Eurofound research report. Publications Office of the European Union. www.eurofound.europa.eu/publications/report/2021/right-to-disconnect-exploring -company-practices [Accessed February 7 2024].

Wood, W. (2019). *Good habits, bad habits*. Farrar, Straus and Giroux.

World Health Organization & International Labour Organization. (2021). *Health and Sage Telework: Technical brief.* https:// www .who .int/ publications/ i/ item/ 9789240040977 [Accessed February 7 2024].

13. Signaling support for work–family balance in order to retain (tele)workers in hybrid work contexts: lessons from the COVID-19 pandemic

Pascale Peters and Melanie de Ruiter

INTRODUCTION

According to McKinsey, the main reason for the increase in voluntary employee turnover during and after the COVID-19 pandemic was not that people were dissatisfied with tangible job resources (e.g. pay and fringe benefits), but that they wanted intangible job resources, such as feeling valued by their organization (De Smet et al., 2021). To meet the "retention challenge", human resource management has been urged to implement policies and practices that are both "human-centric" and "flexible" (De Prins et al., 2015; Moore, 2022). Practices that take account of employee well-being and socio-emotional needs, such as supervisory support and time-spatial flexibility, can make people feel valued (Eisenberger et al., 1986) and may, in turn, enhance job satisfaction and reduce turnover intention (An, 2022; Maan et al., 2020).

Literature that builds on the job demands-resource model (Bakker & Demerouti, 2014) suggests that the relationship between perceived organizational support and job satisfaction can be mediated by factors relating to the boundary between work and nonwork (Baeriswyl et al., 2016), such as work–family balance. The latter is particularly important in view of the intensification of teleworking during the COVID-19 pandemic and since, and the associated blurring of work–nonwork boundaries and the need to cope with atypical work–family situations. Given the need for socio-emotional support, particularly in telework contexts, it is interesting to examine whether this mechanism is contingent on employees' telework frequency (i.e. telework *intensity*) (Allen et al., 2015), as this may also inform future organizational practices.

This study aims to contribute to the conversation on the meaning of (sustainable) human resource management and work–family balance from an organizational behavior perspective in two ways. First, we will focus on perceived organizational support as an important psychological factor in achieving a healthy work–family balance, and its effect on job satisfaction and turnover intention. Specifically, our moderated-mediation model examines how perceived organizational support, which is regarded as a job resource that helps workers to handle demands and which motivates and energizes them, can enhance work–family balance, and whether this psychological process subsequently culminates in increased job satisfaction and reduced turnover intention.

Second, in 'hybrid work contexts', socio-emotional organizational proximity may play an increasingly important role. This study therefore examines how perceived organizational support and telework intensity interact to enhance the motivation process, fostering job satisfaction and reducing turnover intention *through* work–family balance.

THEORY

Work–family Balance

Work–family balance can be defined as "an overall appraisal regarding one's effectiveness and satisfaction with work and family life" (Allen & Kiburz, 2012, p. 373). Job resources, such as organizational support, can prompt a motivational process which energizes employees in both the work and nonwork spheres (Baeriswyl et al., 2016). Support can be conceptualized more generally, such as in terms of emotional or instrumental support during work, or it may focus more specifically on enhancing work–family balance (Straub et al., 2019). Perceived organizational support captures perceptions of both these elements and reflects people's "global beliefs regarding the extent to which the organization values their contributions and cares about their well-being" (Eisenberger et al., 1986, p. 501). It can be expected to improve compatibility between work and family demands and increase positive spillover between work and nonwork. We therefore posit that:

Hypothesis 1a   Perceived organizational support is positively related to work–family balance.

Perceived organizational support is likely to result in employees feeling more effective and satisfied with both their work and family lives, and hence with their job (Maan et al., 2020). Job satisfaction can be defined as a "pleasurable or positive emotional state resulting from the appraisal of one's job or job experiences" (Locke, 1976, p. 1304). Moreover, job satisfaction is known to predict turnover intention (An, 2022), conceived as "a conscious and deliberate willfulness to leave the organization" (Tett & Meyer, 1993, p. 262). Building on the motivational process, Baeriswyl et al. (2016) found that work–family conflict partially mediates the relationship between supervisor support and job satisfaction. Therefore, we posit that:

Hypothesis 1b   *Work–family balance mediates the motivational process, so that perceived organizational support relates positively to work–family balance, which in turn relates positively to job satisfaction, which in turn relates negatively to turnover intention.*

Telework Intensity

Particularly during the pandemic, teleworking may have hindered ongoing organizational socialization, which is important to the development of social knowledge and skills that enable employees to socialize at work and perform their work properly. Higher teleworking intensities may therefore increase stress, undermining the motivation process (Bakker & Demerouti, 2014). At the same time, however, the energizing capacity of perceived organizational support may be particularly important for employees who engage in intensive teleworking. We therefore posit that:

Hypothesis 2a   *The positive relationship between perceived organizational support and work–family balance is moderated by telework intensity, and this relationship is stronger for employees who telework more intensively.*

Hypothesis 2b   *The indirect relationship between perceived organizational support and turnover intention, first through work–family balance and then through job satisfaction, will be stronger among employees who telework more intensively.*

The moderated-mediation model is shown in Figure 13.1.

SAMPLE AND MEASUREMENTS

Data were collected during the COVID-19 pandemic (Winter 2021) using an online questionnaire (in Dutch and English) distributed through social media (e.g. LinkedIn and Facebook) and snowball sampling in an international network of knowledge workers.

After data cleaning, 100 respondents remained: 57 percent male and 43 percent female. Participants' ages ranged from 23 to 66 years (mean = 37.18; standard deviation = 13.42). Most respondents had a high level of education

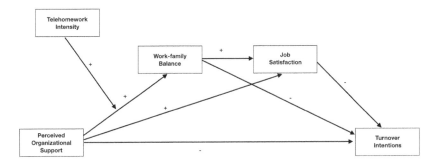

Figure 13.1   Hypothesized moderated-mediation model

(academic education = 42 percent; higher vocational education = 35 percent; postgraduate = 12 percent), 75 percent had a permanent employment contract, and 34 percent had live-in children.

Turnover intention was measured using three items (Mobley et al., 1978), using a five-point Likert scale (1 = strongly disagree to 5 = strongly agree). Perceived organizational support was measured using the eight-item short version by Rhoades et al. (2001) with a seven-point Likert scale (1 = strongly disagree to 7 = strongly agree). Two items were reverse coded. Work–family balance was measured using Allen and Kiburz's (2012) four-item scale with a five-point Likert scale (1 = strongly disagree to 5 = strongly agree). One item was reverse coded. Job satisfaction was measured using four items from COPSOQ II (Pejtersen et al., 2010) with a four-point scale (1 = very satisfied to 4 = very dissatisfied). All items were reversed so that higher scores represented higher job satisfaction. Telework intensity was constructed as a percentage of the total number of weekly home-working hours divided by actual weekly working hours (the sum of hours worked at home, in the office, and at other locations). After confirmatory factor analyses, the measurement model with four factors and 18 items (one item was removed) had the best fit compared to three alternative models.

RESULTS

To test our hypotheses, we used PROCESS version 4.1 Models 6 and 83 (Hayes, 2018) with 5,000 bootstrap samples and mean centering for perceived organizational support and telework intensity. Gender and having children in the household were considered important control variables (e.g. parents with live-in children perceived their work–life balance differently during the

Table 13.1   *Outcomes of the moderated-mediation model for work–life balance*

	WFB (M1)			JS (M2)			TI		
	B	Se	*p*	*B*	se	*p*	*B*	se	*p*
Constant	3.493(2.478)	0.085(0.430)	0.000(0.000)	2.768(1.825)	0.192(0.262)	0.000(0.000)	4.847(6.274)	0.572(0.539)	0.000(0.000)
POS	0.203(0.196)	0.076(0.081)	0.009(0.017)	0.182(0.182)	0.044(0.044)	0.000(0.000)	−0.275(−0.275)	0.080(0.080)	0.001(0.001)
TWI	−0.005	0.003	0.067						
POSxTWI	0.010	0.003	0.001						
WFB				0.069(0.069)	0.053(0.053)	0.197(0.197)	0.048(0.048)	0.090(0.090)	0.598(0.598)
JS							−0.843(−0.843)	0.171(0.171)	0.000(0.000)
	$R^2 = 0.179$ $F_{(3,96)} = 6.978$ p = 0.0003			$R^2 = 0.190$ $F_{(2,97)} = 11.338$ p = 0.0000			$R^2 = 0.387$ $F_{(3,96)} = 20.183$ p = 0.0000		
	($R^2 = 0.057$ $F_{(1,98)} = 5.887$ p = 0.0171)			($R^2 = 0.190$ $F_{(2,97)} = 11.338$ p = 0.0000)			($R^2 = 0.387$ $F_{(3,96)} = 20.183$ p = 0.0000)		
	POS → WFB → TI			POS → JS → TI			POS → WFB → JS → TI		
	Effect	Se	95% Bootstrap CI	Effect	se	95% Bootstrap CI	Effect	se	95% Bootstrap CI
Indirect effect	(0.0094)	(0.0233)	(−0.0319|0.0647)	−0.1532	0.0455	−0.2453|−0.0652	(−0.0115)	(0.0119)	(−0.0389|0.0062)
				(−0.1532)	(0.0455)	(−0.2493|−0.0659)			
Low (−1 SD)	−0.0050	0.0149	−0.0394|0.0227				0.0061	0.0089	−0.0068|0.0286
Medium	0.0097	0.0234	−0.0317|0.0653				−0.0118	0.0125	−0.0427|0.0064
High (+1 SD)	0.0244	0.0555	−0.0747|0.1475				−0.0298	0.0288	−0.0975|0.0167
Index of moderated mediation	0.0005	0.0010	−0.0014|0.0027				−0.0006	0.0005	−0.0018|0.0003

Notes: n = 100. JS = job satisfaction; POS = perceived organizational support; POSxTWI = interaction between perceived organizational support and telework intensity; SD = standard deviation; TI = turnover intention; TWI = telework intensity; WFB = work–family balance. Numbers in parentheses represent Model 6 results. Unstandardized coefficients are presented.

pandemic (Yerkes et al., 2020)). Gender was not significantly correlated with the mediators or outcome variable and was therefore not included as a control. 'Live-in children' was significantly correlated with job satisfaction but was not significantly related to the variables in our analyses. For reasons of parsimony, we present the results without this control (Table 13.1).

In line with Hypothesis 1a, perceived organizational support was positively related to work–family balance ($B = 0.20$, $p = 0.017$). In addition, perceived organizational support was positively related to job satisfaction ($B = 0.18$, $p = 0.000$), and negatively related to turnover intention ($B = −0.28$, $p = 0.001$). Job satisfaction was significantly related to turnover intention ($B = −0.84$, $p = 0.000$). However, contrary to Hypothesis 1b, work–family balance was not significantly related to job satisfaction ($B = 0.07$, $p = 0.197$) and turnover intention ($B = 0.05$, $p = 0.598$). Although the relationship between perceived organizational support and turnover intention was significantly mediated through job satisfaction (B(se) = −0.15(0.05), Cis (−0.2493|−0.0659)), work–

family balance did not mediate the relationships between perceived organizational support and job satisfaction (B(se) = 0.01(0.02), Cis (−0.0319|0.0647)), or the relationships between perceived organizational support, job satisfaction, and turnover intention (B(se) = −0.01(0.01) Cis (−0.0389|0.0062)).

As predicted in Hypothesis 2a, the interaction between perceived organizational support and telework intensity on work–life balance was significant (B = 0.01, p = 0.001). More specifically, the positive relationship between perceived organizational support and work–family balance was higher for employees with higher telework intensity. The index of moderated mediation was nonsignificant (index(se) = −0.0006, (0.00) Cis (−0.0018|0.0003)). Hence no support was found for Hypothesis 2b.

CONCLUSION

As we expected, perceived organizational support can enhance work–family balance, particularly when workers engage in more teleworking. Although perceived organizational support was an important factor in job satisfaction and turnover intention, in contrast to the literature (An, 2022; Baeriswyl et al., 2016), in our study, we did not find that the positive relationship between perceived organizational support and work–family balance triggered a process that culminated in increased job satisfaction and reduced turnover intention, regardless of employees' telework intensity.

What insights does our study provide for the future? Our data were collected during the COVID-19 lockdown when many employees were confined to their homes, not because they wanted to be but due to a government mandate. Employees may have considered their work–family balance during the COVID-19 pandemic as a temporary situation, and it therefore may not have affected job satisfaction or turnover intention. Moreover, our respondents were relatively young, with a high level of education, and less than half of them had live-in children. They might have found other working conditions, such as learning and development opportunities at work, more important than work–family balance (due to the stage they were at in their careers) in relation to job satisfaction and turnover intention.

Implementing human resource management practices and leadership styles that signal intangible job resources, such as approval, recognition, voice, and respect (De Prins et al., 2015), can be expected to foster a process that motivates and energizes workers (Bakker & Demerouti, 2014) and that may subsequently lead to positive work and family outcomes, even after the COVID-19 pandemic. Since work–family balance was not a factor that carried sufficient weight to provide higher job satisfaction and retain employees within the context of our study, it would be interesting to examine the same model in the post-pandemic period, when teleworking is likely to have been more intensive than before the pandemic but on a more voluntary basis. Moreover, future research could employ a longitudinal design to measure causal relationships and consider career-stage differences, as work–family balance may be contingent on such factors.

REFERENCES

Allen, T. D., & Kiburz, K. M. (2012). Trait mindfulness and work–family balance among working parents: The mediating effects of vitality and sleep quality. *Journal of Vocational Behavior, 80*, 372–379.

Allen, T. D., Golden, T. D., & Shockley, K. M. (2015). How effective is telecommuting? Assessing the status of our scientific findings. *Psychological Science in the Public Interest, 16*(2), 40–68.

An, Z. (2022). Research on cross-cultural conflict and employee's turnover intention in Chinese multinational enterprises. *Open Journal of Business and Management, 10*, 1221–1244.

Baeriswyl, S., Krause, A., & Schwaninger, A. (2016). Emotional exhaustion and job satisfaction in airport security officers: Work–family conflict as mediator in the job demands–resources model. *Frontiers in Psychology, 7.* Doi 10.3389/fpsyg.2016.00663.

Bakker, A. B., & Demerouti, E. (2014). Job demands–resources theory. In C. Cooper & P. Chen (Eds), *Wellbeing: A complete reference guide* (pp. 37–64). Wiley-Blackwell.

De Prins, P., De Vos, A., Van Beirendonck, L., & Segers, J. (2015). Sustainable HRM for sustainable careers: Introducing the 'Respect Openness Continuity (ROC) model'. In A. De Vos & B. I. J. M. Van der Heijden (Eds), *Handbook of research on sustainable careers* (pp. 319–334). Edward Elgar Publishing.

De Smet, A., Dowling, B., Mugayar-Baldocchi, M., & Schaninger, B. (2021). *How companies can turn the great resignation into the great attraction.* McKinsey.

Eisenberger, R., Huntington, R., Hutchison, S., & Sowa, D. (1986). Perceived organizational support. *Journal of Applied Psychology, 71*(3), 500–507.

Hayes, A. F. (2018). *Introduction to mediation, moderation, and conditional process analysis: A regression-based approach* (2nd ed.). Guilford Press.

Locke, E. A. (1976). The nature and causes of job satisfaction. In M. D. Dunnette (Ed.), *Handbook of Industrial and Organizational Psychology* (pp. 1297–1343). Rand McNally.

Maan, A. T., Abid, G., Butt, T. H., Ashfaq, F., & Ahmed, S. (2020). Perceived organizational support and job satisfaction: A moderated mediation model of proactive personality and psychological empowerment. *Future Business Journal, 6*(1), 1–12.

Mobley, W. H., Horner, S. O., & Hollingsworth, A. T. (1978). An evaluation of precursors of hospital employee turnover. *Journal of Applied Psychology, 63*(4), 408–414.

Moore, S. (2022). *Gartner survey finds only 29% of IT workers have high intent to stay with current employer survey results point to looming IT talent retention issues for CIOs.* Stamford, March.

Pejtersen, J. H., Kristensen, T. S., Borg, V., & Bjorner, J. B. (2010). The second version of the Copenhagen Psychosocial Questionnaire. *Scandinavian Journal of Public Health, 38*(3), 8–24.

Rhoades, L., Eisenberger, R., & Armeli, S. (2001). Affective commitment to the organization: The contribution of perceived organizational support. *Journal of Applied Psychology, 86*(5), 825–836.

Straub, C., Beham, B., & Islam, G. (2019). Crossing boundaries: Integrative effects of supervision, gender and boundary control on work engagement and work-to-family positive spillover. *International Journal of Human Resource Management*, *30*(20), 2831–2854.

Tett, R. P., & Meyer, J. P. (1993). Job satisfaction, organizational commitment, turnover intention, and turnover: Path analyses based on meta-analytic findings. *Personnel Psychology*, *46*(2), 259–293.

Yerkes, M. A., André, S., Beckers, D., Besamusca, J., Kruyen, P., Remery, C., Van der Zwan, R., & Geurts, S. (2020). Intelligent lockdown, intelligent effects? The impact of the Dutch COVID-19 'intelligent lockdown' on gendered work and family dynamics among parents. *Plos One*. DOI: 10.1371/journal.pone.0242249.

14. Balancing work and life at home: a longitudinal analysis of working from home and work–life balance before and during the pandemic

Laura den Dulk, Joëlle van der Meer, Samantha Metselaar, and Brenda Vermeeren

INTRODUCTION

Working from home increased dramatically during the COVID-19 pandemic, and there are strong indications that many employees will continue to work remotely for a substantial proportion of their working hours (Eurofound, 2022). Many employers in the Netherlands also expect working from home to become a structural feature after the pandemic (Centraal Bureau voor de Statistiek, 2021a). Prior to the pandemic, most employees only spent a small proportion of their working hours at home (Centraal Bureau voor de Statistiek, 2021b). We have therefore witnessed not only a substantial increase in the number of employees working from home but also in the intensity of working from home.

Before COVID-19, limited research had been conducted on how the amount of time spent working from home (i.e. the intensity of working from home) affects work outcomes such as work–life balance (Allen et al., 2015). However, some scholars note that after a certain threshold, working from home is no longer beneficial for employee well-being (Beauregard et al., 2019; Golden & Veiga, 2005). The extreme situation brought about by the COVID-19 pandemic, when employees suddenly had to work entirely from home, provides an opportunity to study how the intensity of working from home affects outcomes like work–life balance among employees with and without care responsibilities.

In this chapter, we contribute to existing research by answering the following research question: *How does the intensity of working from home influence the work–life balance of employees with and without care responsibilities over time?* Panel data were used to compare the work–life balance of public-sector employees before COVID-19 (working from home on a voluntary basis) and during the pandemic (having to work from home, when schools and childcare facilities were also closed) (Shirmohammadi et al., 2022). Within this analysis, we differentiate between employees with and without care responsibilities (childcare or informal care responsibilities). With a focus on the public sector, our research findings can provide input for thinking about what future policies on working from home and work–life balance should look like. By adopting this public administration perspective, we aim to help the public sector to achieve its role as model employer (Steijn & Knies, 2021).

THEORETICAL BACKGROUND: THE RELATIONSHIP BETWEEN WORKING FROM HOME AND WORK–LIFE BALANCE

In recent decades, working from home has been viewed as a resource to achieve a healthy work–life balance, even though the relevant empirical find-ings have been inconsistent (Kelliher & De Menezes, 2019). Existing research indicates that working from home is a double-edged sword (Peters et al., 2009) and that we need to address the questions of how and under what conditions working from home contributes to a healthy and sustainable work–life balance (Kelliher & De Menezes, 2019). On the one hand, the possibility of working from home increases employees' autonomy to decide when and where to work, helping them to achieve a healthy work–life balance (Metselaar et al., 2023a). Working from home also reduces commuting time and helps people focus on work without distractions from coworkers. These factors can lead to more temporal resources for other activities. On the other hand, working from home with the aid of communication technology leads to blurred boundaries, making interaction or spillover between life domains more likely. The increasing permeability of the boundaries between domains makes it harder to discon-nect from work, which can result in work intensification and longer working hours (Gajendran & Harrison, 2007; Kelliher & Anderson, 2010). Gajendran and Harrison (2007), however, argue that high-intensity working from home could also translate into more freedom to combine life domains and develop strategies that increase boundary control, such as a dedicated workspace at home and predictable work routines, thereby mitigating the negative impact of blurred boundaries. In their pre-COVID-19 meta-analysis, they found lower work–family conflict among employees who work extensively from home compared to employees who work from home at a low intensity (Gajendran & Harrison, 2007). We may rightly ask whether this was also the case for mandatory homeworking during the pandemic, however. After all, during the pandemic, care demands increased and employees with children may have had difficulty balancing (paid) work with family life. Pandemic restrictions also made the task of caring for people other than children more complicated, both inside and outside the home, because of the need for social distancing (Verbakel et al., 2021).

In addition, COVID-19 research indicates that a dedicated workplace at home, where employees can work without distractions, is a crucial factor in achieving a good work–life balance. However, not all employees are able to create a suitable workspace at home (Metselaar et al., 2023b; Shirmohammadi et al., 2022). Increasing care demands due to home schooling, the closure of childcare facilities, and the scaling back of formal home care, combined with a lack of resources at home and at work, such as a partner or supportive supervisor, could result in a deterioration in work–life balance (Metselaar et al., 2023b).

Because the research findings on the effects of working from home have been inconclusive so far, we take an explorative approach rather than testing specific hypotheses to study the effects of working from home on work–life balance before and during the COVID-19 pandemic. To find out more about the circumstances under which this relationship occurs, we differentiate between employees with and without care responsibilities.

METHODS: WORK–LIFE BALANCE PRE- AND DURING COVID-19

This study used data from two public organizations in the Netherlands: a government agency operating at the national level and a large municipality. Both organizations had policies in place before the pandemic, which allowed employees to work from home if they wished to do so. In both organizations, the same respondents were surveyed at different points in time.

In the government agency, two questionnaires were sent out before the COVID-19 pandemic (in summer 2018 and 2019), followed by a third questionnaire in the winter of 2020–2021, when employees were required to work entirely from home. At that point, schools and daycare facilities were also closed, and social gatherings were prohibited. A panel of 263 respondents took part in all three questionnaires. 37 percent of the respondents were female. Most respondents were between 41 and 55 years old or older than 55 years. 79 percent were living with a partner. About 42 percent were responsible for caring for children living at home. About 26 percent were providing informal care in 2018 and 2019. This increased to 31 percent during COVID-19 (winter of 2020/2021). Before COVID-19, the respondents worked from home for 34 percent (2018) and 37 percent (2019) of their total working hours, respectively, on average.

At the municipality, questionnaires were sent at two different points in time during the COVID-19 pandemic. The same employees were approached in May 2020 and September 2020 (N = 569). Of those respondents, 58 percent were female and the predominant age range was 51 to 55 years (18.9 percent). About 40 percent of the respondents were responsible for caring for children living at home. In May 2020, about 19 percent were providing informal care, and by September 2020 this had increased to 38 percent. In May 2020 there was an "intelligent lockdown" (Yerkes et al., 2020). This involved several restrictions: schools and childcare facilities were (partially) closed, restaurants and cafés were closed, and people were required to work from home and encouraged to avoid close physical contact. By September 2020, schools and childcare facilities were open again, as well as restaurants and cafés.

Measures

Work–life balance was measured using a shortened three-item scale (Abendroth & Den Dulk, 2011) derived from the original five-item scale developed by Valcour (2007). Items were measured on a five-point scale (5 = "very satisfied"). An example item is: "How satisfied are you with the ability to meet the needs of your job and the needs of your personal and family life?" The Cronbach's alpha was above the 0.7 threshold for all timestamps in both organizations. We examined work–life balance over time and compared respondents with care responsibilities (childcare and informal care) and respondents with no such responsibilities. To assess differences in work–life balance over time and between respondents with and without care responsibilities, we conducted a paired samples t-test and independent samples t-test, respectively.

FINDINGS

Government Agency

At the government agency, we see a declining trend in work–life balance score over time. In 2018, the average score was 4.00 (SD = 0.82), in 2019 this was 3.92 (SD = 0.82); during the lockdown in the winter of 2020–2021 it was 3.87 (SD = 0.91). The difference between 2018 and 2020–2021 is significant (t = 2.356, df = 262, $p < 0.05$). When we compare respondents with and without childcare responsibilities, we find that respondents without childcare responsibilities scored significantly higher on work–life balance (M = 4.05) during the lockdown in 2020–2021 than their counterparts with childcare responsibilities (M = 3.50) (t = 4.710, df = 261, $p < 0.001$). No significant differences were found between these groups in 2018 and 2019. With respect to informal care, the t-tests revealed no significant differences in the work–life balance scores of respondents with and without care responsibilities for other people inside or outside their household.

Municipality

The work–life balance of employees of the municipality improved overall. The average score for work–life balance in May 2020 was 3.55 (SD = 0.96), and in September 2020 it was 3.58 (SD = 0.94), although the differences were not significant. Nevertheless, the findings indicate that in May 2020 there were significant differences between respondents with and without childcare responsibilities. Respondents with childcare responsibilities scored lower on work–life balance (M = 3.50) than those with no children living at home (M = 3.68) (t = 4.038, df = 460, p < 0.001). In September 2020, when schools and childcare facilities were open, no significant differences were found between these groups. With respect to informal care, the t-tests for the municipality showed significant differences in work–life balance scores in both May and September 2020 (respectively, t = 4.829, df = 430, p < 0.001 and t = 2.708, df = 158, p < 0.01). Respondents who provided informal care were less satisfied with their work–life balance on average (M = 3.30 in May and M = 3.28 in September) compared with respondents without informal care responsibilities (M = 3.70 in May and M = 3.57 in September).

The findings for both organizations are shown in Figure 14.1. Figure 14.1 also demonstrates the COVID-19 measures that were in force at each timestamp.

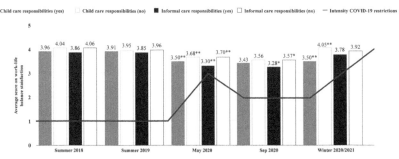

Figure 14.1   *Average score for work–life balance among respondents with and without care responsibilities and the scale of COVID-19 restrictions during 2018–2021*

DISCUSSION

The findings of the longitudinal studies show that on average employees became less satisfied with their work–life balance during the pandemic and that this was particularly true for employees with care responsibilities. We found no large decline in the mean score on work–life balance over time and on average the employees in these two studies were still fairly satisfied with how they could combine work and family demands. Nevertheless, research indicates that even if the magnitude of change is small, a small deterioration in work–life balance negatively affects employee well-being (Van der Meer et al., 2022).

Our findings indicate that employees with children at home find it more difficult to achieve a good work–life balance than employees without childcare responsibilities, in the context of working entirely from home during the pandemic, when schools and childcare facilities were also closed. Increasing care demands due to COVID-19 restrictions might explain this finding (Shirohammadi et al., 2022). Before the pandemic (2018 and 2019) and when schools and childcare facilities were open (September 2020), no significant differences were found between employees with and without care responsibilities.

The study by Yerkes et al. (2022) among working mothers in The Netherlands and Finland with a high level of education found that mothers who continued working at the workplace during the pandemic were better able to combine work and care than mothers who worked from home. This suggests that working from home entirely might be negatively associated with the work–life balance of working parents. In our study, we also checked for differences between men and women, but found no significant difference in work–life balance. However, Yerkes et al. (2022) argue that the Netherlands' dominant "one-and-a-half-earner" model may have mitigated the negative effect of COVID-19 restrictions, because mothers who worked part time were able to take on the extra care responsibilities. This may also explain the relatively small decline in work–life balance between 2018 and 2021. Nevertheless, given that employees are now working from home more than before the COVID-19 pandemic, we need to continue to monitor how the intensity of working from home affects the work–life balance of working parents in relation to care demands and available resources.

With respect to informal care, our findings are less clear. We only found significant differences between those with and without informal care responsibilities at the municipality during the pandemic. We found no similar pattern for informal care in the data from the government agency. This could be because the measures taken to contain the virus played out differently for different groups of informal caregivers. Verbakel et al. (2021) show that, overall, for most informal caregivers the provision of informal care declined, except for the small group that provided informal care at home. Since the need for informal care is likely to increase as our society continues to age, it is important to investigate whether and how working from home affects the work–life balance of employees with informal care responsibilities.

IMPLICATIONS FOR RESEARCH AND PRACTICE

Both studies conducted before and during the pandemic show that intensive care responsibilities can make it harder to achieve a good work–life balance. In addition, we found an overall deterioration in work–life balance over time. Behind this trend, there are likely enormous differences in how and to what extent working entirely from home affects people's work–life balance, depending on the particular constellation of demands and resources people face. For instance, Metselaar et al. (2023b) showed that more work demands combined with increasing care demands as a result of COVID-19 measures led to more work–life conflict and a less favorable work–life balance when there are insufficient resources to deal with these demands. Our findings point in a similar direction and suggest that it is not merely the intensity of working from home that affects employees' work–life balance. Greater awareness of the resources of different groups of employees is important if extensive homeworking is here to stay. More research is therefore needed to inform human resource management policymakers under what conditions more extensive homeworking translates into a more positive work–life balance among employees.

REFERENCES

Abendroth, A. K., & Den Dulk, L. (2011). Support for the work–life balance in Europe: The impact of state, workplace and family support on work–life balance satisfaction. *Work, Employment and Society*, *25*(2), 234–256.

Allen, T. D., Golden, T. D., & Shockley, K. M. (2015). How effective is telecommuting? Assessing the status of our scientific findings. *Psychological Science in the Public Interest*, *16*(2), 40–68.

Beauregard, T. A., Basile, K. A., & Canonico, E. (2019). Telework: Outcomes and facilitators for employees. In R. N. Landers (Ed.), *The Cambridge handbook of technology and employee behavior* (pp. 511–543). Cambridge University Press.

Centraal Bureau voor de Statistiek (2021a). *Ondernemers verwachten dat hybride werken blijft*. November 19. www.cbs.nl/nl-nl/nieuws/2021/46/ondernemers-verwachten-dat-hybride-werken-blijft.

Centraal Bureau voor de Statistiek (2021b). *Werkzame beroepsbevolking: thuiswerken in 2019*. February 16. https://opendata.cbs.nl/#/CBS/nl/dataset/83258NED/table?dl=327E0.

Eurofound (2022). *Fifth round of the living, working and COVID-19 e-survey: Living in a new era of uncertainty*. Publications Office of the European Union.

Gajendran, R. S., & Harrison, D. A. (2007). The good, the bad, and the unknown about telecommuting: Meta-analysis of psychological mediators an individual consequence. *Journal of Applied Psychology, 92*(6), 1524–1541.

Golden, T. D., & Veiga, J. F. (2005). The impact of extent of telecommuting on job satisfaction: Resolving inconsistent findings. *Journal of Management, 31*(2), 301–318.

Kelliher, C., & Anderson, D. (2010). Doing more with less? Flexible working practices and the intensification of work. *Human Relations, 63*(1), 83–106.

Kelliher, C., & De Menezes, L. M. (2019). *Flexible working in organisations: A research overview*. Routledge.

Metselaar, S. A., Den Dulk, L., & Vermeeren, B. (2023a). Teleworking at different locations outside the office: Consequences for perceived performance and the mediating role of autonomy and work-life balance satisfaction. *Review of Public Personnel Administration, 43*, 456–478.

Metselaar, S. A., Den Dulk, L., & Vermeeren, B. (2023b). When home becomes the workplace: Work–life balance experiences during the COVID-19 pandemic. *Contemporary Perspectives in Family Research, 21*(3), 3–30.

Peters, P., Dulk, L. den, & Lippe, T. van der (2009). The effects of time-spatial flexibility and new working conditions on employees' work–life balance: The Dutch case. *Community, Work & Family, 12*(3), 279–298.

Shirohammadi, M., Chan Au, W., & Beigi, M. (2022). Remote work and work–life balance: Lessons learned from the COVID-19 pandemic and suggestions for HRD practitioners. *Human Resource Development International, 25*(2), 163–181.

Steijn, B., & Knies, E. (2021). Introduction. In B. Steijn & E. Knies (Eds), *Research handbook on HRM in the public sector*. Edward Elgar Publishing.

Valcour, M. (2007). Work-based resources as moderators of the relationship between work hours and satisfaction with work–family balance. *Journal of Applied Psychology, 92*(6), 1512–1523.

Van der Meer, J., Vermeeren, B., & Steijn, B. (2022). Well-being during a crisis: A longitudinal study of local government civil servants. *Review of Public Personnel Administration*. https://doi.org/10.1177/0734371X221084104.

Verbakel, C. M. C., Raiber, K., & Boer, A. H. (2021). Verandering in de intensiteit van mantelzorg tijdens de eerste COVID-19 lockdown in 2020 in Nederland. *Mens En Maatschappij, 96*(3), 411–439.

Yerkes M. A., André, S. C. H., Besamusca, J. W., Kruyen, P. M., Remery, C. L. H. S., van der Zwan, R. et al. (2020) "Intelligent" lockdown, intelligent effects? Results from a survey on gender (in)equality in paid work, the division of childcare and household work, and quality of life among parents in the Netherlands during the COVID-19 lockdown. *PLoS ONE, 15*(11), 1–23.

Yerkes, M. A., Remery, C., André, S., Salin, M., Hakovirta, M., & van Gerven, M. (2022). Unequal but balanced: Highly educated mothers' perceptions of work–life balance during the COVID-19 lockdown in Finland and the Netherlands. *Journal of European Social Policy, 32*(4), 376–392.

15. Workplace flexibility and homeworking after COVID-19 in public-sector and private-sector organizations

Pablo Sanabria-Pulido and Palina Prysmakova

INTRODUCTION

Public management theories have shown that the attitudes, environments and rules that dominate the role of public servants in public organizations are different from those in the private sector. Despite these evident differences, the COVID-19 pandemic affected the work–life balance of all employees, regardless of sector or activity, because most organizations had made inadequate preparations to keep their operations running as usual. Some would argue that the effect of the pandemic on organizations, and therefore on employees' work–life arrangements, were similar across many private and public entities, since neither had emergency operation plans in place to deal with a crisis of that scale. Indeed, general administration theories suggest that management, especially human resource management, is a universal approach to all types of organizations (Potcovaru, 2018). There is therefore no need to differentiate between private- and public-sector workers when discussing effective management. According to these generalizing approaches, humans are humans and a workforce is a workforce. In any sector of the economy, people can be divided into X and Y McGregor's motivational groups, or be satisfied step by step by applying the incentives of Maslow's hierarchy. The global COVID-19 pandemic, however, added a new twist to these assumptions. While many organizations in the private sector had various options for shutting down their operations, or at least scaling back, the provision of public services was expected to continue regardless (Ramirez de la Cruz et al., 2020). What is more, the massive demand for public goods and services during the pandemic led to several unique challenges for public organizations and their workforce, thus disrupting their work–life balance in a way unique to public services. The essential role that public employees play in coordinating and implementing an organized government response made their work critical during the COVID-19 pandemic. At a time of widespread tension and uncertainty, there were widespread reports of frontline public workers suffering from fatigue, anxiety, and other mental health problems, while still striving to respond to increasing societal demands during the pandemic.

The impact of COVID-19 was global, with myriad challenges for each nation and society, but the public sector was always in the eye of the storm. Public servants were one of the first lines of defense against an overwhelming public health crisis, and the demand for various public goods surged (e.g., healthcare, safety, mobility, access to food and medicines, etc.). Accordingly, public organizations witnessed increased demand, jeopardizing the work–life balance routine of their employees (Serikbayeva et al., 2021). In this context, new organizational challenges emerged regarding the capacity of public organizations to deliver reliable and consistent services during the COVID-19 pandemic while still maintaining the work–life balance of employees. The differences in the characteristics and environments of public organizations and their workers mean that a public administration perspective regarding the specifics of the public sector is necessary and valuable.

WORKPLACE FLEXIBILITY AS A STRATEGY FOR DEALING WITH SURGING DEMAND DURING CRISES

The first challenge was the universal expectation that public-sector employees, despite the risk to their health, would work faster and perform more effectively than ever before. Such expectations originated from the belief that public-sector employees were genuinely motivated by the desire to serve the public benefit. This concept is also known in the field of public administration as public-service motivation (PSM) (see Prysmakova (2021a) and Sanabria-Pulido (2018) for more on this notion), which implies that public servants would put the needs of others above their own. Another feature of PSM is the expected devotion of public employees to the continuity of public-service provision.

However, human resource practices in public organizations must be redefined and supported in new organizational and operational settings. This is because, due to their reliance on street-level bureaucrats (workers who interact with citizens and have considerable discretion over the dispensation of benefits or public sanctions), many organizations in both public and private settings were expected to protect their employees. One of the critical changes in human resource management was allowing workers to work from home, also known as homeworking. This approach was supposed to allow better mediation of the new challenges of work–life balance. However, when, for instance, parents were obliged to homeschool their children, it was unclear whether public-sector employees' "motivation to serve" would clash with new practices that allowed flexibility in their place of work.

Public-service employees who accepted mandatory homeworking did so in an uncertain work environment characterized by pressure, stress and anxiety (Kramer, 2017), were isolated from their colleagues and had no direct access to service recipients. On the other hand, those who had to continue to work on the frontline and deal directly with the population, such as elderly care workers or police officers, were asked to take the risk of endangering their own wellbeing, with an unknown virus and its possible consequences. Millions of public-service workers worldwide continued their daily work either from home or in the field during COVID-19, often without explicit instructions from the administration or subject to rapidly changing national policies (Fadinger & Schymik, 2020).

Mandatory homeworking accommodated the new personal and family needs of public-sector employees. It was by no means a new approach to human resources, but became much more ubiquitous during the COVID-19 pandemic (Colley & Williamson, 2020). We aim to understand how home-working can work in public-sector organizations, and the advantages and disadvantages that it can bring. In this context, this chapter asks: *What are the pros and cons of working from home in public organizations as opposed to practices in private-sector organizations? Has the context of the pandemic changed those advantages and disadvantages in the particular context of public-sector agencies?*

ADVANTAGES AND DISADVANTAGES OF HOMEWORKING

Even before the COVID-19 pandemic, workplace flexibility was already emerging slowly in modern human capital management practices as a strategy to promote a healthy and sustainable work–life balance. While the pandemic added a new safety dimension, organizations were already looking for ways to actively improve worker satisfaction and motivation, enhance retention, ensure better employee performance while homeworking, and discover new strategies to engage better with new generations of workers. Workers in generations Y and Z see flexibility as a key job attribute and expect organizations to provide jobs that can accommodate their expectations in terms of work schedule, location and monitoring (Sanabria-Pulido, 2018).

We will now outline some of the known benefits of workplace flexibility in the public and private sectors. Some studies have analyzed the general effects of homeworking and workplace flexibility as the new reality that prevails across organizations in all sectors. Fadinger and Schymilk (2020) find that homeworking during COVID-19 was instrumental in reducing infection rates and helped reduce the cost of stay-at-home orders. Similarly, Yang et al. (2023) find that perceived work–life balance improved during the pandemic, even as the physical boundaries between the workplace and home were reduced. More importantly, however, they find that public administration is a sector that, owing to its importance in creating value and enhancing other economic and societal activities, should phase out strict confinement measures as quickly as possible. In other words, homeworking in the context of public-sector organizations could be costly for society as a whole.

There have been peculiarities in adopting workplace flexibility practices in public-sector organizations. More specifically, various studies aiming to disentangle the effects of workplace flexibility in public-sector organizations have focused on the barriers that public-sector organizations face in adopting such practices as widely as private-sector organizations (De Vries et al., 2019; Feeney & Stritch, 2019). Extant scholarship tends to indicate that, rather than being an emerging reality before the pandemic, this practice was an avenue for flexible work, innovation, and the adoption of new technology in human resources practices that emerged on a wider scale in the public sector after the arrival of COVID-19 (De Vries et al., 2018; Pollitt & Hupe, 2011). De Vries et al. (2019) show that homeworking reduced the quality of the work done by public officials because it increased professional isolation and reduced levels of organizational commitment. However, they argue that work engagement was not affected and that higher leader–membership exchange effectively countered the undesirable effects.

In fact, in a pre-pandemic study, De Vries et al. (2019) found that the effects of homeworking in public agencies remained unknown and had not been measured accurately in prior studies. Similarly, Feeney and Stritch (2019) showed that organizational policies such as flexible work schedules and home-working options improve work–life balance in public-sector organizations, but that adoption remains limited. Thus, pre-pandemic studies, although aiming to assess the adoption of homeworking practices, were already beginning to understand how allowing public officials to work from home affected their performance and other organizational outcomes.

However, the pandemic highlighted the importance of keeping public organizations going amid an unprecedented health emergency, and teleworking emerged as a tool with which to do this (Kalwani, 2021). Hence, as the studies reviewed show, public administration scholarship has gradually become more interested in understanding workplace flexibility in public organizations, as witnessed by the growing number of related studies during and after the pandemic. As we can see, a group of studies found either no particular effect or negative effects from adopting such practices in the public sector during the pandemic.

CHALLENGES OF HOMEWORKING IN PUBLIC ORGANIZATIONS

Work–life balance during the pandemic has been affected by new challenges associated with homeworking. The capacities of the organizations and the availability of necessary resources became the cornerstone of this often abrupt transition. Organizations require some resources (technological, human, physical, financial, informational) to carry out the tasks that need to be managed (Hander et al., 2001). Maintaining these resources requires a continuous effort on behalf of the management team so that the tasks can be achieved effectively and regularly. Arguably, during crises the effort required is multiplied and heavily influenced by environmental uncertainty (Kramer, 2017).

Caution should be exercised when responding to the common criticism of low productivity when working from home during the pandemic. In not-for-profit public-service systems, performance evaluation that is based solely on performance indicators "ignores the temporal or causal relationships of the system and offers little insight into understanding systematic effectiveness, sustainability, or generalizability" (Meyer et al., 2012, p. 535). Looking at performance alone is not comprehensive enough. When assessing the effectiveness of delivering public services from a home office, the right question to ask is: "How well did employees perform, given what they had to work with?" This section provides an overview of the main challenges caused by the adoption of homeworking in public-sector organizations based on a qualitative assessment of 14 in-depth interviews with French public officials working in different capacities. The data were collected during the COVID-19 crisis, when homeworking practices had been adopted on an unprecedented scale in different organizations.

Changes in Work Climate

Almost all public-service workers indicated noticeable changes in their work climates. Some of the most prominent changes were unrelated to the switch to a different physical space, such as emotional changes in the recipients of their services, who were also struggling with the situation, making relations more tense. However, many employees felt more distanced from the people they were serving, mainly due to the absence of in-person meetings. Unsurprisingly, this disconnect negatively affected the PSM of those workers (Prysmakova, 2021b).

Changes in Schedule

When they moved from office working to homeworking, the schedules of most public-sector workers also changed. However, the direction of those changes varied. While many felt overburdened as everyday tasks now took longer due to the absence of tools that would have been readily available in their offices, others noticed a reduced workload because of the postponement of activities that could not be done from home, or even the loss of clients. Some employees' schedules conflicted with the additional complications of working from home, such as taking care of their children.

Changes in Communication

Many public employees observed changes in communication – not only the quality of communication, but also a reduction in interaction with other people, as noted earlier. The mass media lamented the scarcity of physical equipment during the first months of the pandemic because it was easier to visualize medical masks or sanitizers. However, seizing the scale of the public sector and its services, the main problems for the stable delivery of public services were the lack of reliable information and insufficient access from home offices (Prysmakova, 2022).

It is alarming that the continuity of public-service provision depended largely on employees' private internet connections, even in less information technology-intensive sectors such as hospitals, social work, and schools (Prysmakova, 2022). A stable connection became crucial for everyday procedures and also to stay in touch and receive updates on policy changes. Nevertheless, it was almost unheard of for organizations to cover employees' internet bills so that they could work from home.

Changes in Performance

Most public-service employees experienced shutdowns of different types that affected their operations. It is impossible to provide an exhaustive list of closures, as these were specific to each profession and service provided. Some examples include a lack of access to research laboratories or fieldwork activities that could not be recreated in home-office settings.

The reduction in performance was ubiquitous across professions: while some maintained their regular in-person operations, others found themselves less busy with normal tasks as their organizations had not organized teleworking effectively. Many services lost their clients in the whirlpool of events and changes. The reduction in organizational performance did not necessarily mean more free time for workers, however. For many, the abrupt switch to homeworking meant that their daily routine demanded more energy than usual.

Implementation of Novelties

Novelties of various types were introduced abruptly into the daily routine of all new teleworkers, such as new work habits, technology, and work design. Most employees had to develop various new work habits in order to continue their work (Prysmakova, 2022).

New technological solutions were introduced across the board, both for those who moved from the company office to a home office and for those who continued working in the field. The types of technology rolled out differed for each respondent, depending on the specifics of their jobs.

Work design was generally modified to accommodate the switch to online working. Many of those who switched to online working believed that the online environment was a poor fit with the in-person nature of their jobs. Many public-service employees raised psychological safety concerns over the new environment (Prysmakova, 2022).

CONCLUSION AND DISCUSSION

Workplace flexibility is on the rise as organizations seek strategies to respond to workers' increasing demands for a healthy and sustainable work–life balance. For a long time, organizations from both the private and public sectors were reluctant to adopt such practices, particularly in the public sector (Kalwani, 2021), because of external legal and societal restrictions and expectations and the importance of individual work motivation in that sector, such as public sector motivation. However, the COVID-19 pandemic and generational changes have accelerated their adoption. Various studies based on data from both public and private organizations confirm this trend and indicate that these practices bring key challenges in terms of adaptation and the changes that organizations need to make to ensure adequate implementation.

According to the literature, adopting more flexible workplace practices has benefits for both organizations and workers, tremendously affecting the work–life balance of the latter. Allowing collaborators to work from different locations and according to their own schedules has been found to be related to greater reported levels of organizational commitment, work satisfaction, and motivation, and ultimately to better performance. Nonetheless, in any attempt to improve employees' work–life balance by enabling full or partial homeworking, public-sector organizations need to be aware that workers can respond in a way that is unique to their context. For instance, it is important to consider the special bond between the beneficiaries of public services and public-service providers and PSM (Prysmakova, 2021b), such as willingness to make sacrifices for the public interest. It is possible that many aspects of public-service work cannot be transferred effectively to a home-office environment.

One way or another, all organizations, particularly those in the public sector, need to move faster in responding to the expectations of new generations of workers who are pursuing a set of job attributes and characteristics that actively improve work–life balance. Public-sector organizations may fall behind if they fail to take action to embrace these new practices. Workplace flexibility comes with massive challenges in terms of planning, strategy, the allocation of resources and commitment from organizational leadership. Whether public-sector organizations will be willing to update their forms of operation in response to the changing needs of a new workforce remains unclear.

REFERENCES

Colley, L., & Williamson, C. D. S. (2020). *Working during the pandemic: From resistance to revolution?* UNSW Canberra Public Service Research Group and CQ University. CRICOS No. 00098G 548493134.

De Vries, H., Tummers, L., & Bekkers, V. (2018). A stakeholder perspective on public sector innovation: Why does position matter? *International Review of Administrative Sciences*, *84*(2), 269–287.

De Vries, H., Tummers, L., & Bekkers, V. (2019). The benefits of teleworking in the public sector: Reality or rhetoric? *Review of Public Personnel Administration*, 39(4), 570–593.

Fadinger, H., & Schymik, J. (2020). The costs and benefits of home office during the COVID-19 pandemic: Evidence from infections and an input–output model for Germany. *Covid Economics*, *9*(24), 107–134.

Feeney, M., & Stritch, J. (2019). Family-friendly policies, gender, and work–life balance in the public sector. *Review of Public Personnel Administration*, *29*(3), 422–448.

Hander, N. R., Gulde, M., Klein, T., Mulfinger, N., Jerg-Bretzke, L., Ziegenhain, U. … & Rothermund, E. (2021). Group-treatment for dealing with the work–family conflict for healthcare professionals. *International Journal of Environmental Research and Public Health*, *18*(21), 11728.

Kalwani, S. (2021). The effect of COVID fatigue on mental health in the public sector organizations: Exploring compassion as a mediator. *Decision*, *48*(4), 403–418.

Kramer, M. W. (2017). Uncertainty management. In A. Farazmand (ed.) *Global encyclopedia of public administration, public policy, and governance*. Springer.

Meyer, A. M., Davis, M., & Mays, G. P. (2012). Defining organizational capacity for public health services and systems research. *Journal of Public Health Management and Practice*, *18*(6), 535–544.

Pollitt, C., & Hupe, P. (2011). Talking about government: The role of magic concepts. *Public Management Review*, *13*, 641–658.

Potcovaru, A. M. (2018). Human resource management in the public versus private sector: A theoretical perspective. *Economics, Management, and Financial Markets*, *13*(3), 203–209.

Prysmakova, P. (2021a). Public service Lala-land: PSM research and its researchers. In T. Bryer (ed.) *Handbook of theories of public administration and management.* Edward Elgar Publishing.

Prysmakova, P. (2021b). Contact with citizens and job satisfaction: Expanding person-environment models of public service motivation. *Public Management Review, 23*(9), 1339–1358.

Prysmakova, P. (2022). Trait or state? Public service motivation and perceived organizational capacity in times of crisis. AIRMAP 11th Conference, June 1–3.

Ramirez de la Cruz, E. E., Grin, E. J., Sanabria-Pulido, P., Cravacuore, D., & Orellana, A. (2020). The transaction costs of government responses to the COVID-19 emergency in Latin America. *Public Administration Review, 80*(4), 683–695.

Sanabria-Pulido, P. (2018). Public service motivation and job sector choice: Evidence from a developing country. *International Journal of Public Administration, 41*(13), 1107–1118.

Serikbayeva, B., Abdulla, K., & Oskenbayev, Y. (2021). State capacity in responding to COVID-19. *International Journal of Public Administration, 44*(11–12), 920–930.

Yang, E., Kim, Y., & Hong, S. (2023). Does working from home work? Experience of working from home and the value of hybrid workplace post-COVID-19. *Journal of Corporate Real Estate, 25*(1), 50–76.

16. When you just can't "let it go": a study of work-to-life conflict and job performance among Dutch public servants

Shelena Keulemans and Peter Kruyen

INTRODUCTION

Changing trends in work and home roles – such as our ever-increasing reliance on digital technologies that ensure structural proximity to the workplace, an aging workforce, and increasing female labor force participation – are forcing changes in how employees find a balance between work and home responsibilities (Beauregard & Henry, 2009; Gisler et al., 2018), increasing the likelihood of work-to-life conflict along the way (Gisler et al., 2018). Work-to-life conflict arises when employees' work role responsibilities make it difficult to meet home role demands (Delanoeije & Verbruggen, 2020).

During the COVID-19 pandemic, many employees were forced to work from home. These arrangements have inspired many organizations to continue encouraging employees to work from home in the post-pandemic era, increasing the prevalence of hybrid work. Hybrid work arrangements can increase work-to-life conflict and reduce employee performance: employees who work from home are more likely to (1) suffer from interruptions in work activity due to family members and (2) suffer from work-to-home interruptions because working from home raises the expectation of employees' constant availability (Wang et al., 2021). Performance-wise, reliance on suboptimal modes of digital communication and collaboration, employee procrastination, and feelings of loneliness can all undermine employee performance (Wang et al., 2021).

In this chapter, we explore the association between work-to-life conflict and job performance in public-sector organizations during the first wave of the COVID-19 pandemic in 2020. The association between work-to-life conflict and job performance is critical for public-sector organizations and public servants alike. Significant budget cuts, staff reductions, the introduction of part-time, fixed, and temporary contracts (Morgan & Allington, 2002), and the adoption of market-like principles have radically changed public servants' work role demands, and all carry a higher risk of work-to-life conflict (Kruyen et al., 2020).

Meanwhile, public-sector organizations face a human capital crisis (Linos, 2018). In particular, an aging workforce combined with a steady decline in the number of people who are interested in pursuing a career in the public sector are making it more difficult to attract and retain personnel (Groeneveld et al., 2009). These circumstances put pressure on public-sector performance. By investigating the association between work-to-life conflict and employee job performance, this chapter provides public-sector organizations with some potential pointers on how to safeguard employee performance and work–life balance in a sustainable way.

To theorize about work-to-life conflict, we draw from insights into work-to-life conflict, work-to-family conflict, and work–life balance. To explore the association between work-to-life conflict and job performance, we focus on two dimensions of job performance: task performance and contextual performance (e.g., Odle-Dusseau et al., 2012). We distinguish between these two performance types because previous studies have provided mixed insights into the association between work-to-life conflict and job performance (e.g., Allen et al., 2000; Aryee, 1992; Netemeyer et al., 1996), suggesting that this association may differ for different dimensions of job performance.

THEORY

Work-to-life conflict arises at the work–life interface and occurs when the work domain interferes with the home domain (Gisler et al., 2018). Home domain demands stem from family roles as well as other non-work roles, such as friends, sports, home responsibilities, and community roles, such as volunteering (e.g., Delanoeije & Verbruggen, 2020; Russo et al., 2016).

Work-to-life conflict can be time-based or strain-based (Delanoeije & Verbruggen, 2020). Time-based work-to-life conflict occurs when the time spent on the work role simply leaves employees with too little time to fulfill their home role demands (Delanoeije & Verbruggen, 2020). Strain-based conflict occurs when work roles trigger stress or strain that make it difficult to fulfill those home role demands (Delanoeije & Verbruggen, 2020), reducing individuals' ability to focus on home-life events (e.g., Sirgy & Lee, 2018).

Job performance refers to "behaviors or actions that are relevant to the goals of the organization, and under control of the individual" (Koopmans et al., 2013, p. 23). Multiple scholars distinguish between the technical and social elements of job performance (e.g., Abramis, 1994; Odle-Dusseau et al., 2012). Technical elements relate to how employees perform, handle job demands, and reach the right decisions (Abramis, 1994). These elements come together in *task performance* – i.e., "activities specific to the functioning and continuance of organizational processes" (Odle-Dusseau et al., 2012, p. 30).

Social elements are reflected in *contextual performance*. Contextual performance involves "behaviors that support the organizational, social, and psychological environment in which the technical core must function" (Borman & Motowidlo, 1993, p. 73). Contextual performance thus refers to activities that foster the "broader psychological and social environment of an organization" (Odle-Dusseau et al., 2012, p. 30).

Scholars tend to assume a negative association between work-to-life conflict and job performance (e.g., Mukarram et al., 2012; Russo et al., 2016; Wijayati et al., 2020), with Russo et al. (2016) suggesting that work-to-life conflict reduces employees' positive energy and psychological availability at work. Positive energy gives employees a sense of harmony and fulfilment because they experience consistency between how their life is and how they would like it to be. This affective state generates positive energy because it creates the optimal psychological, physical, and environmental circumstances for employees to thrive. As a result, positive energy motivates employees to take actions with positive implications for the organization.

A sense of harmony simultaneously acts as a buffer against negative and distracting thoughts that can arise from a felt work-to-life conflict, and against the frustrations fostered by discrepancies between an individual's actual life and their desired life (Russo et al., 2016). These thoughts deplete employees' psychological and physical resources because negative cognitions and feelings demand a coping response from employees, which costs energy. The resources that negative thoughts consume can no longer be expended on positive work outcomes (Demerouti et al., 2010). Efforts to self-regulate the negative thoughts that arise from work-to-life conflict consequently undermine both task performance and contextual performance (Demerouti et al., 2010).

Similar arguments apply to the assumed negative association between work-to-life conflict and job performance through employees' psychological availability. Psychologically available employees are ready "to engage in a specific role despite the distractions caused by the participation in other roles" (Russo et al., 2016, p. 176). Psychological availability therefore reflects an employee's resources to personally engage in multiple roles at a particular moment (Russo et al., 2016). Because work-to-life conflict reduces employees' psychological availability at work, they will presumably be less able to fulfill their work role.

We expect these associations to be stronger for contextual performance than task performance. When employees experience work-to-life conflict, they need to make choices regarding what to expend their limited resources on. Employees are more likely to be evaluated on task performance than contextual performance, and so employees under strain are more strongly incentivized to invest in the requirements of task performance than contextual performance (Allen et al., 2000). In addition, contextual performance is inherently non-task-related as it relates to the broader context of work (Organ, 1997). Consequently, contextual performance behavior is reminiscent of organizational citizenship behaviors (Organ, 1997). Employees experiencing work-to-life conflict may be unwilling or unable to go the extra mile for their organization (Allen et al., 2000).

These expectations lead to the following hypotheses:

Hypothesis 1   *Public servants who experience higher work-to-life conflict are more likely to have lower job performance than public servants who experience lower work-to-life conflict.*

Hypothesis 2   *The negative association between work-to-life conflict and job performance is stronger for contextual performance than task performance.*

METHODS

To explore the association between work-to-life conflict and performance, we used survey data collected in the Netherlands in the spring of 2020, during the first wave of the COVID-19 pandemic. The respondents were civil servants on the e-mail list of *Binnenlands Bestuur*, a fortnightly magazine for public servants in the Netherlands, mainly knowledge workers. Of the total pool of respondents ($n = 3,307$), we removed eight respondents who stated that they had not been working in the previous few months.

Work-to-life conflict was tapped by a three-item measure ($\alpha = 0.89$, mean = 6.01, sd = 2.79) adapted from Greenhaus et al. (2006), where the individual items contain elements of both time and strain conflict. A sample item is: "My work makes it difficult for me to take my responsibilities and participate in activities at home." Exploratory factor analysis showed a clear unidimensional structure. Job performance was assessed using the six-item "task performance" scale ($\alpha = 0.77$, mean = 23.98, sd = 3.87) and the eight-item "contextual performance" scale ($\alpha = 0.81$, mean = 31.40, sd = 3.87) from the Individual Work Performance Questionnaire (Koopmans et al., 2013). Sample items are: "To what degree are you able to perform your work well with minimal time and effort?" (i.e., task performance) and "To what degree do you develop creative solutions for new problems?" (i.e., contextual performance). Exploratory factor analysis showed a simple structure for two separate components providing some validity evidence for the existence of two separate constructs (i.e., task performance and contextual performance). All three scales used a five-point answering scale ranging from "not at all" to "to a large extent."

We conducted linear regression analyses using both types of performance as the dependent variable. In these regression analyses, we controlled for age (mean = 52.27, sd = 9.59), gender (i.e., 52.12 percent of respondents identified as female, 43.91 percent as male, and 0.16 percent as other), the formal number of working hours as specified in the contract (mean = 33.43, sd = 4.81), the extent to which respondents worked at home (1.15 percent of respondents indicated that they almost never worked at home, 1.75 percent less than 20 percent of the time, 1.37 percent between 20 and 40 percent, 2.55 percent between 40 and 60 percent, 4.45 percent between 60 and 80 percent, 20.87 percent more than 80 percent, and 53.10 percent of the respondents stated that they almost always worked at home), and the required (educational) level of the job (i.e., 3.27 percent vocational education, 48.51 percent degree from a university of applied sciences, and 42.39 percent academic degree). Primary and secondary education levels were excluded from this measurement as almost all government jobs in the Netherlands require a degree from a university of applied sciences or higher.

Based on initial data inspection, we excluded the five respondents who had indicated their gender as "other" because of the small number of respondents in this category. We also removed ten respondents who indicated they had a formal contract of more than 40 working hours, which is against Dutch law, and very likely an erroneous response. We used pairwise deletion for the other variables in the regression analyses, leaving us with a final sample of 3,024 respondents.

RESULTS

Table 16.1 shows the results of the linear regression analysis for both task performance and contextual performance, confirming our hypothesis. Respondents experiencing higher levels of work-to-life conflict reported significantly lower levels of both task performance and contextual performance, but when we controlled for the other variables in the model, the effect on task performance was stronger. With respect to the control variables, older respondents reported both higher task performance and contextual performance, while male respondents reported lower contextual performance but not task performance. Respondents contracted to work a higher number of hours reported higher levels of both types of performance. Similarly, respondents working in jobs requiring a higher educational level reported higher performance. Finally, the reported extent of homeworking had no effect on task performance, but did have a significant negative effect on contextual performance.

*Table 16.1   Task performance and contextual performance (regression
                   results)*

Variable	b	SE	β	t-value	p-value
Task performance					
Intercept	21.32	0.87	0.00	24.59	0
Work-to-life conflict	−0.44	0.02	−0.36	−19.81	0
Age	0.07	0.01	0.18	9.16	0
Gender	−0.18	0.15	−0.02	−1.17	0.24
Formal working hours	0.04	0.02	0.05	2.50	0.01
Educational level	0.45	0.13	0.07	3.52	0
Extent of homeworking	0.05	0.06	0.02	0.86	0.39
Contextual performance					
Intercept	27.55	1.17	0.00	23.48	0
Work-to-life conflict	−0.07	0.03	−0.04	−2.20	0.03
Age	0.06	0.01	0.11	5.32	0
Gender	−1.17	0.21	−0.12	−5.58	0
Formal working hours	0.09	0.02	0.09	4.11	0
Educational level	0.79	0.17	0.09	4.59	0
Extent of homeworking	−0.23	0.08	−0.06	−2.85	0

Notes: b = regression coefficient; SE = standard error; β = standardized regression coefficient.

CONCLUSION AND DISCUSSION

This chapter set out to explore the association between work-to-life conflict
and job performance among public servants, one of the largest employee
groups across countries. Our hypothesis that work-to-life conflict is negatively
associated with job performance in this group was confirmed. Contrary to our
expectations, however, the negative association between work-to-life conflict and job performance was stronger for task performance than contextual
performance.

Two alternative explanations may account for the latter. Firstly, our
respondents are mainly knowledge workers with a strong capacity for innovation, which is a defining feature of contextual performance (e.g., Koopmans
et al., 2013). Indeed, contextual performance is sometimes part of their job
description, and our respondents may therefore prioritize some elements of
contextual performance over task performance. Secondly, duties relating to
task performance require immediate (cognitive) resources, while work activities that might contribute to contextual performance are less time-dependent.
Thus, if work-to-life conflict arises, employees may compromise on duties that

contribute to task performance but there is no direct need to compromise on work activities that contribute to contextual performance.

This study has some methodological limitations. We assessed work-to-life conflict and job performance through self-reports. Although it is common to assess job performance in studies of work-to-life conflict through self-reporting (e.g., Aryee, 1992; Netemeyer et al., 1996), it is sensitive to bias: individuals may be incentivized to overestimate or underestimate their performance – overestimating performance to maintain a favorable self-image, or underestimating performance because of socialization into lower performance expectations, which is often the case among women and people of color (e.g., Buchanan & Selmon, 2008). Furthermore, we investigated the effects of work-to-life conflict on job performance using a cross-sectional research design.

We acknowledge that previous studies have also yielded mixed findings regarding the association between work-to-life conflict and job performance (Allen et al., 2000), with some scholars finding a negative or no association between these constructs and others concluding a negative association between conflict in some life domains but not in others (e.g., Aryee, 1992; Netemeyer et al., 1996). Further research is therefore needed to advance our knowledge of the boundary conditions of the association between work-to-life conflict and job performance, including differences across employee groups. In this regard, it would be interesting to investigate the potential moderating effects of age, gender, and the other control variables that we included in our study and which were found to correlate with job performance.

Based on our research, we would advise organizations to invest in enabling employees to fulfill their non-work roles, such as by granting employees the right to not be disturbed outside regular office hours, and by offering flexible working hours and the option of taking care leave. Supervisors play an important role, not only by providing employee support but also by acting as a role model. Such investment can have a positive influence on employees' well-being and quality of life. These resources can help employees to manage their work and non-work roles and strengthen individuals' ability to accomplish organizational objectives, thus contributing to their job performance (Odle-Dusseau et al., 2012).

REFERENCES

Abramis, D. J. (1994). Relationship of job stressors to job performance: Linear or an inverted-U? *Psychological Reports*, *75*(1 Pt 2), 547–558.

Allen, T. D., Herst, D. E. L., Bruck, C. S., & Sutton, M. (2000). Consequences associated with work-to-family conflict: A review and agenda for future research. *Journal of Occupational Health Psychology*, *5*(2), 278–308.

Aryee, S. (1992). Antecedents and outcomes of work–family conflict among married professional women: Evidence from Singapore. *Human Relations*, *45*(8), 813–837.

Beauregard, T. A., & Henry, L. C. (2009). Making the link between work–life balance practices and organizational performance. *Human Resource Management Review*, *19*(1), 9–22.

Borman, W. C., & Motowidlo, S. J. (1993). Expanding the criterion domain to include elements of contextual performance. In N. Schmitt & W. C. Borman (Eds), *Personnel selection in organizations* (pp. 71–98). San Francisco, CA: Jossey Bass.

Buchanan, T., & Selmon, N. (2008). Race and gender differences in self-efficacy: Assessing the role of gender role attitudes and family background. *Sex Roles*, *58*, 822–836.

Delanoeije, J., & Verbruggen, M. (2020). Between-person and within-person effects of telework: A quasi-field experiment. *European Journal of Work and Organizational Psychology*, *29*(6), 795–808.

Demerouti, E., Bakker, A. B., & Voydanoff, P. (2010). Does home life interfere with or facilitate job performance? *European Journal of Work and Organizational Psychology*, *19*(2), 128–149.

Gisler, S., Omansky, R., Alenick, P. R., Tumminia, A. M., Eatough, E. M., & Johnson, R. C. (2018). Work–life conflict and employee health: A review. *Journal of Applied Biobehavioral Research*, *23*(4), 1–46.

Greenhaus, J. H., Allen, T. D., & Foley, S. (2006). *Work–family balance: Exploration of a concept*. Families and Work Conference, Provo.

Groeneveld, S., Steijn, B., & Van der Parre, P. (2009). Joining the Dutch civil service: Influencing motives in a changing economic context. *Public Management Review*, *11*(2), 173–189.

Koopmans, L., Bernaards, C. M., Hildebrandt, V. H., Van Buuren, S., Van der Beek, A. J., & De Vet, H. C. W. (2013). Development of an individual work performance questionnaire. *International Journal of Productivity and Performance Management*, *62*(1), 6–28.

Kruyen, P. M., Keulemans, S., Borst, R., & Helderman, J.-K. (2020). Searching for the renaissance bureaucrat: A longitudinal computer-assisted study of personality traits in government vacancies. *International Journal of Public Sector Management*, *33*(1), 22–44.

Linos, E. (2018). More than public service: A field experiment on job advertisements and diversity in the police. *Journal of Public Administration Research and Theory*, *28*(1), 67–85.

Morgan, P., & Allington, N. (2002). Has the public sector retained its "model employer" status? *Public Money and Management*, *22*(1), 35–42.

Mukarram, A., Akbar, A., Jan, Z., & Gul, A. (2012). Work life conflict impact on females' job performance: A study of primary level female school teachers in Pakistan. *European Journal of Business and Management*, *4*(20), 74–83.

Netemeyer, R. G., Boles, J. S., & McMurrian, R. (1996). Development and validation of work–family conflicts and work–family conflict scales. *Journal of Applied Psychology*, *81*(4), 400–410.

Odle-Dusseau, H. N., Britt, T. W., & Greene-Shortridge, T. M. (2012). Organizational work–family resources as predictors of job performance and attitudes: The process of work–family conflict and enrichment. *Journal of Occupational Health Psychology*, *17*(1), 28–40.

Organ, D. W. (1997). Organizational citizenship behavior: It's construct clean-up time. *Human Performance*, *10*(2), 85–97.

Russo, M., Shteigman, A., & Carmeli, A. (2016). Workplace and family support and work–life balance: Implications for individual psychological availability and energy at work. *Journal of Positive Psychology, 11*(2), 173–188.

Sirgy, M. J., & Lee, D.-J. (2018). Work–life balance: An integrative review. *Applied Research Quality Life, 13*, 229–254.

Wang, B., Liu, Y., Qian, J., & Parker, S. K. (2021). Achieving effective remote working during the COVID-19 pandemic: A work design perspective. *Applied Psychology, 70*(1), 16–59.

Wijayati, T., Achmad, D. K., & Karwanto, K. (2020). Emotional intelligence, work family conflict, and job satisfaction on junior high school teacher's performance. *International Journal of Higher Education, 9*(1), 179–189.

PART IV

Working parents

17. Returning to work after childbirth: maternal experiences and spillover-crossover effects on the infant

Roseriet Beijers

INTRODUCTION

Given the rise in employment participation among mothers, and the length of maternity leave in many countries, many mothers have to resume work within a few months of giving birth. Although the transition back to work can bring positive emotions, in their book *The second shift* Hochschild and Machung (2012) show that the return to work after maternity leave is not always easy. The return to work involves many stressors for mothers: they need to get used to being separated from their infant, combine work and family responsibilities, and readjust to work. Although many mothers go through this transition, work–family studies on the postpartum work resumption period are few and far between. The studies that have investigated mothers' experiences of returning to work are mainly qualitative in nature and based on small samples (see e.g. Brand & Barreiro-Lucas, 2014; Nichols & Roux, 2004). Moreover, these studies have focused on maternal well-being rather than considering the potential consequences for the infant. After describing the experiences and emotions around the return to work among a large sample of mothers in the Netherlands, I will present a theoretical model to encourage and guide future studies into the possible consequences of stress in mothers resuming work for the infant.

WORK RESUMPTION EXPERIENCES OF DUTCH MOTHERS

In the Netherlands, around 170,000 babies are born every year. As in many other Western countries, pregnancy leave ends 10–12 weeks postpartum and most Dutch mothers return to work within a few months of childbirth. To understand how mothers feel during this period, a survey based mainly on open

Table 17.1   Sample descriptives mothers

	Percentage
Number of children	
First child	52.9
≥ Two children	47.1
Length of maternity leave	
0–2 months	2.8
3–5 months	78.1
≥ 6 months	19.1
Number of working days	
1–2 days	8.0
3–4 days	83.7
≥ 5 days	8.3
Number of working days partner	
1–2 days	2.2
3–4 days	41.0
≥ 5 days	56.8
Most frequent professional sectors mother	
Healthcare	29.0
Management and advice	24.2
Education	14.0

Note: N = 372.

questions was created and distributed through various channels, just before the COVID-19 pandemic. In total, 372 mothers participated who had returned to work in the previous two years (see Table 17.1).

First, mothers were asked the following open question: "How do you look back on the period when you returned to work?" Around 20 percent of the mothers shared positive experiences (e.g. "Wonderful to see my colleagues again" and "Nice to do something for myself"). By contrast, 65 percent of the mothers mentioned only negative experiences. For example, mothers wrote: "I found this period terribly difficult. I was not ready, mentally and physically" and "I was tired from the sleepless nights and found it very difficult to combine work and family life." The remainder (15 percent) reported both positive and negative experiences.

Next, we asked mothers to indicate, on a scale from 1 to 10, how they experienced their return to work. On average, mothers gave a low score ($M = 5.4$; $SD = 2.2$), with about half reporting a 5 or lower. Mothers who gave a higher score had taken a significantly longer period of leave, had more working hours, had more children, and worked in the professional sector of "management and advice." The correlation coefficients were significant but small, suggesting that many mothers struggling with the transition back to work and stress due to resuming work cannot be narrowed down to a particular group of mothers or professional sector.

Finally, we asked mothers what could have led them to increase their score by one point. The most frequently mentioned factors related to the following themes: (1) more support from employer/colleagues (27.5 percent), including options for working from home, more understanding and acceptance, and less pressure; (2) longer leave (27.3 percent), including partner leave and unpaid leave; and (3) build-up/adjustments at work after leave (26.7 percent), including building up tasks/hours/days more gradually, no evenings or irregular shifts, and the ability to work flexibly.

WHAT ABOUT THE INFANT?

Concerns about how maternal work might impact child development arose in the 1970s when the prevalent view of gender roles (i.e. female caregiver and male breadwinner) came into conflict with the increasing number of women who continued working after childbirth. Nevertheless, decades of research produced little evidence of the net effects of maternal employment on child development (Repetti & Wang, 2014).

These studies focused on the objective parameters of employment, such as the timing and number of hours worked by mothers, and not on subjective work experiences. However, during the first 1,000 days of an infant's life, covering the period between conception and the child's second birthday, infants are known to be highly sensitive to their environment, including the well-being of their mothers and primary caregivers (e.g. Hughes et al., 2017).

Spillover-crossover Processes

The spillover-crossover model hypothesizes that stress in the work domain will first spill over into the home domain and subsequently cross over from the employee to others at home (Bakker & Demerouti, 2013). According to this model, the primary mechanism by which maternal work resumption stress could affect the infant is through its impact on parenting quality. Indeed, research on the work–family interface has provided evidence that work stress affects parenting quality, as indicated by reduced positivity and increased negativity and harshness (see e.g. Danner-Vlaardingerbroek et al., 2013; Malinen et al., 2017; Shimazu et al., 2020).

However, most of the studies were carried out in families with older children, long after the mothers concerned had resumed work. Since the period of returning to work is characterized by new stressors and parental adaptation processes, it is possible that short-term adaptations are made that may adversely affect the child or the family in the long term. For example, a mother might decide to reduce working hours, or even to stop working, which increases her financial dependence on her partner. Furthermore, I argue that, next to parenting quality, maternal work resumption stress can affect the child through its impact on nutrition quality.

Nutrition Quality: Breastfeeding and Milk Consumption

The World Health Organization recommends exclusive breastfeeding for the first six months of an infant's life, followed by breastfeeding supplemented with complementary foods until the age of two (World Health Organization, 2003). These recommendations stem from the undeniable long-term health benefits for infant and mother that are associated with breastfeeding (Rollins et al., 2016; Victora et al., 2016). Despite these recommendations, many countries do not achieve the goals of (exclusive) breastfeeding. In the Netherlands, for example, breastfeeding is most frequently discontinued in the first two months of life, and only 39 percent of mothers exclusively breastfeed their infant up to the age of six months (TNO, 2015).

Among the factors known to affect breastfeeding practices, women working is one of the main reasons for not breastfeeding or early weaning (Rollins et al., 2016; Thulier & Mercer, 2009). For example, women who plan to return to work after childbirth are less likely to start breastfeeding, and short maternity leave increases the likelihood of early weaning (Guendelman et al., 2009; Mirkovic et al., 2014). It remains unclear to what extent stress among mothers resuming work contributes to women's decision to wean early or not to breastfeed at all. Are mothers struggling with work–life balance tempted to remove breastfeeding from their to-do list?

The stress experienced by mothers when resuming work could also affect milk composition. Besides water and nutrients, human milk contains many other constituents, including immune factors, microbes, and hormones. These biological constituents are hypothesized not only to affect the physical health of the infant, but also the developmental programming of cells, tissues, and organs that impact the offspring's phenotype. The hypothesis that lactating mothers send physiological information about their environment, including stress factors, to the infant, so that the infant develops a behavioral profile that matches that (future) environment, is known as *Lactocrine Programming* (de Weerth et al., 2022).

Indeed, some studies have found indications that milk composition is associated with maternal mental health and general stress, though these studies are few in number and the results are not always consistent. For example, one recent study found no differences in cortisol concentrations – the main end product of the stress-responsive hypothalamic–pituitary–adrenal axis – in milk between mothers with and without psychiatric complaints (Romijn et al., 2021); however, in another study, higher maternal stress was found to be associated with higher milk cortisol concentrations (Aparicio et al., 2020), while relaxation therapy reduced milk cortisol concentrations in a randomized controlled trial (Mohd Shukri et al., 2019). Despite such interesting results, human milk is one of the most understudied biological systems in the life sciences (de Weerth et al., 2022).

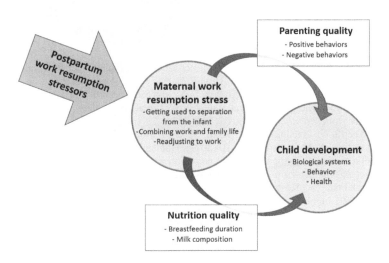

Figure 17.1   Theoretical model showing the two pathways through which maternal work resumption stress could independently impact child development

CONCLUSION

Although many mothers return to work after pregnancy and face numerous stressors – including getting used to being separated from their baby, combining working and family life, and readjusting to work – work–family studies on the postpartum work resumption period are scarce. Those studies that have investigated the return to work after maternity leave indicate that it is challenging across different countries with different leave policies. However, more quantitative, longitudinal, cross-cultural, and experimental studies are needed to discover under which conditions mothers experience the return to work as stressful, and how mothers can successfully adapt. Such studies should also include the possible consequences of maternal work resumption stress for parenting, nutrition, and infant development. The model presented in this chapter aims to guide and encourage future studies in this direction (see Figure 17.1). Evidence that stress caused by returning to work involves risks for mother and infant provides a moral, political, and public health imperative to undertake efforts to mitigate possible consequences.

REFERENCES

Aparicio, M., Browne, P. D., Hechler, C., Beijers, R., Rodríguez, J. M., de Weerth, C., & Fernández, L. (2020). Human milk cortisol and immune factors over the first three postnatal months: Relations to maternal psychosocial distress. *PloS One*, 15.

Bakker, A. B., & Demerouti, E. (2013). The spillover-crossover model. In J. G. Grzywacz & E. Demerouti (eds) *New frontiers in work and family research*. Psychology Press, pp. 54–70.

Brand, H., & Barreiro-Lucas, J. (2014). Return-to-work experiences of female employees following maternity leave. *African Journal of Employee Relations*, 38, 69–92.

Danner-Vlaardingerbroek, G., Kluwer, E. S., van Steenbergen, E. F., & van der Lippe, T. (2013). The psychological availability of dual-earner parents for their children after work. *Family Relations*, 62, 741–754.

de Weerth, C., Aatsinki, A. K., Azad, M. B., Bartol, F. F., Bode, L., Collado, M. C., Dettmer, A. M. ... & Beijers, R. (2022). Human milk: From complex tailored nutrition to bioactive impact on child cognition and behavior. *Critical Reviews in Food Science and Nutrition*, 63(26), 7945–7982.

Guendelman, S., Kosa, J. L., Pearl, M., Graham, S., Goodman, J., & Kharrazi, M. (2009). Juggling work and breastfeeding: Effects of maternity leave and occupational characteristics. *Pediatrics*, 123, 38–46.

Hochschild, A., & Machung, A. (2012). *The second shift: Working families and the revolution at home*. Penguin.

Hughes, K., Bellis, M. A., Hardcastle, K. A., Sethi, D., Butchart, A., Mikton, C. ... & Dunne, M. P. (2017). The effect of multiple adverse childhood experiences on health: A systematic review and meta-analysis. *Lancet Public Health*, 2, E356–E366.

Malinen, K., Ronka, A., Sevon, E., & Schoebi, D. (2017). The difficulty of being a professional, a parent, and a spouse on the same day: Daily spillover of workplace interactions on parenting, and the role of spousal support. *Journal of Prevention & Intervention in the Community*, 45, 156–167.

Mirkovic, K. R., Perrine, C. G., Scanlon, K. S., & Grummer-Strawn, L. M. (2014). In the United States, a mother's plans for infant feeding are associated with her plans for employment. *Journal of Human Lactation*, 30, 292–297.

Mohd-Shukri, N. H., Wells, J., Eaton, S., Mukhtar, F., Petelin, A., Jenko-Pražnikar, Z., & Fewtrell, M. (2019). Randomized controlled trial investigating the effects of a breastfeeding relaxation intervention on maternal psychological state, breast milk outcomes, and infant behavior and growth. *American Journal of Clinical Nutrition*, *110*, 121–130.

Nichols, M. R., & Roux, G. M. (2004). Maternal perspectives on postpartum return to the workplace. *Journal of Obstetric, Gynecologic & Neonatal Nursing*, *33*, 463–471.

Repetti, R. L., & Wang, S. W. (2014). Employment and parenting. *Parenting: Science and Practice*, *14*, 121–132.

Rollins, N. C., Bhandari, N., Hajeebhoy, N., Horton, S., Lutter, C. K., Martines, J. C. … & Victora, C. G. (2016). Why invest, and what it will take to improve breastfeeding practices? *Lancet*, *387*, 491–504.

Romijn, M., van Tilburg, L., Hollanders, J. J., van der Voorn, B., de Goede, P., Dolman, K. M., … & Finken, M. (2021). The association between maternal stress and glucocorticoid rhythmicity in human milk. *Nutrients*, *13*, 1608.

Shimazu, A., Bakker, A. B., Demerouti, E., Fujiwara, T., Iwata, N., Shimada, K. … & Kawakami, N. (2020). Workaholism, work engagement and child well-being: A test of the spillover-crossover model. *International Journal of Environmental Research and Public Health*, *17*, 6213.

Thulier, D., & Mercer, J. (2009). Variables associated with breastfeeding duration. *Journal of Obstetric, Gynecologic, and Neonatal Nursing*, *38*, 259–268.

TNO. (2015). *Peiling melkvoeding van zuigelingen 2015*. Leiden: TNO.

Victora, C. G., Bahl, R., Barros, A. J. D., Franca, G. V. A., Horton, S., Krasevec, J. … & Rollins, N. C. (2016). Breastfeeding in the 21st century: Epidemiology, mechanisms, and lifelong effect. *Lancet*, *387*, 475–490.

World Health Organization. (2003). *Global strategy for infant and young child feeding*. Geneva: World Health Organization.

18. Engaged fathers: towards a fatherhood premium or penalty?

Marc Grau-Grau and Stéfanie André

INTRODUCTION

This chapter aims to shed more light on heterogeneity among fathers at work and how their caring behaviors may have potential work consequences. The scholarly literature in this domain tends to present men and women, and consequently fathers and mothers, as two broad categories and researchers study the differences between both groups, in many cases overlooking the heterogeneity within gender groups (Gerson, 2004). This chapter therefore applies a "gender lens" to look beyond gender differences to understand diversity among one specific group: working fathers.

Working fathers are a very interesting group for at least three reasons. First, fatherhood is in transition. This transition implies a reconfiguration of central priorities and work–family dynamics and is leading to a double and possibly contradictory call: to be a breadwinner and a nurturing dad. This double call may undermine work–family balance among working fathers. By work–family balance, we do not mean an absence of conflict or equal involvement in the work and family domains, but rather the capacity or agency to combine work and family roles according to one's personal values at a given moment (Greenhaus & Allen, 2011). Second, fatherhood is receiving growing political, academic, and media interest, probably explained by the impact of engaged fatherhood on children (Kotelchuck, 2021), on gender equality (Grau-Grau & Bowles, 2022), and on fathers themselves (Grau-Grau, 2023). Third, fathers are a very heterogeneous group whose diversity and richness have not been fully explored.

For mothers, the terms "involved" or "engaged" are rarely used because involvement and engagement are implicit in the concept of motherhood (Ladge & Humberd, 2022). The need to add the terms "involved," "engaged," or "nurturing" for fathers demonstrates the disparity and diversity of attitudes among fathers. The emergence of father typologies supports this argument (Cooper, 2000; Halrynjo, 2009; Hanlon, 2012; Kaufman, 2013; Tanquerel &

Table 18.1   *Types of fathers*

	Time with children	Discourse in public	Discourse in private	Primary role (exposed)	Career adjustments
Traditional	Low	Normative	Normative	Earner	None
Transitional	Medium	Normative	Non-normative	Earner	Minor
Engaged-breadwinner	Medium	Hybrid	Non-normative	Earner > carer	Major
Engaged-nurturer	High	Non-normative	Non-normative	Carer	Major

Grau-Grau, 2020). This new categorization generally places fathers into three groups: traditional, in transition, and engaged.

Some studies suggest that engaged fathers experience similar work–life balance challenges to mothers (Humberd et al., 2015). At the same time, some significant differences exist between involved fathers and mothers (Ladge & Humberd, 2022): fathers generally return to work quickly after becoming a parent (Grau-Grau, 2020); fathers have fewer role models for their work–family aspirations (Ladge & Greenberg, 2019); and engaged fathers may be judged even more harshly than women because they contradict *more* prevailing expectations and stereotypes. In fact, these work consequences are not a reality for all working fathers, so this theoretical chapter presents four types of fathers and work consequences associated with different caring behaviors.

FOUR TYPES OF FATHERS

Our theoretical model includes four types of working fathers (see Table 18.1). By distinguishing two types of engaged fathers, we expand the triple typology of working fathers (Cooper, 2000; Halrynjo, 2009; Hanlon, 2012; Kaufman, 2013; Tanquerel & Grau-Grau, 2020) who seem to coexist simultaneously: traditional, in transition, and engaged fathers.

Traditional fathers spend less time with their children than other fathers, have normative discourses at home and work, prioritize their role as earners, and do not make any career adjustments following the birth of a child (Kaufman, 2013). Transitional fathers have higher caregiving aspirations than traditional fathers, but do not spend as much time with their families as they would like. They have non-normative discourse in private but normative in public, and may make some minor career adjustments after the birth of a child (Kaufman, 2013). Finally, engaged fathers spend more time with their children than other fathers; they talk openly about their practices and responsibilities at home, and they can make major adjustments in their careers for their families, such as moving to another sector if necessary (Kaufman, 2013).

Based on the role prioritization model (Haines & Stroessner, 2019), we assume that there are two types of engaged fathers (engaged-breadwinner and engaged-nurturer). An engaged father is considered an "engaged-breadwinner" if his primary identity as a carer *complements* his primary identity as an earner. According to the role prioritization model, as long as a person appears to prioritize the normative roles for their gender, it is acceptable – or even desirable – to engage in atypical gender behavior. This type of father would therefore experience positive work implications, as presented in the following sections. On the other side, an engaged father is considered an "engaged-nurturer" if his primary identity as a carer *substitutes* his primary identity as an earner. In this case, if fathers prioritize a non-normative role, they may experience negative consequences at work. Developing the "engaged-breadwinner" and "engaged-nurturer" categories, based on the role prioritization model, could help to disentangle different work consequences based on different caregiving behaviors. So, according to our new categorization, we propose that:

Hypothesis 0.1   *Traditional fathers spend less time with their children than other types of fathers. Both public and private discourses are normative. Their priority is work, and they do not make any adjustments to their professional careers after the birth of their child.*

Hypothesis 0.2   *Transitional fathers spend more time with their children than traditional fathers but less than engaged fathers. They spend less time with the children than they would like. They maintain a non-normative discourse in private and a normative one in public. They prioritize family and work, although in the eyes of organizations they look like traditional fathers. They may make minor career adjustments after a child is born.*

Hypothesis 0.3   *Engaged-breadwinner fathers spend more time with their children than traditional or transitional fathers. Their discourse in private is non-normative, and in public, they prioritize normative gender roles without hiding atypical gender behaviors at home. If necessary, they may make major changes in their professional career after the birth of a child.*

Hypothesis 0.4   *Engaged-nurturer fathers spend more time with their children than traditional or transitional fathers. Their private and public discourses are non-normative, and they openly prioritize their family and their role as caregivers. If necessary, they may make major changes in their professional career after the birth of a child.*

Table 18.2   Work implications

Type of father	Ideal worker norm	Use of flexible work arrangements	Fatherhood premium	Penalty
Traditional	+++	+	+++	+
Transitional	+++	++	++	+
Engaged-breadwinner	++	++	++	+
Engaged-nurturer	+	+++	+	+++

Note: Level of adherence/use/importance (+ = low; ++ = medium; +++ = high).

In the rest of the chapter, we will argue how these four types of fathers may experience the implications of their approach to fatherhood (see Table 18.2).

IDEAL WORKER NORM

Although job positions are typically presented as abstract positions with no specific gender or possessor, organizations are not gender-neutral (Acker, 1990). Gendered organizations imply a systematic advantage for a particular gender group. While it is true that gendered organizations affect women negatively, we assume that they may also impact negatively on men who openly challenge hegemonic masculinity and the ideal worker norm as engaged-nurturer fathers.

The ideal worker norm is defined as the belief that the ideal worker is totally committed to the job to the point, if necessary, of neglecting family and personal needs (Blair-Loy, 2003). Although the notion of an ideal worker does not match many employees' aspirations (Davies & Frink, 2014), it remains prevalent in many organizations, which encourages many male employees to try to pass as ideal workers to avoid career penalties (Reid, 2015). This is the case for transitional and engaged-breadwinner fathers. This reality has many consequences for some working fathers, especially those who aspire to be fully engaged with their families like engaged-nurturer fathers because, as will be explained later, they violate the ideal worker norm. So, according to this, we propose the following:

Hypothesis 1.1   *Traditional fathers, who prioritize work, embrace the notion of the ideal worker.*
Hypothesis 1.2   *Transitional fathers, who pass as traditional fathers, embrace the notion of the ideal worker.*
Hypothesis 1.3   *Engaged-breadwinner fathers, who communicate openly their atypical behaviors at home while prioritizing their primary role as a worker, embrace the notion of the ideal*

worker, in some sense. Their role as caregiver complements the role of ideal worker.

Hypothesis 1.4   *Engaged-nurturer fathers, who communicate openly their*
                     atypical behaviors at home while prioritizing their primary
                     role as caregivers, violate the notion of the ideal worker.
                     Their role as caregiver replaces that of the ideal worker.

FLEXIBLE WORK ARRANGEMENTS

We are witnessing the democratization of flexible work arrangements. Work–
life balance is a real need for many contemporary parents. This is explained
by many factors, such as the rise of dual-earner couples, technologies that blur
the boundaries between work and family, and the COVID-19 pandemic. In
the face of this contemporary challenge, companies are offering flexible work
arrangements that may have important implications for health, as explored in
this edited volume. These policies are necessary, but they need to be accompanied by family-supportive behaviors from managers (Cooper & Baird, 2015),
together with a work–family balance culture (Thompson et al., 1999). Without
these, employees may feel compelled not to take up flexible work arrangements, especially in order to engage in care responsibilities. Leslie et al. (2012)
show how supervisors interpret employees' flexible work arrangements as
signals of high or low productivity, depending on the reasons to which the use
of the flexible work arrangements can be attributed.

We therefore assume that taking up flexible work arrangements in order
to engage in care is still penalized by many organizations that lack a strong
work–family balance culture and managers with family-friendly behaviors.
Given this context, we argue that traditional fathers are the least likely
to make use of flexible work arrangements, followed by transitional and
engaged-breadwinner fathers, in order to avoid violating the notion of ideal
worker. As empirical evidence shows, engaged-nurturer fathers may suffer
from a flexibility stigma, which is the belief that making use of flexible work
arrangements is related to lower commitment and productivity (Coltrane et
al., 2013). For example, Rudman and Mescher (2013) found that men who
requested family leave are viewed as higher on feminine traits and lower on
masculine traits, which is predictive of a greater risk of penalties. Accordingly,
we propose the following:

Hypothesis 2.1   *Traditional fathers, who embrace the notion of the ideal*
                     worker, will rarely make use of flexible work arrangements,
                     as this would violate the notion of the ideal worker.
Hypothesis 2.2   *Transitional fathers, who pose as traditional fathers and*
                     embrace the notion of the ideal worker, will make moderate

use of flexible work arrangements to avoid unmasking themselves.

Hypothesis 2.3   *Engaged-breadwinner fathers, who publicly prioritize their role as workers while communicating openly their atypical gender behaviors at home, will make use of flexible work arrangements to a moderate extent, to avoid contradicting part of their discourse.*

Hypothesis 2.4   *Engaged-nurturer fathers, who prioritize their role as caregivers, will use flexible work arrangements when necessary.*

FATHERHOOD PREMIUM

Becoming a parent is associated with work implications but these differ by gender. Fathers tend to experience a "fatherhood premium" through an increased chance of promotion, more hiring opportunities, or higher earnings. Women, by contrast, generally face a motherhood penalty in terms of earnings, hiring, and promotion opportunities (Correll et al., 2007; Hodges & Budig, 2010). However, empirical evidence also shows significant intragroup variations. For example, a study that compared Australia, the United Kingdom, and the United States showed that the lowest-earning men actually face a small but significant fatherhood penalty, rather than a premium (Cooke, 2014).

Another group that is subject to fatherhood penalties is single fathers (Steffens et al., 2019). According to the study by Steffens et al. (2019), work-related impressions and stereotypes play an important role. Childcare remains a family domain, and single fathers therefore violate traditional social roles *more* than single mothers, resulting in a fatherhood penalty. Similarly, other studies found that impressions of fathers who take parental leave are more negative than mothers who do so (Vinkenburg et al., 2012), and that men are punished more than women for long spells of unemployment (Smith et al., 2005). These cases reinforce the idea that men who deviate from male stereotypes may be penalized *more* in the labor market than women, who, according to stereotyping research, are expected to be more involved in and committed to childcare. We might anticipate, then, that men who contradict or challenge their social role or the ideal worker norm might also be judged more harshly than women as they contradict prevailing expectations and stereotypes more. This would imply that engaged-nurturer fathers may not enjoy the fatherhood premium that other fathers do. We therefore propose the following:

Hypothesis 3.1   *Traditional fathers, who embrace the notion of the ideal worker and do not make use of flexible work arrangements,*

	are more likely to benefit from a fatherhood premium than other fathers.
Hypothesis 3.2	*Transitional fathers, who embrace the notion of the ideal worker and make moderate use of flexible work arrangements, may benefit from a fatherhood premium.*
Hypothesis 3.3	*Engaged-breadwinner fathers, who embrace the notion of the ideal worker in some sense and make moderate use of flexible work arrangements, may benefit from a fatherhood premium.*
Hypothesis 3.4	*Engaged-nurturer fathers, who violate the notion of the ideal worker and make use of flexible work arrangements, are less likely to benefit from a fatherhood premium than other fathers.*

PENALTIES

Engaged fatherhood might be seen as a counter-stereotypical behavior that could result in backlash effects, such as reduced hiring or promotion opportunities (career penalties), as shown in Table 18.2. However, some research shows that engaged fathers sometimes avoid this backlash effect (Fleischmann & Sieverding, 2015). One potential explanation for this could be the role prioritization model (Haines & Stroessner, 2019) presented previously. This model argues that as long as a person appears to prioritize the normative roles for their gender, it may be acceptable, or even desirable, to engage in atypical gender behaviors (Haines & Stroessner, 2019). Accordingly, backlash effects might be avoided if gender-atypical behaviors are seen as complementary to traditional gender norms rather than replacing them. In other words, the role prioritization model implies that backlash effects will not occur if the primary gender role is fulfilled well. We therefore expect that being an involved father will not imply a significant backlash effect or fatherhood penalty if the father fulfills his primary role as a worker first. According to this model, then, engaged fathers can escape wage penalties *only* if they are committed to earning (engaged-breadwinner fathers) and their role as engaged fathers complements the notion of ideal worker. However, if engaged fathers explicitly challenge hegemonic masculinity and the ideal worker norm by expressing a non-normative discourse, and their primary role as carer substitutes that of breadwinner, they may suffer career penalties just as many women do, and in some cases, with a greater intensity because they contradict the expectations, stereotypes, and gender norms around them even *more*, as suggested by some authors (Steffens et al., 2019). We therefore propose the following:

Hypothesis 4.1   *Traditional fathers, who embrace the notion of the ideal worker and do not make use of flexible work arrangements, are less likely to experience career penalties than other groups.*

Hypothesis 4.2   *Transitional fathers, who embrace the notion of the ideal worker and make moderate use of flexible work arrangements, are less likely to experience career penalties than engaged-nurturer fathers.*

Hypothesis 4.3   *Engaged-breadwinner fathers, who embrace the notion of the ideal worker in some sense and make moderate use of flexible work arrangements, are less likely to experience career penalties than engaged-nurturer fathers.*

Hypothesis 4.4   *Engaged-nurturer fathers, who violate the notion of the ideal worker and make use of flexible work arrangements, are more likely to experience career penalties than other types of fathers.*

CONCLUSION

In this chapter, we have aimed to enrich the work–life literature by exploring how different types of working fathers with varying caregiving behaviors may experience different work consequences. Fatherhood is in transition, and this transition has been accelerated by the COVID-19 pandemic, bringing fathers to new crossroads (Hodkinson & Brooks, 2022). Empirical evidence suggests that fathers are showing more caregiving ambition than previously, but many organizations are still not helping their employees to foster a healthy work–life balance. Riley Bowles and her colleagues suggest three working principles that can be applied to organizations that aim to support working fathers (Bowles et al., 2022). Reluctant companies may make small interventions among their employees to understand the implications of different caring behaviors among working fathers.

This new framework encourages research that aims to identify heterogeneity within gender groups. More specifically, our propositions can be used to analyze different work implications among different types of working fathers. Empirical data may help us to understand this framework better, and the realities, tensions, aspirations, and consequences of different types of working fathers.

ACKNOWLEDGMENT

This publication is part of the project "Fathers Combining Work and Care" with project number VI.Veni.211S.046 of the NWO talent program VENI 2021 which is financed by the Dutch Research Council.

REFERENCES

Acker, J. (1990). Hierarchies, jobs, bodies: A theory of gendered organizations. *Gender & Society*, *4*(2), 139–158.

Blair-Loy, M. (2003). *Competing devotions: Career and family among women executives.* Cambridge, MA: Harvard University Press.

Bowles, H. R., Kotelchuck, M., & Grau-Grau, M. (2022). Reducing barriers to engaged fatherhood: Three principles for promoting gender equity in parenting. In M. Grau-Grau, M. Las Heras, & H. R. Bowles (Eds), *Engaged fatherhood for men, families and gender equality: Healthcare, social policy, and work perspectives* (pp. 299–325). Cham: Springer.

Coltrane, S., Miller, E. C., Dehaan, T., & Stewart, L. (2013). Fathers and the flexibility stigma. *Journal of Social Issues*, *69*(2), 279–302.

Cooke, L. P. (2014). Gendered parenthood penalties and premiums across the earnings distribution in Australia, the United Kingdom, and the United States. *European Sociological Review*, *30*(3), 360–372.

Cooper, M. (2000). Being the "go-to guy": Fatherhood; masculinity; and the organization of work in Silicon Valley. *Qualitative Sociology*, *23*(4), 379–405.

Cooper, R., & Baird, M. (2015). Bringing the "right to request" flexible working arrangements to life: From policies to practices. *Employee Relations*, *37*(5), 568–581.

Correll, S. J., Benard, S., & Paik, I. (2007). Getting a job: Is there a motherhood penalty? *American Journal of Sociology*, *112*(5), 1297–1339.

Davies, A. R., & Frink, B. D. (2014). The origins of the ideal worker: The separation of work and home in the United States from the market revolution to 1950. *Work and Occupations*, *41*(1), 18–39.

Fleischmann, A., & Sieverding, M. (2015). Reactions toward men who have taken parental leave: Does the length of parental leave matter? *Sex Roles*, *72*(9–10), 462–476.

Gerson, K. (2004). Understanding work and family through a gender lens. *Community, Work & Family*, *7*(2), 163–178.

Grau-Grau, M. (2020). Return-to-work for fathers. A group with specific needs? In M. Karanika-Murray, & C. Cooper (Eds), *Navigating the return-to-work experience for new parents.* New York: Routledge.

Grau-Grau, M. (2023). Fatherhood involvement as a source of human flourishing. In M. Las Heras, M. Grau-Grau, & Y. Rofcanin (Eds), *Human flourishing: A multidisciplinary perspective on neuroscience, health, organizations and arts* (pp. 149–162). Cham: Springer.

Grau-Grau, M., & Bowles, H. R. (2022). Launching a cross-disciplinary and cross-national conversation on engaged fatherhood. In M. Grau-Grau, M. Las Heras, & H. R. Bowles (Eds), *Engaged fatherhood for men, families and gender equality. Healthcare, social policy, and work perspectives* (pp. 1–12). Cham, Switzerland: Springer.

Greenhaus, J. H., & Allen, T. D. (2011). Work–family balance: A review and extension of the literature. In J. C. Quick & L. E. Tetrick (Eds), *Handbook of occupational health psychology* (pp. 165–183). Washington, DC: American Psychological Association.

Haines, E. L., & Stroessner, S. J. (2019). The role prioritization model: How communal men and agentic women can (sometimes) have it all. *Social and Personality Psychology Compass*, *13*(12), 1–12.

Halrynjo, S. (2009). Men's work–life conflict: Career, care and self-realization: Patterns of privileges and dilemmas. *Gender, Work and Organization*, *16*(1), 98–125.

Hanlon, N. (2012). Care in masculinities studies. In N. Hanlon (Ed.), *Masculinities, care and equality* (pp. 1–28). London: Palgrave Macmillan.

Hodges, M. J., & Budig, M. J. (2010). Who gets the daddy bonus? Organizational hegemonic masculinity and the impact of fatherhood on earnings. *Gender & Society*, *24*(6), 717–745.

Hodkinson, P., & Brooks, R. (2022). Caregiving fathers and the negotiation of crossroads: Journeys of continuity and change. *British Journal of Sociology*, September, 36–50.

Humberd, B., Ladge, J. J., & Harrington, B. (2015). The "new" dad: Navigating fathering identity within organizational contexts. *Journal of Business and Psychology*, *30*(2), 249–266.

Kaufman, G. (2013). *Superdads: How fathers balance work and family in the 21st century*. New York: New York University Press.

Kotelchuck, M. (2021). The impact of father's health on reproductive and infant health and development. In M. Grau-Grau, M. Las Heras Maestro, & H. R. Bowles (Eds), *Engaged fatherhood for men, families and gender equality: Healthcare, social policy, and work perspectives* (pp. 31–61). Cham: Springer.

Ladge, J. J., & Greenberg, D. (2019). *Maternal optimism: Forging a positive path through work and motherhood*. New York: Oxford University Press.

Ladge, J. J., & Humberd, B. K. (2022). Impossible standards and unlikely trade-offs: Can fathers be competent parents and professionals? In M. Grau-Grau, M. Las Heras, & H. R. Bowles (Eds), *Engaged fatherhood for men, families and gender equality. Healthcare, social policy, and work perspectives* (pp. 183–196). Cham: Springer.

Leslie, L. M., Flaherty Manchester, C., Park, T.-Y., & Ahn Mehng, S. I. (2012). Flexible work practices: A source of career premiums or penalties? *AMJ*, *55*, 1407–1428.

Reid, E. (2015). Embracing, passing, revealing, and the ideal worker image: How people navigate expected and experienced professional identities. *Organization Science*, *26*(4), 997–1017.

Rudman, L. A., & Mescher, K. (2013). Penalizing men who request a family leave: Is flexibility stigma a femininity stigma? *Journal of Social Issues*, *69*(2), 322–340.

Smith, F. I., Tabak, F., Showail, S., Parks, J. M. L., & Kleist, J. S. (2005). The name game: Employability evaluations of prototypical applicants with stereotypical feminine and masculine first names. *Sex Roles*, *52*(1), 63–82.

Steffens, M. C., Preuß, S., & Scheifele, C. (2019). Work-related impression formation: Reviewing parenthood penalties and investigating a "fatherhood penalty" for single fathers. *Basic and Applied Social Psychology*, *41*(5), 287–304.

Tanquerel, S., & Grau-Grau, M. (2020). Unmasking work–family balance barriers and strategies among working fathers in the workplace. *Organization*, *27*(5), 680–700.

Thompson, C. a., Beauvais, L. L., & Lyness, K. S. (1999). When work–family benefits are not enough: The influence of work–family culture on benefit utilization, organizational attachment, and work–family conflict. *Journal of Vocational Behavior*, *54*(3), 392–415.

Vinkenburg, C. J., van Engen, M. L., Coffeng, J., & Dikkers, J. S. E. (2012). Bias in employment decisions about mothers and fathers: The (dis)advantages of sharing care responsibilities. *Journal of Social Issues*, *68*(4), 725–741.

19. "Dadpreneurship": a new practice among second-generation Chinese-Dutch entrepreneurs to achieve work–life balance

Yidong Tao and Caroline Essers

INTRODUCTION

There has recently been an attempt to conduct more research involving the themes of male entrepreneurs and fatherhood (Eräranta & Moisander, 2011). Kelan (2008), for instance, asks why male entrepreneurs with children are never described as "dadpreneurs," in contrast to the frequently used term "mumpreneur" (Ekinsmyth, 2013), which seems to point to a gendered subtext in the literature on entrepreneurship. Unlike female entrepreneurs' identities, which are bound up in their everyday activities as both mothers and entrepreneurs (Duberley & Carrigan, 2012), the multiple identities of male entrepreneurs who are also fathers are rarely mentioned or discussed.

This chapter focuses on a special group: second-generation male entrepreneurs of Chinese origin in the Netherlands. The Chinese represent one of the largest groups of ethnic-minority business owners in the Netherlands. A report presented by the Netherlands Institute for Social Research in 2011 explores the progress made by the second-generation Chinese compared to their first-generation counterparts. Second-generation Chinese people believe that the household is a shared responsibility of both men and women, and women should not have to give up working when they have a child. They are much less traditional in their views on gender roles than first-generation Chinese (Gijsberts et al., 2011). Recently, the second generation has been found to differ from the first generation in that they seem to be actively seeking a better work–life balance than the first generation (Tao et al., 2021).

This chapter challenges the notion of masculinity by revealing parenthood practices and emphasizing the domestic responsiveness of men in the context of ethnic-minority entrepreneurship. Secondly, it highlights this newly emerging shift in gender attitudes among the Chinese community in the Netherlands.

And thirdly, it shows how they are achieving a sustainable work–life balance by negotiating different gender role expectations in both family and business.

THEORETICAL BACKGROUND

Scholars of entrepreneurship have recognized that the long-standing masculine archetype of the entrepreneur is being challenged (Marlow & Martinez Dy, 2018). Masculine and feminine are in fact highly fluid concepts (Butler, 2004; Kelan, 2010). Hearn and Collinson (2018) assert that the notion of "universal, essential and singular" masculinity should be abandoned (p. 11). Critical scholars point out that it seems that men's experiences and expectations of domestic life do not matter (Özbilgin et al., 2011). The long-standing assumption that "men do not suffer from gender oppression" neglects the fact that men, as a group, are heterogeneous and have a wide range of diverse identities (Murray, 2015, p. 2). Marlow and Martinez Dy (2018, p. 10) suggest that the use of the term "dadpreneurship" could be one way of highlighting that "the gendering of entrepreneurial activity" is becoming a more common daily practice than mainstream assumptions of "the risk-taking adventurer." This gender performance can also be interpreted as a form of undoing gender, as individuals move away from traditional gender roles in certain circumstances (Kelan, 2010; Reid, 2018).

METHOD

This is a small-scale qualitative study of second-generation Chinese-Dutch male entrepreneurs. A qualitative approach was chosen because the aim was to illustrate the various ways in which members of this group construct their identities as entrepreneurs and achieve a sustainable work–life balance, and how gender roles have evolved and influenced this process, rather than generalizing across the whole group of entrepreneurs of Chinese origin. Empirical data were collected through in-depth life-story interviews conducted with 24 Chinese-Dutch entrepreneurs, which were derived from a larger research project that concerns the multiple identities of entrepreneurs of Chinese ancestry in the Netherlands. During the interviews, the participants were first asked to provide some general information about their business. We then followed McAdams' life-story interview protocol (McAdams, 2008) to ask the interviewees to reflect on their life as if it were a book with chapters, to focus on messages received from their families and peers regarding gender, ethnicity, culture, generation, and entrepreneurship, and to discuss the most important scenes in each chapter with respect to identity construction. The interviewees were also asked to elaborate on the most important events and people in their lives (Essers, 2009, p. 149).

Each interview lasted for around 90 minutes. The interviews were recorded with permission, the collected narratives transcribed verbatim, and all personal identifiers removed. The coding process was created through ATLAS.ti Mac (Version 1.5.0), as well as any interpretation of the data to complete our work. We adopted thematic analysis and first coded all 24 stories to find the common themes and patterns mentioned by the interviewees. We focused on the ways in which they accounted for the experiences relating to entrepreneurship and other social categories, for example, how they talked about being an entrepreneur, a second-generation Chinese person, a male, and a father in the Dutch context. Subsequently, these subthemes were analyzed with discourse analysis (Potter & Wetherell, 1987) in order to deepen our understanding of the identity-construction process. We have selected two second-generation narratives that contained the most illustrative passages to explain how "dad-preneurship" is practiced in daily life based on atypical gender patterns, how different role expectations stemming from both family and entrepreneurship are negotiated, and how a sustainable work–life balance is achieved. The names of both entrepreneurs have been anonymized in this study.

RESULTS

In this section, we present two typical examples of our interviewees, and use the term "dadpreneur" to describe them in order to emphasize the domestic responsibilities of men and highlight this newly emerging shift in gender patterns. Chan is an example of how "dadpreneurs" perform their roles as entrepreneur and father simultaneously, and how they maintain a healthy and sustainable work–life balance. Chan is the owner of a three-star hotel. His wife is also second-generation Chinese and has a regular full-time job. They have two kids, aged four and two years. Chan identifies more as Dutch than as Chinese, saying "I think I am more like a Dutchman, regarding most aspects of the culture, language and experiences." Once the business was established and stable, Chan was able to run the business using a laptop. He thus manages to combine entrepreneurship and fatherhood. Chan says:

> In our family, we both work outside and we both take care of kids. But at the moment the balance is perhaps that I take more care of the kids. The kids go to daycare from Monday to Friday. I pick up both kids, go to the supermarket, do grocery shopping for the home, go back home, cook a meal and feed the kids so they have eaten enough. They need to go to bed at eight o'clock, and after that my wife comes back. In the morning, I also take the kids to daycare.

Chan's narrative provides evidence that in this family, the husband acts as the main caregiver. Being a father and an entrepreneur at the same time, Chan combines these two roles well. Compared to his wife who has a full-time job,

Chan has more flexibility with respect to time management and physical presence in the workplace. They share domestic work flexibly, depending on who can adapt their schedule or according to preference. What is interesting is that Chan's narrative emphasizes that "in our family, we both work outside and we both take care of the kids," which we interpret as a narrative technique to make other members of the Chinese community believe that he does not provide more childcare than his spouse, as this would challenge the traditional gender norm in the Chinese community. What also needs to be addressed here is that Chan only started to practice "dadpreneurship" when his business had become stable, in order to ensure that his parental responsibility would not undermine the development of his business. Compared to "mumpreneurs," who embark on entrepreneurship in order to combine the demands of motherhood with owning a business, the "dadpreneurs" we interviewed do not deliberately set out to combine fatherhood and entrepreneurship from the outset. Rather, they take on the main responsibility for childcare when they feel able to because their businesses is stable. Chan therefore feels no conflict between the roles of father and entrepreneur, but does experience a good balance between work and family.

Another "dadpreneur," Andy, tells a different story. Andy runs a courier company and his wife is first-generation Chinese, working as an accountant in his company. Regarding his ethnicity, he emphasizes that "I will be Chinese forever." Andy became a father after his company was well established. He talks about his current daily routine:

> I get up at 6 o'clock every morning, cook breakfast for my daughter, dress her and take her to daycare. This makes me feel full of energy, because as a father, I feel really proud that I can do something for my daughter first thing in the morning. After that, I go to work.

Here, like Chan, Andy elaborates on his daily routine of preparing and taking his daughter to childcare. He also expresses the positive feeling of doing his duty as a father. However, Andy's thoughts on gender roles are fairly traditional:

> In a family, the husband should work outside the home and the wife should do domestic tasks at home. This is the division of labor in a harmonious Chinese family. I am not saying that women have to stay at home and are not allowed to work. She can find a job, but the focus is family … When a man comes back home and sees the house is clean and comfortable, there is a hot meal on the table and the kids are happily playing, how nice life is … So, I still think Chinese women should focus on their family, go back to the family and care for their family properly. This is their primary responsibility. And men work hard outside the home.

Andy describes his ideal family life, which is traditional. He expects to have a traditional Chinese family, which is consistent with his Chinese identity. His main role and goal is working hard in his business. It is interesting that when discussing his gender role expectations, he uses mainly collective nouns rather than the first-person pronoun, suggesting that he believes that these gender expectations are part of a broader social category, and do not only apply to him and his family. Here, his ethnicity and gender identity co-exist in order to build a Chinese male entrepreneurial identity. However, he then explains that the reason he takes more responsibility for childcare is his wife's inability to do domestic tasks. He seems resigned to this, saying: "My wife does not know how to cook nor how to clean. She has no idea about housework. I have to do everything. I don't complain because a lot of young Chinese women are like her." He talks about his wife's inability to cook and clean, which are assumed to be the duties of women in a family. He then attributes his wife's incapability to a more general phenomenon that many Chinese young women cannot handle housework. However, he also states that he appreciates his work–life balance and is quite satisfied with his quality of life and ability to combine fathering with running a business.

However, Andy's words are not consistent with his actions. On the one hand, he expresses a firm belief in the idea of gender complementarity where men and women each have their main responsibilities in the domains of work and home. It is obvious that he continues to believe in traditional gender roles, even though he is second-generation Chinese. On the other hand, his behavior – such as taking responsibility for everyday routines and childcare – do not reflect those traditional gender roles. Reflecting on this apparent contradiction, we note that Andy's gender expectations are fairly traditional but his actual performance of the identity of father is totally different. In conclusion, on the one hand, both Chan and Andy have taken on fairly non-traditional gender roles by performing more parental duties at home than their spouses, and combining this with their professional activities. However, these practices seem to have emerged for different reasons and based on different convictions, and what is more, we notice that neither of them chose to be entrepreneurs for family reasons, but began to practice fatherhood when their companies were already well established.

DISCUSSION

In this study, we have used two lively examples to show how the second-generation Chinese male entrepreneurs that we interviewed take responsibility for childcare and domestic duties. On the one hand, they fit their work around the rhythm of children's school and leisure activities. Currently, a positive image of masculinity usually includes the ability to earn an adequate income, but does not yet include men as primary homemakers (Acker, 2012). How these second-generation Chinese male entrepreneurs maintain their masculinity when taking care of their children is an interesting phenomenon. The interviewees became "dadpreneurs" only once their businesses were established and did not sacrifice their business for the purpose of parenthood. This is consistent with another study which showed that fathers (unlike mothers) are unlikely to emphasize family reasons for choosing entrepreneurship, but rather are primarily concerned with their provider role responsibilities (Hilbrecht & Lero, 2014). However, the pattern with Chan and Andy is different. Fathers like Chan break out of the breadwinner model and position themselves as "breadsharers" (Reid, 2018, p. 723), sharing both work and family responsibilities with their wives in an egalitarian way. In doing so, and by performing gender differently, they are challenging the still predominant gender roles in Chinese families. Interestingly, men like Andy do not give up being the primary breadwinner and still maintain traditional gender expectations within the family.

By exploring these examples of "dadpreneurship," this chapter contributes to critical studies of masculinity by revealing parenthood practices in the context of ethnic-minority entrepreneurship. This analysis of "dadpreneurs" helps to broaden our ideas around masculinity. Both women who are entrepreneurs and men with primary childcare responsibilities challenge the traditional gender binary, as entrepreneurship is not traditionally associated with women and taking care of children is not closely associated with men. These men live their lives between Dutch culture and Chinese culture, at the complex intersection of gender and ethnicity, with ethnic identity playing a role at the intersection of multiple identities.

While in this chapter we have reflected on the diversity of second-generation Chinese entrepreneurs by describing the everyday experiences of two "dadpreneurs," we suggest that more research is needed to explore how both genders within this particular Chinese community and other ethnic communities are doing and undoing gender in the context of entrepreneurship. This would enable a deeper and more nuanced understanding of second-generation entrepreneurs of Chinese and other ethnic origins in the Netherlands, both female and male, and of how masculinity and femininity are being practiced and experienced in combination with entrepreneurship.

REFERENCES

Acker, J. (2012). Gendered organizations and intersectionality: Problems and possibilities. *Equality, Diversity and Inclusion: An International Journal*, 31(3), 214–224.
Butler, J. (2004). *Undoing Gender*. London: Routledge.

Duberley, J., & Carrigan, M. (2012). The career identities of "mumpreneurs": Women's experiences of combining enterprise and motherhood. *International Small Business Journal*, 31(6), 629–651.

Ekinsmyth, C. (2013). Managing the business of everyday life: The roles of space and place in "mumpreneurship." *International Journal of Entrepreneurial Behaviour and Research*, 19(5), 525–546.

Eräranta, K., & Moisander, J. (2011). Psychological regimes of truth and father identity: Challenges for work/life integration. *Organization Studies*, 32(4), 509–526.

Essers, C. (2009). Reflections on the narrative approach: Dilemmas of power, emotions and social location while constructing life-stories. *Organization*, 16(2), 163–181.

Gijsberts, M., Huijnk, W., & Vogels, R. (2011). *The Chinese in the Netherlands. Van horeca naar hogeschool*. Den Haag: Sociaal en Cultureel Planbureau.

Hearn, J., & Collinson, D. (2018). *Oxford Research Encyclopedia of Business and Management*. DOI:10.1093/acrefore/9780190224851.013.55.

Hilbrecht, M., & Lero, D. S. (2014). Self-employment and family life: Constructing work–life balance when you're "always on." *Community, Work and Family*, 17(1), 20–42.

Kelan, E. (2008). Bound by stereotypes? *Business Strategy Review*, 19(1), 4–7.

Kelan, E. (2010). Gender logic and (un)doing gender at work. *Gender, Work and Organization*, 17(2), 174–194.

Marlow, S., & Martinez Dy, A. (2018). Annual review article: Is it time to rethink the gender agenda in entrepreneurship research? *International Small Business Journal*, 36(1), 3–22.

McAdams, D. P. (2008). *The Life Story Interview*. Evanston, IL: Northwestern University.

Murray, R. (2015). Too much presence? Men's interests and male intersectionality. European Conference on Politics and Gender, Uppsala, pp. 11–13.

Özbilgin, M. F., Beauregard, T. A., Tatli, A., & Bell, M. P. (2011). Work–life, diversity and intersectionality: A critical review and research agenda. *International Journal of Management Reviews*, 13(2), 177–198.

Potter, J., & Wetherell, M. (1987). *Discourse and Social Psychology: Beyond Attitudes and Behaviour*. London: Sage.

Reid, E. M. (2018). Straying from breadwinning: Status and money in men's interpretations of their wives' work arrangements. *Gender, Work and Organization*, 25(6), 718–733.

Tao, Y., Essers, C., & Pijpers, R. (2021). Family and identity: Intersectionality in the lived experiences of second-generation entrepreneurs of Chinese origin in the Netherlands. *Journal of Small Business Management*, 59(6), 1152–1179.

20. Work–family balance and mental well-being across Europe: does a supportive country context matter?

Mark Visser, Gerbert Kraaykamp, and Stéfanie André

INTRODUCTION

In the literature on quality of life, work–family balance – a particular form of work–life balance – has a prominent place because it is considered one of the most salient dimensions of life satisfaction (Joseph Sirgy & Lee, 2018). Work–family balance denotes a successful combination of work and family demands, while work–family conflict indicates incompatibilities between a person's work and family roles (Hochschild, 1997). The primary explanations for a good work–family balance are found in people's resources and restrictions in the work and family domain. For instance, high work demands, such as non-standard work hours and a high workload, can lead to work–family conflict, while the outsourcing of childcare and household tasks or partner support may help to achieve a healthy and sustainable work–family balance (Allen et al., 2000).

Prior studies on the consequences of work–family balance found that re-conciling work and family responsibilities promotes well-being (Greenhaus & Powell, 2006). By contrast, an imbalance between work and family has an adverse impact on people's physical and mental health (Allen et al., 2000; Borgmann et al., 2019). This negative effect of work–family conflict on physical and mental health is usually understood in terms of time squeeze, stress, and reduced energy. Turning to cross-national studies, research has found that the average work–family balance differs between countries (Crompton & Lyonette, 2006). This variation is largely explained by differences in work conditions, working time regulations, policies that support childcare, and welfare state regimes (Anttila et al., 2015; Lunau et al., 2014; Notten et al., 2017; Taiji & Mills, 2020). However, little is known about whether these policy indicators and the cultural context of a country reinforce the positive effects of work–family balance on people's well-being. Our research question is therefore: *To what extent is the positive association between work–family balance and mental well-being moderated by a country's institutional and cultural context?*

To answer this question, we will explore whether this plays out differently for men and women, since men and women will presumably respond differently to a country's institutional and cultural context (André et al., 2013). To assess the national contexts, we focus on family policies (i.e. childcare and parental leave arrangements) and gender egalitarianism (i.e. norms that support equal rights, roles, and responsibilities for men and women). Although these concepts are correlated, their influence is likely to differ. Including both of these contextual aspects is novel and will shed light on the relative importance of the institutional context versus the cultural context when it comes to the relationship between work–family balance and mental well-being. Our sociological perspective helps us to understand the complex macro–micro links between the institutional and cultural context in a given country, people's work–family balance and their mental well-being. Furthermore, our approach could explain differences between men and women with respect to these links, because institutional arrangements may work differently for them and because societies project different expectations onto men and women depending on the level of gender egalitarianism.

THEORY

Few studies have examined whether the spill-over relationship between work–family balance and well-being varies across societal contexts, and even fewer have used a multilevel design to explain such variation (for an exception, see Hagqvist et al., 2017). The strongest association between work–family balance and self-reported health is observed in Nordic welfare state regimes, while the association is weaker in conservative and liberal welfare states (Mensah & Adjei, 2020). The limited empirical evidence available on the role of gender egalitarianism is mixed: one study found that work–family balance is more beneficial for well-being in gender-egalitarian cultures (Haar et al., 2014), while another study found exactly the opposite (Hagqvist et al., 2017).

How can we understand the interplay between the macro and micro levels in theoretical terms? Socialization theory posits that as children we learn how men and women should behave. Socialization takes place in households, schools, but also in society at large. The institutional and cultural context is thus expected to influence people (Bolzendahl & Myers, 2004). If the country context is conducive, this could lead to a stronger positive relationship between work–family balance and mental well-being because people feel supported in their choice to combine work and family life in a healthy and sustainable way. This could even serve as a buffer against the negative spill-over effects of work–family conflict, because a supportive country context signals that work–family balance is worth achieving. Hence, our hypothesis is that family policies that support both men and women in combining work and family (i.e. the dual-earner/dual-carer model) and gender-egalitarian cultures foster an environment that reduces interference between work and family and magnifies the positive spill-over effect of work–family balance on a person's mental well-being.

METHOD

We used data from round 5 of the European Social Survey, conducted in 2010, which included an extensive module on work, family, and well-being. We selected employed respondents aged 18–65 years with a partner, and removed data from Israel, Russia, and Ukraine because no information on family policies was available for those countries. Multiple Imputation by Chained Equations was performed to deal with missing values on all individual-level variables. Our analytical sample consisted of 13,886 individuals across 24 European countries. Multilevel analyses were performed in SPSS version 29.

The outcome variable – mental well-being – was measured using three items, all of which asked how often respondents had experienced a certain feeling in the past two weeks: "I have felt cheerful and in good spirits," "I have felt calm and relaxed," and "I have felt active and vigorous." Answer categories were: at no time, some of the time, less than half of the time, more than half of the time, most of the time, and all of the time. A scale was created by taking the average across the items (Cronbach's alpha = 0.80).

Work–family balance was also measured using multiple items. Respondents were asked how often they "continued worrying about work problems when you are not working," "feel too tired after work to enjoy the things you would like to do at home," "find that your job prevents you from giving the time you want to their partner or family," "find that your partner or family get fed up with the pressure of your job," "find that your family responsibilities prevent you from giving the time you should to your job," and "find it difficult to concentrate on work because of your family responsibilities." There were five possible answers, ranging from always to never. Again, we took the mean score across these items to create a scale (Cronbach's alpha = 0.79).

Three moderating variables at the country level were included. First, the extent to which a country supports childcare was proxied by the participation rate in formal childcare or pre-school for children younger than age 3 in 2010 (Eurostat, n.d.). Second, we added the duration of paid leave in calendar days per country in 2010, distinguishing between paid maternity leave plus paid parental leave for the mother, paid paternity leave plus paid parental leave for the father and shared leave (World Bank, n.d.). Third, to measure gender egal-itarianism, we combined two items available in the European Social Survey data, namely: "A woman should be prepared to cut down on paid work for the sake of her family" and "When jobs are scarce, men should have more right to a job than women." We created a dichotomous variable with score 1 indicating gender-egalitarian norms, which referred to respondents who either disagreed or strongly disagreed with both statements. We then aggregated this variable, creating a country-level variable that reflected the proportion of people in a country that hold gender-egalitarian norms. Descriptive statistics for all variables are available upon request.

RESULTS

Table 20.1 shows the results of the linear multilevel regression analysis of mental well-being. Model 1 shows that work–family balance is positively and strongly associated with mental well-being. If a person were to move from a score of 0 to a score of 4 on the work–family balance scale, that person's mental well-being would be predicted to increase by $(4 \times 0.47 =) 1.88$ – i.e. almost two scale points on a scale that ranges from 0 to 5. The interaction between work–family balance and sex was non-significant (results not shown here), indicating that work–family balance has a similar effect on the mental well-being of both men and women.

In Models 2 to 4, we added cross-level interaction terms between work–family balance and our indicators of a supportive country context. Because support for childcare and gender egalitarianism are multicollinear (Pearson r correlation $= 0.83$), we excluded gender egalitarianism from Model 2 and support for childcare from Models 3 and 4. The results indicate that the positive relationship between work–family balance and mental well-being is moderated by a country's cultural context, but not by a country's institutional context. The higher the level of gender egalitarianism, the stronger the positive effect of work–family balance on mental well-being. The effect of work–family balance on well-being is positive and statistically significant across the entire range of gender egalitarianism, so even in countries where traditional, non-egalitarian gender norms are more common, work–family balance is still positively related to mental well-being – just less strongly.

We also estimated the cross-level interactions separately for men and women. It could also be the case that some of the previous null findings are because diverging effects for men and women cancel each other out. Importantly, however, the results of this analysis confirmed the main results: only gender egalitarianism moderates the positive association between work–family balance and mental well-being, and it does so similarly for men and women.

Table 20.1   Linear multilevel analysis of mental well-being, unstandardized coefficients

	Model 1	Model 2	Model 3	Model 4
Intercept	2.91***	2.91***	2.92***	2.91***
WFB	0.47***	0.47***	0.47***	0.48***
WFB* childcare		0.00		
WFB* paid leave mother			0.00	
WFB* paid leave father			0.00	
WFB* paid leave shared			0.00	
WFB* gender egalitarianism				0.18*
Childcare (country)	0.00	0.01***		
Paid leave mother (country)	0.00	0.00	0.00	0.00
Paid leave father (country)	−0.00	−0.00	−0.00	−0.00
Paid leave shared (country)	0.00	0.00	0.00	0.00
Gender egalitarianism	0.08		0.50***	0.35**
Female	−0.09***	−0.09***	−0.09***	−0.09***
Age (/10)	−0.24***	−0.24***	−0.24***	−0.24***
Age (/10) squared	0.03**	0.03**	0.03**	0.03**
Migrant	0.04	0.04	0.04	0.04
Education				
Low	Ref.	Ref.	Ref.	Ref.
Intermediate	0.01	0.01	0.01	0.01
Height	0.01	0.01	0.01	0.01
Occupation				
Managers	0.27***	0.28***	0.27***	0.27***
Professionals	0.24***	0.24***	0.24***	0.24***
Technicians and associate professionals	0.19***	0.19***	0.19***	0.19***
Clerical support workers	0.13***	0.13***	0.13***	0.12***
Service and sales workers	0.18***	0.18***	0.18***	0.18***
Skilled agricultural, forestry and fishery workers	0.29***	0.29***	0.29***	0.28***
Craft and related trades workers	0.13***	0.13***	0.13***	0.13***
Plants and machine operators, and assemblers	0.15***	0.15***	0.15***	0.15***
Armed forces	0.37**	0.37**	0.38**	0.38**
Elementary occupations	Ref.	Ref.	Ref.	Ref.
Working hours				
1–31 hours	Ref.	Ref.	Ref.	Ref.

	Model 1	Model 2	Model 3	Model 4
32–40 hours	0.12***	0.12***	0.12***	0.12***
40+ hours	0.20***	0.20***	0.20***	0.20***
Education partner				
Low	Ref.	Ref.	Ref.	Ref.
Intermediate	0.07**	0.07**	0.06**	0.06**
High	0.11***	0.10***	0.10***	0.10***
Working hours partner				
Low	Ref.	Ref.	Ref.	Ref.
Intermediate	0.08**	0.08**	0.08**	0.08**
High	0.06**	0.06**	0.06**	0.06**
Children in the household	0.07**	0.07**	0.07**	0.07**
Children in the household				
None	Ref.	Ref.	Ref.	Ref.
Youngest child 0-3 years	0.08**	0.09**	0.09**	0.09***
Youngest child 4-12 years	0.05	0.05*	0.05*	0.05*
Youngest child 13-17 years	0.03	0.03	0.03	0.03
Youngest child 18+ years	−0.02	−0.02	−0.01	−0.01
Variance level 2 (country)	0.79	0.79	0.79	0.79
Variance level 1 (individual)	0.01	0.01	0.01	0.01
Variance WFB (random slope)		0.00	0.00	0.00

Note: * $p < 0.05$, ** $p < 0.01$, *** $p < 0.001$. WFB = work–family balance.

DISCUSSION

This chapter set out to answer the question of whether the positive relationship between work–family balance and mental well-being is moderated by a country's institutional and cultural context. Confirming prior studies (Allen et al., 2000; Borgmann et al., 2019; Greenhaus & Powell, 2006), we established that work–family balance does indeed have a positive spill-over effect on mental well-being, which we found for both men and women. A novel empirical finding is that this positive spill-over is stronger in countries where gender-egalitarian norms are more prevalent, which partly confirms our hypothesis and is in line with the study of Haar et al. (2014). We conclude that it is a country's cultural context rather than its institutional arrangements that matters when comparing the relationship between work–family balance and mental well-being between countries, and equally so for men and women.

However, we must be aware that the moderating role of gender egalitarianism is modest compared to the independent impact of work–family balance on well-being. Therefore, we should not disregard institutional arrangements that support the dual-earner/duel-carer model, because policies that support childcare promote work–family balance (Notten et al., 2017), which in turn has a strong positive effect on mental well-being, particularly among parents. Moreover, it is likely that such institutional arrangements are present in more gender-egalitarian countries. All in all, it seems more promising to promote work–family balance directly rather than strengthening the positive spill-over effects of work–family balance through a country's cultural context, primarily because changing the culture of a country is so much harder.

One interesting avenue for future studies is to examine to what extent homeworking, which has become a requirement for many workers as a result of the COVID-19 pandemic, has improved or worsened work–family balance and what effect it has had on mental well-being and for whom. While working remotely may enhance flexibility and productivity, there are challenges to navigate here, too (Wheatley, 2017). For example, people may struggle to preserve a healthy boundary between their work and family life when working at home. Even in gender-egalitarian countries, it may be the case that households, in particular those with young children, revert to a more gender-traditional division of paid and unpaid work if homeworking becomes the new standard. Future research is invited to examine how this subsequently affects mental well-being and to what extent a country's institutional and cultural context play a role in this.

REFERENCES

Allen, T. D., Herst, D. E. L., Bruck, C. S., & Sutton, M. (2000). Consequences associated with work-to-family conflict: A review and agenda for future research. *Journal of Occupational Health Psychology*, *5*(2), 278–308.

André, S., Gesthuizen, M., & Scheepers, P. (2013). Support for traditional female roles across 32 countries: Female labour market participation, policy models and gender differences. *Comparative Sociology*, *12*(4), 447–476.

Anttila, T., Oinas, T., Tammelin, M., & Nätti, J. (2015). Working-time regimes and work–life balance in Europe. *European Sociological Review*, *31*(6), 713–724.

Bolzendahl, C. I., & Myers, D. J. (2004). Feminist attitudes and support for gender equality: Opinion change in women and men, 1974–1998. *Social Forces*, *83*(2), 759–789.

Borgmann, L.-S., Rattay, P., & Lampert, T. (2019). Health-related consequences of work–family conflict from a European perspective: Results of a scoping review. *Frontiers in Public Health*, *7*(189), 1–12.

Crompton, R., & Lyonette, C. (2006). Work–life "balance" in Europe. *Acta Sociologica*, *49*(4), 379–393.

Eurostat. (n.d.). Children aged less than 3 years in formal childcare. https://ec.europa.eu/eurostat/web/products-datasets/-/tepsr_sp210 [Accessed July 8 2022].

Greenhaus, J. H., & Powell, G. N. (2006). When work and family are allies: A theory of work–family enrichment. *Academy of Management Review, 31*(1), 72–92.

Haar, J. M., Russo, M., Suñe, A., & Ollier-Malaterre, A. (2014). Outcomes of work–life balance on job satisfaction, life satisfaction and mental health: A study across seven cultures. *Journal of Vocational Behavior, 85*(3), 361–373.

Hagqvist, E., Gådin, K. G., & Nordenmark, M. (2017). Work–family conflict and well-being across Europe: The role of gender context. *Social Indicators Research, 132*(2), 785–797.

Hochschild, A. R. (1997). *The time bind: When work becomes home and home becomes work.* New York: Metropolitan Books.

Joseph Sirgy, M., & Lee, D.-J. (2018). Work–life balance: An integrative review. *Applied Research in Quality of Life, 13*(1), 229–254.

Lunau, T., Bambra, C., Eikemo, T. A., van der Wel, K. A., & Dragano, N. (2014). A balancing act? Work–life balance, health and well-being in European welfare states. *European Journal of Public Health, 24*(3), 422–427.

Mensah, A., & Adjei, N. K. (2020). Work–life balance and self-reported health among working adults in Europe: A gender and welfare state regime comparative analysis. *BMC Public Health, 20*(1052), 1–14.

Notten, N., Grunow, D., & Verbakel, E. (2017). Social policies and families in stress: Gender and educational differences in work–family conflict from a European perspective. *Social Indicators Research, 132*(3), 1281–1305.

Taiji, R., & Mills, M. C. (2020). Non-standard schedules, work–family conflict, and the moderating role of national labour context: Evidence from 32 European countries. *European Sociological Review, 36*(2), 179–197.

Wheatley, D. (2017). Employee satisfaction and use of flexible working arrangements. *Work, Employment and Society, 31*(4), 567–585.

World Bank. (n.d.). Gender statistics. https:// databank .worldbank .org/ source/ gender -statistics/Series/ [Accessed July 8 2022].

PART V

Work–life balance and retirement

21. Sustainable work–life balance after retirement

Klaske Veth

INTRODUCTION

As a result of increasing life expectancy but also for financial reasons, many of us will have to work until later in life. To better understand the challenge of work–life balance for all workers, we need to include the growing group of those who continue to work beyond the statutory retirement age (known as 'bridge workers'). A few studies have examined late-career issues (e.g., Veth et al., 2018), and based on these I will address questions such as which factors contribute to decisions about whether or not to continue working beyond the statutory retirement age, and to what extent financial constraints impact sustainable work–life balance. In the past, retirement was seen as a predictable and permanent exit from full-time work into full-time leisure (Kojola & Moen, 2016; Sullivan & Ariss, 2019). Nowadays, however, for many workers, 'retirement' actually means semi-retirement, and a combination of paid work and leisure time (Moen & Flood, 2013). Although conclusive insights are still lacking, based on initial studies in this domain, this chapter summarizes what we know so far.

Definitions

Continuing to work after retirement is linked to concepts such as 'bridge employment' or 'bridge work', drawing on the idea of a bridge or gradual transition between a person's working life and a life without work. This usually involves part-time work (Shultz, 2003). To better understand the dynamics underlying the retirement process, it is essential to understand the context in which the transition from work to retirement takes place, as well as the drivers behind decisions on continuing to work beyond the statutory retirement age.

Why Examine This Group of Employees?

Due to the growing number of bridge workers and the ever tighter labor market, scientists and human resources professionals alike wish to understand why and how workers engage in bridge work from both a quantitative and qualitative perspective. A deeper understanding of the decision-making process around retirement and bridge work through its antecedents is important for older workers who wish to transition smoothly to full retirement, and for organizations that can benefit from retaining skilled and experienced employees. Let us first look at the most common theories that help explain why workers continue to work beyond the statutory retirement age (or not).

THEORIES ON BRIDGE EMPLOYMENT

There are a number of theoretical perspectives regarding how work-related and non-work-related factors influence people's decisions around bridge employment.

Role theory emphasizes the importance of role loss and the transition process from work to retirement. According to Ashforth (2001), role identity influences the behavior and decisions of a worker. This identity may involve simultaneously losing or weakening work roles and strengthening roles in family and the community (Barnes-Farrell, 2004). Role theory states that role transition can have positive or negative consequences, depending on whether the role transition is desirable and consistent with the values and goals of the worker (e.g., Wang, 2007).

Continuity theory emphasizes adapting to changes and a consistent pattern over time (Atchley, 1989). It suggests that older people try to preserve and maintain existing internal and external structures in order to avoid stress and disruption. In continuity theory, retirement is seen as an opportunity to define a new life and work strategy, as well as to maintain social contacts and lifestyle.

Finally, the life-course perspective (Elder, 2007) represents a dynamic view of human development. It emphasizes the importance of the contextual embedding and interdependence of life spheres such as the effect of individual characteristics, work-related (psychological) variables, and private-related variables in decision-making about retirement (Elder & Johnson, 2003).

THE ANTECEDENTS OF BRIDGE EMPLOYMENT

From previous theories concerning the retirement process, we can identify a number of factors that can influence people's decision to engage in bridge work: the antecedents. Based on various studies, the following categories or levels of antecedents can be outlined (e.g., Wang et al., 2009): (1) personal factors at the individual level (micro); (2) work or organizational factors (meso); and (3) societal influences (macro), which are beyond the scope of this chapter.

Firstly, at the individual level, age has often been studied as an antecedent. The propensity to engage in bridge work decreases with age (e.g., Adams & Rau, 2004; Dingemans, 2016), since as they age workers become more motivated to find bridge work that corresponds with their own values and interests. Their own promotion opportunities matter less (Erdogan et al., 2011) as they realize that their career has already peaked. Secondly, employees with a university degree (Kim & DeVaney, 2005) or higher-education degree (Wang et al., 2008) are more likely to engage in bridge work than to retire completely (Dingemans, 2016). This group usually has a retirement income, which makes bridge employment more of a free choice for them. For bridge workers who live close to the poverty line, by contrast, bridge employment may not be a matter of choice. Thirdly, health status is another predictor that is related to age to some extent. In general, poor health correlates negatively with bridge employment. Fourthly, according to Dingemans (2016), only 15 percent of bridge workers indicate that they continue to work mainly for financial reasons. This involves more than income as a predictor; this is also about investment assets, debts, or the spouse's income (e.g., Dingemans, 2012). Lastly, Moen et al. (2001) report that men are more likely to engage in bridge work, while women are more likely to engage in volunteer work, provide care to relatives, or engage in leisure activities (Petkoska & Earl, 2009). Delving into these research results in more detail reveals that more single women in the self-employed category continue to work beyond the statutory retirement age, while significantly more married men continue in paid employment than married women.

At the work and organizational level, some other variables can affect the decision as to whether to continue working or not. Firstly, the world of work is changing rapidly and becoming more complex. This transformation is affecting work and organizations, and can lead to chronic work stress. This factor would certainly discourage people from continuing to work, especially in the same field, but it remains unclear whether work stress also deters people from seeking work in a different field (Gobeski & Beehr, 2009; Wang et al., 2008).

Wang et al. (2008) also find that retirement planning is an antecedent to the decision-making process around bridge work, in the sense that retirees who – with the support of their organization in the form of coaching and retirement training programs – have thought more about their future retirement before they actually retire are less likely to engage in bridge employment and instead opt for full retirement.

Now that we have a clearer picture of the antecedents of bridge work, it is at least as important to investigate its consequences, in particular its consequences for a sustainable work–life balance after retirement.

CONSEQUENCES OF BRIDGE EMPLOYMENT

This section explores why people continue to work beyond the statutory retirement age. There are two common assumptions here: people work to earn more money; or they do it to give their life more purpose (intrinsic motivation). These assumptions mimic the manifest and latent functions of employment outlined by Jahoda (1995). Manifest functions are the obvious and expected aspects, while latent functions are less overt and maybe even unintended. The consequences of bridge work can be very closely related to the antecedents. For instance, financial incentives may be a reason for continuing to work after retirement, and bridge work also impacts the financial situation after retirement.

Engaging in bridge work for financial reasons almost certainly influences the work–life balance of bridge workers. Only 15 percent indicate that they mainly continue working for financial reasons alone (Dingemans, 2016), but this group experiences a decline in life satisfaction (Dingemans & Henkens, 2014) since this is a form of involuntary working. These are often less-educated employees, and they also have the lowest chance of finding employment beyond the statutory retirement age, which increases their risk of poverty in old age. A larger group of bridge workers is made up of those with valuable and specific knowledge which employers wish to retain. It is therefore mainly the better-educated and healthier people who continue working voluntarily after retirement and who experience a modest improvement in their work–life balance.

The five latent functions of bridge work are more psychological or sociological in nature: working provides workers with (1) identity, (2) social contact, (3) collective purpose, (4) activity, and (5) time structure (Beehr & Bennett, 2015). First, work fulfills the latent function of identity. Retirees often experience a shift in their identity. They may identify with their new status as 'retiree' or they may continue to identify with their previous job (e.g., 'I am a retired professor') or with their former employer ('I used to work for FrieslandCampina'). They may also identify with their new bridge job. Whatever the case may be, a switch from a regular job to a bridge job will affect that sense of identity. Second, humans are social animals, and most people seek out the company of others for pleasure and social support. In the transition to the retirement phase, Haslam et al. (2019) outline how sustainable work–life balance improves when people are able to maintain existing social contacts or acquire new ones. Veth et al. (2018) also show that bridge workers benefit from good relationships with their manager and colleagues. Third, humans seek out the company of others to complete collective tasks, fulfilling the fourth latent function of keeping active. Fifth, bridge work covers the latent function of structure, implicitly helping to provide people with a daily and weekly routine.

In the end, working people tend to perform better on these latent functions, especially compared to those who are unemployed, and as a result they have a better work–life balance (Selenko et al., 2011), but not necessarily better than retirees (e.g., Paul & Batinick, 2010). This depends on what retirees need in terms of stress reduction, expect in terms of life satisfaction, and how they adjust to life after retirement (Paul & Batinick, 2010; Selenko et al., 2011). Hence, people who retire from a job with poor working conditions experience greater improvements in mental health after retirement. Those who continue working voluntarily reported that this was based on their intrinsic motivation: they enjoy working and are not yet ready to fully retire. Their work–life balance is therefore better than that of those who are required to fully retire (Dingemans & Henkens, 2014). Context is everything: the way in which people retire has an influence on their experiences of retirement (Wheaton, 1990). Retiring from a stressful or 'alienating' job appears to come as a relief, for instance (Oshio & Kan, 2017; Stenholm & Vahtera, 2017), leading to improvements in both mental and perceived general health (Van den Bogaard et al., 2016).

CONCLUSIONS

In view of the current shortage of workers, research and practical implications can be derived from previous findings. From bridge retirement theories and the first studies on bridge work, we now know that different antecedents can work out differently in terms of work–life balance. Factors like health and educational level are positively associated with a positive work–life balance. Promoting healthy lifestyle interventions, healthy workplaces, training programs on the job, and improving challenging work content might therefore be beneficial for all (potential) bridge workers. Financial considerations appear to be a double-edged sword in that they affect the retirement decision-making process and also have immediate consequences after retirement. So, with good insight and financial support, it seems that there is a world to win through bridge work, particularly for lower-paid workers who would otherwise risk ending up close to the poverty line after their statutory retirement. In addition, since less attention seems to be paid to the growing group of older workers of lower socio-economic status, more dialogue is needed. We now know that retirement planning which implies an anticipation of the (working) future has an impact on the post-retirement phase regardless of the form. It would therefore seem beneficial for both employers and (potential) bridge workers to initiate a dialogue in areas such as stress reduction, maintaining social contacts, collective (purposeful) goals, staying active, and maintaining a structure. Although scientific studies in this field remain scarce, some of the insights provided in this chapter can support both employers and (potential) bridge workers, helping them to stay healthy and maintain a sustainable work–life balance, even after retirement (or semi-retirement!).

REFERENCES

Adams, G., & Rau, B. (2004). Job seeking among retirees seeking bridge employment. *Personnel Psychology, 57*(3), 719–744.

Ashforth, B. (2001). *Role transitions in organizational life: An identity-based perspective*. Mahwah, NJ: Lawrence Erlbaum.

Atchley, R. C. (1989). A continuity theory of normal aging. *The Gerontologist, 29*(2), 183–190.

Barnes-Farrell, J. L. (2004). Older workers. In J. Barling, E. K., Kelloway, & M. Frone (Eds), *Handbook of work stress* (pp. 431–454). Thousand Oaks, CA: Sage.

Beehr, T. A., & Bennett, M. M. (2015). Working after retirement: Features of bridge employment and research directions. *Work, Aging and Retirement, 1*(1), 112–128.

Dingemans, E. (2012). Bridge employment after early retirement: A bridge to better postretirement well-being of older adults? RM thesis.

Dingemans, E. (2016). Working after retirement: Determinants and consequences of bridge employment. Doctoral thesis.

Dingemans, E., & Henkens, K. (2014). Involuntary retirement, bridge employment, and satisfaction with life: A longitudinal investigation. *Journal of Organizational Behavior, 35*(4), 575–591.

Elder, G. H. (2007). Life course perspective. *The Blackwell Encyclopedia of Sociology.*

Elder, G. H., & Johnson, M. K. (2003). The life course and aging: Challenges, lessons, and new directions. In R. Settersten, Jr. (Ed.), *Invitation to the life course: Toward new understandings of later life* (pp. 49–81). Abingdon: Routledge.

Erdogan, B., Bauer, T. N., Peiró, J. M., & Truxillo, D. M. (2011). Overqualified employees: Making the best of a potentially bad situation for individuals and organizations. *Industrial and Organizational Psychology, 4*(2), 215–232.

Gobeski, K. T., & Beehr, T. A. (2009). How retirees work: Predictors of different types of bridge employment. *Journal of Organizational Behavior: The International Journal of Industrial, Occupational and Organizational Psychology and Behavior, 30*(3), 401–425.

Haslam, C., Steffens, N. K., Branscombe, N. R., Haslam, S. A., Cruwys, T., Lam, B. C., ... & Yang, J. (2019). The importance of social groups for retirement adjustment: Evidence, application, and policy implications of the social identity model of identity change. *Social Issues and Policy Review, 13*(1), 93–124.

Jahoda, G. (1995). The ancestry of a model. *Culture & Psychology, 1*(1), 11–24.

Kim, H., & DeVaney, S. A. (2005). The selection of partial or full retirement by older workers. *Journal of Family and Economic Issues, 26*(3), 371–394.

Kojola, E., & Moen, P. (2016). No more lock-step retirement: Boomers' shifting meanings of work and retirement. *Journal of Aging Studies, 36*, 59–70.

Moen, P., & Flood, S. (2013). Limited engagements? Women's and men's work/volunteer time in the encore life course stage. *Social Problems, 60*(2), 206–233.

Moen, P., Plassmann, V., & Sweet, S. (2001). *The Cornell midcareer paths and passages study.* Ithaca, NY: Cornell University, Bronfenbrenner Life Course Center.

Oshio, T., & Kan, M. (2017). The dynamic impact of retirement on health: Evidence from a nationwide ten-year panel survey in Japan. *Preventive Medicine, 100,* 287–293.

Paul, K. I., & Batinick, B. (2010). The need for work: Jahoda's latent functions of employment in a representative sample of the German population. *Journal of Organizational Behavior, 31,* 45–64.

Petkoska, J., & Earl, J. K. (2009). Understanding the influence of demographic and psychological variables on retirement planning. *Psychology and Aging, 24*(1), 245.

Selenko, E., Batinic, B., & Paul, K. (2011). Does latent deprivation lead to psychological distress? Investigating Jahoda's model in a four-wave study. *Journal of Occupational and Organizational Psychology, 84*(4), 723–740.

Shultz, K. S. (2003). Bridge employment: Work after retirement. In G. Adams & T. Beehr (Eds), *Retirement: Reasons, Processes, and Results* (pp. 214–241). Cham: Springer.

Stenholm, S., & Vahtera, J. (2017). Does retirement benefit health? *Preventive Medicine, 100,* 294–295.

Sullivan, S. E., & Al Ariss, A. (2019). Making sense of different perspectives on career transitions: A review and agenda for future research. *Human Resource Management Review, 31*(1), 100727.

Van den Bogaard, L., Henkens, K., & Kalmijn, M. (2016). Retirement as a relief? The role of physical job demands and psychological job stress for effects of retirement on self-rated health. *European Sociological Review, 32*(2), 295–306.

Veth, K. N., Van der Heijden, B. I. J. M, Korzilius, H. P., De Lange, A. H., & Emans, B. J. (2018). Bridge over an aging population: Examining longitudinal relations among human resource management, social support, and employee outcomes among bridge workers. *Frontiers in Psychology, 9,* 574.

Wang, M. (2007). Profiling retirees in the retirement transition and adjustment process: Examining the longitudinal change patterns of retirees' psychological well-being. *Journal of Applied Psychology, 92*(2), 455.

Wang, M., Zhan, Y., Liu, S., & Shultz, K. S. (2008). Antecedents of bridge employment: A longitudinal investigation. *Journal of Applied Psychology, 93*(4), 818.

Wang, M., Adams, G. A., Beehr, T. A., & Shultz, K. S. (2009). Bridge employment and retirement. In S. G. Baugh & S. E. Sullivan (Eds), *Maintaining focus, energy, and options over the career* (pp. 135–162). Charlotte, NC: Information Age Publishing.

Wheaton, B. (1990). Life transitions, role histories, and mental health. *American Sociological Review,* 209–223.

22. Balancing retirement age and termination of employment

Mark Heemskerk

INTRODUCTION

Retirement is closely linked to work–life balance. Many people tend to see retirement as a natural path to stopping work: the moment at which one 'officially' becomes old. Many countries provide pensions as income security in an old age. European Union (EU) case law shows that many European countries have a system in which retirement is linked to termination of employment. This chapter focuses on the legal relation between retirement age, termination of employment, and age discrimination – rules which affect the work–life balance of workers. The relationship between retirement age and age discrimination is based on EU legislation and can therefore be widely applied. The relationship between retirement age and termination of employment varies between member states. That being said, it may be interesting for people in other jurisdictions to read about how the Dutch system functions.

THE STATUTORY RETIREMENT SYSTEM AND RETIREMENT AGE

Many countries provide an old age pension to ensure income security. The retirement system is often based on national legislation and so the statutory retirement age varies between countries. At the time of writing, in the spring of 2023, strikes are occurring in France because of the government's intention to raise the retirement age from 62 years to 64 years. Many other countries have already raised their retirement age. The Dutch government offers residents income security from the state pension age, which, for almost 50 years, was 65 years. From 2013 onwards the statutory retirement age was raised. People are living longer. This is good news. However, it also means that providing income security for pensioners is becoming more expensive. The state pension is a pay-as-you-go system. Due to ageing and degrowth, there are ever fewer young people to pay for the statutory old-age pensions of ever more older people, who are also living longer. This is a heavy financial burden. The aging population and increasing life expectancy mean people need to work for longer. The old-age dependency ratio is rising. The same amount of work needs to be done by fewer workers. Furthermore, more people will require care, pushing up the amount of work that needs to be done still further.

The increase in the state retirement age is legally linked to the average remaining life expectancy. As of 2024, the state pension age of 67 years will no longer rise by one year for each additional year of life expectancy, but by eight months. This slower rise in the state pension age is designed to ensure that older workers are able to reach retirement age in good health. In the eyes of the law, a person of that age is old. The statutory retirement age is often the end point in a person's working life, but in reality many will already have left the employment market before then. Some people look forward to that moment eagerly, while others would prefer to continue working, either for financial reasons or simply because they enjoy it.

RETIREMENT AGE AND TERMINATION OF EMPLOYMENT

Agreed Retirement Age in the Employment Contract

For many employees, the retirement age is the final date in their employment contract. Around 85 percent of Dutch employees have a supplementary pension in addition to the statutory pension. This is a pension agreed between employer and employee. The combination of the state pension (first pillar) and the supplementary pension (second pillar) is, together with the level of income, one of the reasons why the Netherlands is considered to have one of the best pension systems in the world. People have a lifelong income after reaching retirement age.

An employment contract constitutes the entrance ticket to the supplementary pension of the second pillar. The vast majority of Dutch employment contracts include a pension agreement. In practice, many pension plans are tax-driven and, for this reason, the most commonly used retirement age for pension plans coincides with the fiscal retirement age of 68 years used for pension accrual. However, there is no legal obligation for this to be set at 68 years. There are also pension plans with retirement ages of 65 or 67. Almost all pension reg-ulations include the possibility of early retirement. People can then choose to (partially) retire early – possibly in order to achieve or maintain a healthy and sustainable work–life balance. However, this has the effect of reducing the pension paid out, pro rata, based upon an actuarial recalculation. The old age pension cannot be lowered, creating a (temporary) pension gap. So in reality there is more than one retirement age, and there is no clear answer as to the question of what the retirement age actually is (see Table 22.1). These different retirement ages often lead to disputes between employees and employers about the end date of employment contracts.

Table 22.1   Different concepts of the retirement age

Definition	Source	Age
Pensionable age	Statutory retirement age	66 years 10 months (2023)
Pensionable age pension scheme	Pension scheme	68
Fiscal pensionable age	Dutch tax law	68 years (2022)
Pension dismissal age	Negotiated	Statutory retirement age or higher (judges 70)
Early retirement date	Choice of employee	Flexible

Is the Retirement Age a Reasonable Ground for Dismissal?

The basic principle of Dutch labor law is that termination by the employer without the employee's consent is only possible if there are reasonable grounds for this. However, the law sees reaching the retirement age as a valid reason for termination of employment, and the employer has the legal power to use the retirement age to terminate the employment contract.

The employment contract can end in two ways when the retirement age is reached: (1) by operation of law through a written retirement dismissal clause (in Dutch: *pensioenontslagbeding*); or (2) by notice given by the employer (retirement notice, in Dutch: *pensioenopzegging*).

The legal difference is that with a retirement dismissal clause, the employment contract ends automatically, and the employer is not therefore required to give notice. The employment contract stipulates that the employment contract ends by operation of law upon reaching the retirement age. The Dutch Supreme Court confirmed that an employment contract entered into for an indefinite period may end by operation of law. The idea is that both employer and employee have mutually agreed (upon signing the employment contract) on the retirement age as the end date.

Interpretation of Retirement Age as Pension Termination Date

As mentioned above, the concept of retirement age regularly leads to disputes about the end date of employment contracts. The classic disagreement occurs when the employer interprets the term retirement age as meaning the state pension age but the employee believes they can continue working until 68 years. Some interpretation of the retirement age is then required. This has led to several rulings. In one of those cases, the court concluded that the parties' intention had been the state pension age. Clarification of the applicable retirement age and the termination of employment is desirable in order to avoid litigation.

AGE DISCRIMINATION AND TERMINATION OF EMPLOYMENT

The Legal Justification for Dismissal at the Statutory Retirement Age

Across the EU, there have been many legal cases of employees asking whether mandatory retirement is in line with age discrimination as laid down in the European Framework Directive (2000/78/EC). Although this directive leaves national provisions determining the pensionable age intact, this does not mean that the termination of the employment contract is exempt. Termination of employment due to reaching retirement age falls within the scope of the prohibition on age discrimination, and it therefore has to be objectively justified (ECJ 16 October 2007).

National legislation has to comply with European law. Employers cannot simply refer to the statutory provisions for employees. Not only are courts required to interpret the law in conformity with the directive, but European case law also shows that judges have to, if necessary, disapply national provisions that are contrary to the general principle of equal treatment on the grounds of age. This also applies to the relationship between employee and employer. In a dispute between individuals, the employer cannot successfully rely on legal certainty and a legal provision that is discriminatory (CJEU 19 April 2016). In short, there has to be a justification for employers to dismiss employees when they reach retirement age.

Established European case law seems to confirm that pension dismissal at the state pension age is objectively justified. For example, in ECJ 16 October 2007, the European Court of Justice (ECJ) ruled that the Spanish pension dismissal may be an appropriate and necessary means of regulating the national labor market, in particular to combat unemployment (advancement). It is important in this respect that pension dismissal is linked to an (adequate) old-age pension. The ECJ also ruled that member states and social partners have a wide margin of appreciation in deciding which social and employment policy objective they want to pursue specifically and through which measures they want to achieve this objective. However, the measures may not go beyond what is appropriate and necessary to achieve the objective pursued (compare ECJ 5 March 2009). Nevertheless, this broad margin of appreciation gives social partners and legislators a great deal of legal leeway for pension dismissal at the state pension age. Age-related dismissal is not allowed in the case of an excessive infringement (ECJ 12 October 2010). Provided there is a statutory old-age pension that is deemed to be sufficient, however, it is not easy to prove an excessive infringement.

The appeal of a fixed and objective age limit is that it prevents uncomfortable conversations about older workers who are no longer performing as well as they once did. Not everyone has the self-awareness to recognize that they are no longer competent to do their job. These arguments seem to have sufficient legal merit. At the same time, they impede those who are able to and would like to continue working, meaning that their potential may be lost. Experienced workers with valuable knowledge and skills could be disappearing from the labor market.

RELATION BETWEEN LEGAL RETIREMENT FRAMEWORK AND WORK–LIFE BALANCE

The law – both national and international – provides a legal retirement framework for people and institutions. The set of rules in place can be used to create a work–life balance for society as a whole and for individuals. Those who know the rules on retirement and the financial effect of their choices are better equipped for making decisions on (early) retirement, although clearly personal circumstances are the most relevant factor when making such decisions. Early retirement generally leads to a lower income. The presence of a statutory retirement age and state pension is often deemed to be a valid reason for employers to terminate employment. The effect of mandatory retirement is that employees have no choice but to stop working. However, continuing to work is possible.

A number of rules that prevent employers from continuing to employ workers beyond the state pension age have been eliminated in the Dutch legal framework. For example, employers are not liable to pay severance pay when an employee reaches the state pension age. These kinds of rules are supposed to enable employees to continue working for their employers after the retirement age.

CONCLUSION

The retirement age is a pivotal moment for the work–life balance of employees. It is a natural moment at which to stop working – the moment when one officially becomes old. Many countries provide income security at the retirement age. That is supposed to remove any financial need to continue working, but the downside may be that the retirement age can also be a valid reason for terminating employment. The work–life balance shifts from 'work' towards 'life', but this may happen involuntarily, depending on the national rules regarding retirement and termination of employment. Employers in several countries can use the statutory retirement age as valid grounds for dismissal. The idea is that there is no need to work because people receive a state pension.

At the same time, the statutory retirement age is moving ever upward. In the Netherlands, it was 65 years until 2013 and will be 67 years in 2024. The statutory retirement age will rise by eight months for every additional year of average life expectancy. This slower rate of increase in the state pension age is designed to ensure that older workers are able to reach retirement age in a healthy manner, and could therefore contribute to a healthy and sustainable work–life balance. Wherever you live, your retirement age and rules on termination of employment will affect your work–life balance.

REFERENCES

ECJ 16 October 2007, ECLI:EU:C:2007:604 (*Palacios*).
ECJ 5 March 2009, ECLI:EU:C:2009:128 (Age Concern).
ECJ 12 October 2010, ECLI:EU:C:2010:601 (Rosenbladt).
ECJ 19 April 2016, ECLI:EU:C:2016:278 (*Rasmussen*).

PART VI

Individual strategies for fostering work–life balance

23. Taking care of your own wellbeing

Marjolein van de Pol

INTRODUCTION

Humans have been thinking about the pursuit of happiness throughout their history, and even the Greek philosopher Socrates explored the question of 'what makes life worthwhile?' Human beings have a fundamental tendency towards personal growth (Ryan et al., 2019) and, when asked, most people mention subjective wellbeing or happiness as the most important priority in life.

However, in post-war society, the main focus has shifted to the pursuit of success. Although success may contribute to happiness, this is not guaranteed. Indeed, the desire for (professional) success can undermine subjective wellbeing and disrupt not only the healthy balance between work demands and personal life demands, but also our physical and mental health.

Subjective wellbeing plays a protective role in maintaining both physical and mental health (Steptoe et al., 2015). However the opposite is also true: people with (chronic) illnesses show increased levels of stress and lower subjective wellbeing (Sprangers et al., 2000). Increased stress levels are relevant to all disease, not only psychological issues like depression or anxiety, but also diabetes, cardiovascular diseases or auto-immune disorders (Steptoe et al., 2015). Understanding subjective wellbeing and the ability to foster resilience can therefore take us a long way in the pursuit of a healthy life and a healthy work–life balance.

Since the late 1990s, two renowned psychologists, Martin Seligman and Mihaly Csikszentmihalyi, have been working on 'positive psychology': the scientific study of how to live our lives well (Seligman & Csikszentmihalyi, 2000). Positive psychology originates from the humanistic psychology of Abraham Maslow, among others, and it encourages an emphasis on wellbeing (Maslow, 1954; Seligman & Csikszentmihalyi, 2000).

The positive psychology movement has examined many factors that can potentially contribute to individual and societal wellbeing, and have developed a 'wellbeing theory' that consists of six elements: (1) positive emotions; (2) engagement or flow; (3) relationships; (4) meaning or purpose; (5) accomplishment or achievement; and (6) vitality and health (PERMA-V) (Seligman, 2018).

An important disclaimer in this regard is the complexity and uniqueness of each individual, which makes it impossible to do justice to the complexity of each individual's subjective wellbeing. In this chapter, we therefore present evidence-based recommendations based on the positive psychology of the 'wellbeing theory', which can serve as a basis for improving subjective wellbeing and fostering resilience. These recommendations can help individuals to cope better with stress and challenges in their work and personal lives, thus supporting a healthy work–life balance.

WELLBEING THEORY: THE 'PERMA-V' MODEL

As outlined in the previous section, the wellbeing theory provides six core elements of a person's subjective wellbeing and happiness. Each of these six elements contributes to subjective wellbeing, is pursued for its own sake, and can be defined and measured independently of the other elements. There is still some debate about the relative importance of each element, but the overall theory is widely accepted (Wagner et al., 2020). Research has shown significant positive associations between each individual element and subjective wellbeing and life satisfaction (Kovich et al., 2022). Proactively working on elements of the model also reduces psychological distress in individuals (Kern et al., 2015).

Positive Emotions

Regularly experiencing positive emotions is perhaps the most obvious foundation for subjective wellbeing (Alexander et al., 2021). Whenever you feel good, you feel positive. Positive emotion goes beyond just smiling, and involves real emotions and the ability to stay optimistic, regardless of how bad your past experiences may have been, and to look forward to whatever the future may hold (Seligman, 2011). In evolutionary terms, our brains are wired to survive, but not to thrive (Alexander et al., 2021). It is therefore necessary to consciously reflect on what has gone well on a particular day. Indeed, writing down what went well during the day in a daily journal is a proven method of fostering resilience (Morris, 2020).

In our media-saturated society, there is an emphasis on apparently constant pleasure and enjoyment, which some have dubbed 'toxic positivity' (Goodman, 2022). This is certainly not what is meant by pleasure in the PERMA-V model. Rather, pleasure refers to the fulfillment of physical needs (i.e. food and drink, shelter, safety), while enjoyment is the satisfaction and fulfilment derived from doing something joyful. A positive outlook can promote robust relationships, working environments, and recreational activities. Optimism and positivity have many health benefits (Goodman et al., 2018). Practicing gratitude (Emmons & McCullough, 2003), writing down or verbally expressing what you are thankful for, and savoring experiences (the simple act of stepping out of your own experience) and truly valuing these as they are happening – all these practices help to magnify the effect of positive emotions (Armenta et al., 2022; Jose et al., 2012).

Engagement or Flow

Engagement refers to the process of becoming engrossed or absorbed in an activity. It is consistent with Csikszentmihalyi's concept of 'flow' (Csikszentmihalyi, 1990). Flow includes the loss of self-consciousness and complete absorption in an activity. In other words, it is living in the present moment and focusing entirely on the task at hand. Activities that have the right balance between challenge and skill can bring about a state of heightened engagement or flow, and flood the body with neurotransmitters and hormones that elevate the sense of subjective wellbeing. Engagement helps us to remain present and comes about through activities where we find calm, focus, and joy. This may be work, making music, sport, outdoor activity, dancing, or a hobby (Bonaiuto et al., 2016). Research on engagement has found that individuals who sought to channel their strengths in new ways on a daily basis for a week felt happier and less depressed after six months (Seligman et al., 2005).

Relationships

Relationships and social connections involve feeling supported, loved, and valued by others, and they are therefore crucial to a meaningful life. Humans are social animals and hard-wired to bond with and depend on other humans (Seligman, 2011). This is not just something we want, but something we need, and it helps us to feel safe, valued, wanted, and included. Positive relationships with parents, siblings, peers, work colleagues, and friends with similar interests and aspirations are a key ingredient in emotional support and joy. People who have strong romantic and other social relationships are happier than people who lack strong relationships (Diener et al., 2018). Joining a class or group that interests you or getting in touch with people you have not spoken to for a while will therefore positively reinforce those relationships (Siedlecki et al., 2014; Wagner et al., 2020). To achieve true friendships, unplugging from devices and consciously engaging in dialogue (first trying to understand, then trying to make yourself understood) is a helpful first step.

Meaning or Purpose

Meaning or purpose relates to the 'why' of life. Finding meaning means belonging and/or serving something bigger than ourselves (Seligman, 2011). Having a purpose in life helps individuals to focus on what is really important in the face of potential challenges (Bronk & Mitchell, 2022). Religion and spirituality, working for a good company, raising children, volunteering for a good cause, or expressing ourselves creatively can all provide meaning or purpose (Manco & Hamby, 2021), depending on our personal values. People who report having a purpose in life live longer and report higher levels of subjective wellbeing (Czekierda et al., 2017). Getting involved in a cause or organization that matters to you (i.e. planetary health, a local community center) (Tang et al., 2022) or trying something new to discover what inspires you contribute to subjective wellbeing and foster resilience (Steptoe, 2019).

Accomplishment or Achievement

People take pride in things that they have accomplished (Gander et al., 2016; Ryan & Deci, 2000). Accomplishment is also known as achievement, mastery, or competence (Seligman, 2011) and drives individuals to achieve more, leading to positive feelings. Accomplishments strengthen our subjective wellbeing when they are tied to intrinsic goals or personal improvement. Achieving intrinsic goals (such as growth and connection) leads to larger gains in wellbeing than extrinsic goals such as making money or achieving fame (Ryan et al., 2019). Setting both short- and long-term goals, reflecting on past successes, and celebrating achievements with loved ones therefore positively influence wellbeing (Gander et al., 2016).

Vitality and Health

Vitality refers to a feeling of living and flourishing. It is essential to our wellbeing and includes various areas of human functioning, including physical health, mental health, and performance (Lavrusheva, 2020). Research suggests that most things that have a negative effect on physical health or mood also have a negative effect on vitality (Wunsch et al., 2017). Smoking, poor diet, lack of physical activity, bad sleep quality, negativity, and a stressful environment are all negatively associated with vitality (and health) (Stranges et al., 2014). Fostering vitality and health is essential to building resilience and the ability to bounce back from adversity or challenging periods (Carver et al., 2010).

MISCONCEPTIONS ABOUT SUBJECTIVE WELLBEING

We can all improve subjective wellbeing by addressing the six elements out-lined above. However, there remains a lack of knowledge in this regard, and people (and scientists) value subjective wellbeing differently. From a scientific point of view, subjective wellbeing is an ongoing state that ebbs and flows and can be influenced by the way people live their lives (Diener et al., 2018). Many people assume that if a person has the right upbringing and education, works hard, and settles down, then subjective wellbeing will automatically follow. These factors *may* contribute to subjective wellbeing, but are no guar-antee. Indeed, some of the main research findings regarding lasting subjective wellbeing contradict many common misconceptions in this area (Gilbert et al., 1998; Lyubomirsky et al., 2005).

Money and Material Goods

The relationship between money and subjective wellbeing is complex (D'Ambrosio et al., 2020; Dunn et al., 2020). Although poverty is associated with hardship, many studies have shown that once people have enough money to live a comfortable life (i.e. shelter, food, the occasional fun activity), subjec-tive wellbeing does not increase any further as income increases (Kahneman & Deaton, 2010). One way in which money *can* help improve wellbeing is when it is used for meaningful social activities rather than material goods (Gilovich & Kumar, 2015). Furthermore, research shows that spending money on others promotes the subjective wellbeing of the spender (Dunn et al., 2008).

Marriage

High-quality relationships increase our overall subjective wellbeing (Diener et al., 2018); however, societal pressure to find the perfect partner, get married, have kids, and 'live happily ever after' does not. This pressure perpetuates the unrealistic expectation that an individual can experience complete happiness in every way, all at once.

Choice

Choice means autonomy and options for pursuing meaning in life. However, choice is a double-edged sword. Having too much choice can lead to 'choice overload' and regrets regarding decisions made. When a person is presented with too many options, their ability to make decisions is undermined, and research shows that decisions are exhausting and can negatively influence cognitive abilities (Schwartz, 2005). It is therefore better to reduce choices regarding minor details and focus on personal satisfaction instead.

Success (Such as Good Grades or Job)

People tend to believe that once an end goal has been achieved, true subjective wellbeing will follow. However, the end result often only provides subjective wellbeing in the short term; in reality, it is the process of working on something you enjoy and moving towards your goal that really improves wellbeing. Research shows that there is a major difference between how happy people expect to be when they achieve good school grades or get a new job and how much subjective wellbeing these things actually bring (Levine et al., 2012).

Control (if only …) and Social Comparison

'If only I had good grades, more money, a six-pack … If only I was famous … If only I could change this one thing in my partner … I know I'd be happy then.' Why do the majority of people hanker after wealth, fame, or power? It is because of the incorrect assumption that these things will provide subjective wellbeing. In fact, all too often, people are distracted into trying to maximize the things that have no intrinsic value in themselves. Social media also plays a role in this (Malik et al., 2021).

Social media tempts users into social comparison with other users. Social comparison influences our self-esteem, because we derive our sense of self from comparing ourselves with others (Buunk & Gibbons, 2007; Warrender D, 2020). Real-world social comparison usually involves one individual and just a few other people, but the digital realm of social media presents almost limit-less potential for people to compare themselves with others. Negative social comparison and 'fear of missing out' (the idea that someone else is having a better time or is more successful than you, based on what you are shown of their lives on social media) can impact our wellbeing negatively.

BUILDING RESILIENCE

One thing that is certain in life is that we will all face trauma, adversity, and other stressors that will challenge our subjective wellbeing. Resilience is the ability to adapt successfully to difficult or challenging life experiences. Resilient people tend to maintain a more positive outlook and cope with stress more effectively, which not only enhances their subjective wellbeing but their health, too (Steptoe et al., 2015). Actively practicing and training the techniques described above and avoiding common pitfalls positively influences subjective wellbeing, while also building resilience. Research has shown that although some people seem to be resilient by nature, these behaviors can also be learned.

Develop a Growth Mindset

People with a growth mindset feel that their skills and intelligence can be improved with effort and persistence. A growth mindset means seeing difficulties as a challenge, rather than as debilitating, and recognizing that failure and mistakes can be lessons learned and opportunities for growth (Yeager et al., 2019).

Although people may differ in their innate aptitudes, interests, and temperaments, everyone can change and grow through application and experience. Every experience has the power to teach you something important, so look for the lesson in every situation. Recall how you have coped with difficulties in the past. Consider your past behavior and identify the skills and strategies that helped you through difficult times. This helps you to acquire the habits that foster resilience. Small changes can, when performed consistently, lead to massive improvements (Clear, 2021). Habits are actions that you do often and without even thinking about, which is why a small daily action can have a powerful effect on your life. The choice between chatting briefly to a neighbor in the street every day or walking past without saying anything may seem trivial now, but the former leads to an expanding network of relationships, while the latter leaves us more isolated.

Seek Help

Seeking help when you need it is crucial to building resilience. Anybody can feel stuck sometimes or feel they are not doing so well. It is important to talk to a health professional for guidance in such situations. Talking about things with others can help people to understand the challenges they are facing (Yeager et al., 2019).

Be Proactive

Proactive people do not ignore problems but foster self-discovery by identifying what can be done. Taking the initiative fosters motivation and purpose, even during stressful periods in life (Covey, 1991), as it involves focusing energy and attention on the things that we can influence (rather than on things that are outside our control). It can take time to recover from a major setback in life and figure out what needs to be done, but working out what to focus on is always the first step.

CONCLUSION

In our success-oriented society, taking care of our own wellbeing can be a challenge, but it is crucial for health. The positive psychology of 'wellbeing theory' and evidence-based advice offered in this chapter can help people to improve their subjective wellbeing, foster resilience and provide a basis for a healthy work–life balance.

REFERENCES

Alexander, R., Aragon, O., Bookwala, J., Cherbuin, N., Gatt, J., Kahrilas, I. et al. (2021). The neuroscience of positive emotions and affect: Implications for cultivating happiness and wellbeing. *Neuroscience and Biobehavioral Reviews*, *121*, 220–249.

Armenta, C. N., Fritz, M., Walsh, L., & Lyubomirsky, S. (2022). Satisfied yet striving: Gratitude fosters life satisfaction and improvement motivation in youth. *Emotion*, *22*(5), 1004–1016.

Bonaiuto, M., Mao, Y., Roberts, S., Psalti, A., Ariccio, S., Ganucci Cancellieri, U., & Csikszentmihalyi, M. (2016). Optimal experience and personal growth: Flow and the consolidation of place identity. *Frontiers in Psychology*, *7*.

Bronk, K. C., & Mitchell, C. (2022). Considering purpose through the lens of prospection. *Journal of Positive Psychology*, *17*(2), 281–287.

Buunk, A. P., & Gibbons, F. X. (2007). Social comparison: The end of a theory and the emergence of a field. *Organizational Behavior and Human Decision Processes*, *102*(1), 3–21.

Carver, C. S., Scheier, M. F., & Segerstrom, S. (2010). Optimism. *Clinical Psychology Review*, *30*(7), 879–889.

Clear, J. (2021). *Atomic habits: Tiny changes, remarkable results*. Random House.

Covey, S. R. (1991). The seven habits of highly effective people. *National Medical-Legal Journal*, *2*(2), 8.

Csikszentmihalyi, M. (1990). *Flow: The psychology of optimal experience*. Harper & Row.

Czekierda, K., Banik, A., Park, C., & Luszczynska, A. (2017). Meaning in life and physical health: Systematic review and meta-analysis. *Health Psychology Review*, *11*(4), 387–418.

D'Ambrosio, C., Jäntti, M., & Lepinteur, A. (2020). Money and happiness: Income, wealth and subjective well-being. *Social Indicators Research*, *148*(1), 47–66.

Diener, E., Seligman, M. E. P., Choi, H., & Oishi, S. (2018). Happiest people revisited. *Perspectives on Psychological Science*, *13*(2), 176–184.

Dunn, E. W., Aknin, L. B., & Norton, M. (2008). Spending money on others promotes happiness. *Science*, *319*(5870), 1687–1688.

Dunn, E. W., Whillans, A. V., Norton, M., & Aknin, L. (2020). Prosocial spending and buying time: Money as a tool for increasing subjective well-being. *Advances in Experimental Social Psychology*, *61*, 67–126.

Emmons, R. A., & McCullough, M. E. (2003). Counting blessings versus burdens: An experimental investigation of gratitude and subjective well-being in daily life. *Journal of Personality and Social Psychology*, *84*, 377–389.

Gander, F., Proyer, R. T., & Ruch, W. (2016). Positive psychology interventions addressing pleasure, engagement, meaning, positive relationships, and accomplishment increase well-being and ameliorate depressive symptoms: A randomized, placebo-controlled online study. *Frontiers in Psychology*, *7*, 686.

Gilbert, D. T., Pinel, E. C., Wilson, T., Blumberg, S., & Wheatley, T. (1998). Immune neglect: A source of durability bias in affective forecasting. *Journal of Personality and Social Psychology*, *75*, 617–638.

Gilovich, T., & Kumar, A. (2015). We'll always have Paris: The hedonic payoff from experiential and material investments. *Advances in Experimental Social Psychology*, *51*, 147–187.

Goodman, F. R., Disabato, D. J., Kashdan, T., & Kauffman, S. (2018). Measuring well-being: A comparison of subjective well-being and PERMA. *Journal of Positive Psychology*, *13*(4), 321–332.

Goodman, W. (2022). *Toxic positivity*. Hachette.

Jose, P. E., Lim, B. T., & Bryant, F. (2012). Does savoring increase happiness? A daily diary study. *Journal of Positive Psychology*, *7*(3), 176–187.

Kahneman, D., & Deaton, A. (2010). High income improves evaluation of life but not emotional well-being. *Proceedings of the National Academy of Sciences*, *107*(38), 16489–16493.

Kern, M. L., Waters, L. E., Adler, A., & White, M. (2015). A multidimensional approach to measuring well-being in students: Application of the PERMA framework. *Journal of Positive Psychology*, *10*(3), 262–271.

Kovich, M. K., Simpson, V. L., Foli, K., Hass, Z., & Phillips, R. (2022). Application of the PERMA model of well-being in undergraduate students. *International Journal of Community Wellbeing*, 1–20.

Lavrusheva, O. (2020). The concept of vitality: Review of the vitality-related research domain. *New Ideas in Psychology*, *56*.

Levine, L. J., Lench, H. C., Kaplan, R., & Safer, M. (2012). Accuracy and artifact: Reexamining the intensity bias in affective forecasting: Correction to Levine et al. (2012). *Journal of Personality and Social Psychology*, *103*, 772.

Lyubomirsky, S., Sheldon, K. M., & Schkade, D. (2005). Pursuing happiness: The architecture of sustainable change. *Review of General Psychology*, *9*(2), 111–131.

Malik, A., Dhir, A., Kaur, P., & Johri, A. (2021). Correlates of social media fatigue and academic performance decrement: A large cross-sectional study. *Information Technology & People*, *34*(2), 557–580.

Manco, N., & Hamby, S. (2021). A meta-analytic review of interventions that promote meaning in life. *American Journal of Health Promotion*, *35*(6), 866–873.

Maslow, A. H. (1954). *Motivation and personality*. Harper & Brothers.

Morris, M. H. (2020). Write it out! CPR for the soul. *Nursing Clinics of North America*, *55*(4), 475–488.

Ryan, R. M., & Deci, E. L. (2000). Self-determination theory and the facilitation of intrinsic motivation, social development, and well-being. *American Psychologist*, *55*(1), 68–78.

Ryan, R. M., Ryan, W., Di Domenico, S., & Deci, E. (2019). The nature and the conditions of human autonomy and flourishing: Self-determination theory and basic psychological needs. In *The Oxford handbook of human motivation*, 2nd ed. (pp. 89–110). Oxford University Press.

Schwartz, B. (2005). *The paradox of choice*. HarperCollins.

Seligman, M. E. (2011). *Flourish: A visionary new understanding of happiness and well-being*. Hachette.

Seligman, M. E. (2018). PERMA and the building blocks of well-being. *Journal of Positive Psychology*, *13*(4), 333–335.

Seligman, M. E., & Csikszentmihalyi, M. (2000). Positive psychology. An introduction. *American Psychologist*, *55*(1), 5–14.

Seligman, M. E. P., Steen, T. A., Park, N., & Peterson, C. (2005). Positive psychology progress: Empirical validation of interventions. *American Psychologist*, *60*(5), 410–421.

Siedlecki, K. L., Salthouse, T. A., Oishi, S., & Jeswani, S. (2014). The relationship between social support and subjective well-being across age. *Social Indicators Research*, *117*(2), 561–576.

Sprangers, M. A., de Regt, E. B., Andries, F., van Agt, H., Bijl, R., de Boer, J., Foets, M. et al. (2000). Which chronic conditions are associated with better or poorer quality of life? *Journal of Clinical Epidemiology*, *53*(9), 895–907.

Steptoe, A. (2019). Happiness and health. *Annual Review of Public Health*, *40*(1), 339–359.

Steptoe, A., Deaton, A., & Stone, A. (2015). Subjective wellbeing, health, and ageing. *Lancet*, *385*(9968), 640–648.

Stranges, S., Samaraweera, P. C., Taggart, F., Kandala, N.-B., & Stewart-Brown, S. (2014). Major health-related behaviours and mental well-being in the general population: The Health Survey for England. *BMJ Open*, *4*(9), e005878.

Tang, J., Li, X.-c., & Zhang, X. (2022). The eudemonic wellbeing of volunteers in a public health emergency: COVID-19 in China. *Frontiers in Psychology*, *13*.

Wagner, L., Gander, F., Proyer, R., & Ruch, W. (2020). Character strengths and PERMA: Investigating the relationships of character strengths with a multidimensional framework of well-being. *Applied Research in Quality of Life*, *15*(2), 307–328.

Warrender, D., & Milne, R. (2020). How use of social media and social comparison affect mental health. *Nursing Times*, *116*(3), 56–59.

Wunsch, K., Kasten, N., & Fuchs, R. (2017). The effect of physical activity on sleep quality, well-being, and affect in academic stress periods. *Nature and Science of Sleep*, *9*, 117–126.

Yeager, D. S., Hanselman, P., Walton, G., Murray, J., Crosnoe, R., Muller, C. et al. (2019). A national experiment reveals where a growth mindset improves achievement. *Nature*, *573*(7774), 364–369.

24. Impact of strategies and interventions for improving work–life balance

Marjolein van de Pol and Ron Hameleers

INTRODUCTION

Over the past 75 years, major changes have occurred in work and society that may influence work–life balance (Schaufeli et al., 2009). The workforce has changed dramatically, and now includes more women, more single parents, and more dual earners. Work intensity has also increased, while work–non-work boundaries have become blurred due to the advent of 24/7 communication technology. People need to work faster, harder, and for longer hours, and autonomy is often limited (Schaufeli et al., 2009).

All this means that maintaining a healthy work–life balance and balancing professional and personal life can be challenging. Empirical evidence suggests that an imbalance between work and life not only reduces life satisfaction, but individual health as well (Albrecht et al., 2020; Gribben & Semple, 2021; Sirgy & Lee, 2018). Society, employers, and employees all have a responsibility for achieving a healthy work–life balance and putting work–life balance on the agenda, and this benefits society as a whole. The evidence regarding the factors that play a role in work–life balance is solid, but evidence on the effectiveness of individual, workplace, and social strategies and interventions designed to improve work–life balance remains relatively scarce. In recent years, various intervention studies have been done, but many studies suffer from methodological shortcomings and a lack of long-term follow-up or general-izability, as was shown in two recent review studies by Rashmi and Kataria (2021b) and Suto et al. (2022).

The aim of this chapter is therefore to discuss practical strategies and interventions that have a proven effect on work–life balance. To this end, we combined those studies from the reviews mentioned above, which showed useful interventions to improve work–life balance through evidence-based strategies for preventing burnout (Aronsson et al., 2017; Maslach & Leiter, 2008; Schaufeli et al., 2009) and increasing wellbeing (Brand et al., 2017; Burnett, 2016). We distinguish between individual strategies and interventions on the one hand and employer and company culture strategies and interventions on the other. The social factors that can play a role in creating a healthy work–life balance are discussed in other chapters in this book.

INDIVIDUAL STRATEGIES AND INTERVENTIONS TO IMPROVE WORK–LIFE BALANCE

Find a Job that Suits You

Many factors can influence an individual's perceptions of their work–life balance, but the time they have available for personal interests, obligations, and recreation often positively or negatively mediates their overall assessment. Finding a job that matches one's values, interests, personality, and competencies is therefore crucial when it comes to finding work that suits one's personal circumstances (Albrecht et al., 2020; Gribben & Semple, 2021).

When a job feels draining to the employee, it also becomes harder to engage in non-work activities, and vice versa. People do not need to like every aspect of their job, but there does need to be enough interest to maintain motivation. Individuals also have different priorities, which may be context-dependent and may change over time. This affects which jobs suit an individual best at a certain point in their life: parents may need informal care, or traveling for work may be difficult, for example. Being open and reassessing one's needs regularly are essential in finding a good balance.

Depending on the field of work, irregular working hours may be required, and workers must therefore decide whether their own biorhythm can cope with irregular working hours (Brauner et al., 2020).

Most people also aspire to do meaningful work that reflects their values and interests (Aronsson et al., 2017; Burnett, 2016). This notion leads many people to feel 'stuck' in a job that is unfulfilling or to continue searching for their 'perfect job'. These beliefs are dysfunctional, however, and based on the assumption that there is an 'ideal' job for everyone. To counteract this, Burnett and Evans have developed a tool called 'building a life compass' in order to help people find a job – and a life – that suits them (Burnett, 2016).

The Life Compass

Building a 'life compass' consists of two elements; a 'life view' and a 'work view'. The life view focuses on questions such as: What is important to you? How do you relate to other people? How important is money to you? What gives your life meaning? The work view focuses on questions such as: Why do you work? What makes work good or bad? Identifying discrepancies between the two perspectives can prevent clashes and improve work–life balance. This method of building a life compass and designing your life is a proven method that can be used throughout various stages of life.[1]

Acceptance

Many people have unrealistically high expectations regarding work–life balance. They imagine doing a productive day's work, going home on time, and having enough energy to spend time with friends and family or to take part in a social impact project. It sounds too good to be true, and indeed it nearly always is (Aronsson et al., 2017; Danzig, 1981; Schaufeli et al., 2009). In reality, all too often a bad day at work, a bad night's sleep, or a simple lack of energy throw a spanner in the works.

It is therefore important not to strive for perfection every day, but for a realistic schedule. Some days the focus may be more on work, while on other days there may be time and energy left over to engage in hobbies, spend time with loved ones, or just do nothing and relax. Balance is achieved over time, not every day. Workers need to embrace imperfection and be gentle with themselves. Gratitude exercises can help to achieve acceptance (see Chapter 23 in this volume).

Prioritizing

How do we find a good balance between work and life? Zooming out, the answer is simple: 'set clear priorities!' Unfortunately, in real-life settings sticking to our priorities is challenging (Rashmi & Kataria, 2021b). No matter how clearly we have defined our priorities, new things require our attention every day. One method of dealing with such situations is to ask the following question four times: 'Do I have to do this now?' This apparently simple question becomes very powerful when you ask it four times, emphasizing a different word each time.

1. DO I have to do this now? Or can I choose to say no? (And if I can say no, do I want to say no?)
2. Do I have to do this now? Am I the right person for this, or could somebody else do it? (Is there a smart way to delegate the task?)
3. Do I have to do THIS now? Would it not be better to invest my time in something higher on my priorities list? Is this really the best use of my time and attention right now?

---

[1]	To find out more, we advise readers to read the book *Designing your life* or follow the associated course (Burnett 2016).

4. Do I have to do this NOW? Is this really the best way to spend my time right now? Does this need to be done NOW, or can it wait? Is there perhaps something more important to do right now?

If one of the answers to this magic question is 'no', the task is not currently a priority. It is probably better to focus your attention and energy on something else. However, this can be quite difficult in practice. Declining lunch with a colleague is probably easier than saying 'no' to your boss who wants to delegate an important task to you. Fortunately, as with many difficult things, 'practice makes perfect'. You can start practicing by prioritizing at a low level (e.g. unplugging your phone for a few hours of undisturbed work, or not responding immediately to an email from your boss that is addressed to multiple people). Starting low, going slowly, and practicing often can help you to adopt behaviors that will help you to prioritize. Setting priorities goes beyond choosing which task is most important now. It is also about taking care of your health and, for example, spending enough time with family and friends. Prioritizing your health will make you a better employee, who will miss less work and be happier and more productive. Working too much stops people getting better, and can mean they have to take more days off in the future (Schaufeli et al., 2009). Prioritization is a tool for finding the right balance, not a panacea. It should be seen in conjunction with other strategies, such as company policy and social factors (see below).

Investing in Social Support

Social support both at work from colleagues and outside work from family, friends, and partners is an important resource in maintaining a good work–life balance. Social support involves more than hands-on help with performing tasks; it also means advice and information. The single most important aspect of social support, however, is emotional support in the form of someone to share your thoughts and feelings with (Schaufeli et al., 2009).

Taking Breaks and Disconnecting

Breaks are important. Research has shown that performance deteriorates when we work for too long without interruption or when were are online for too long (Launspach, 2022). The brain needs some time to disconnect and relax between tasks, and taking a break allows us to recover and enables new thoughts and ideas to emerge. Regularly interrupting work and disconnecting digital devices is good for concentration, memory, and job satisfaction. Disconnecting can mean something simple like practicing transit meditation on your daily commute instead of checking work emails (Malik et al., 2021;

Launspach, 2022). Other ways to build breaks into your life are adding regular coffee breaks to your diary, scheduling time for a walk between appointments, or commuting by bike. It is advisable to spend time on non-work activities, such as exercise or personal hobbies that give you time away from your work role (Rashmi & Kataria, 2021b; Launspach, 2022).

Employer Strategies for Improving Work–Life Balance

The drive for improved performance in recent decades has had an unintended consequence: a hyper-competitive and individualistic working environment. This is damaging to the wellbeing of both employees and employers, and counterproductive to creating a future-proof workforce. Employers who are committed to providing an environment that supports work–life balance for their employees can reduce costs and absenteeism and enjoy a more loyal workforce, as we will discuss in the following paragraphs.

Flexible Work Arrangements

Job autonomy is an employee's ability to make decisions about how they carry out their work without being monitored excessively. Such decisions may involve the amount of work done, the way that work is done, and when certain things are done. In some fields of work, job autonomy might be lower due to stricter regulations (e.g. medicine, police). However, research shows that employees who are granted even a limited measure of *autonomous decision making* ('play room'), and who have the security of a back-up (a manager who is always available for consultation), experience more control over their work, manage their time better, and meet professional and personal commitments more effectively and efficiently (Alarcon, 2011; Aronsson et al., 2017; Quirk et al., 2021; Rashmi & Kataria, 2021b).

Flexible working hours and teleworking are also known to improve job autonomy. A possible downside of flexibility and teleworking is the blurring of the lines between work and non-work (OECD, 2019; Rashmi & Kataria, 2021b). Employers and employees need to agree on clear criteria to prevent this. Dialogue and coordination are crucial in this regard (Gribben & Semple, 2021; Rashmi & Kataria, 2021b; Sirgy & Lee, 2018; Suto et al., 2022).

Supportive Environment

A supportive work environment is a workplace that fosters and encourages a good work–life balance through goals and values that are shared profession-ally and personally. Supervision and workplace support affect employees' behaviors, attitudes, and expectations, and shape their ability to achieve a good balance. Research has shown us how to be a supportive manager (Rashmi & Kataria, 2021b):

Align values and manage expectations
In the company's mission statement or value statement, a focus on wellbeing sends a clear message to employees. Be a *role model* in this regard, and know what your employees are striving for. Not everyone has the same work–life balance goals. Talk to employees about their objectives and decide how to reinforce job motivation and commitment. Help employees to manage resources and reduce conflicts between professional and personal obligations.

Be a role model
Set a good example. Do not be a manager who is 'top of the class' but one who facilitates and allows the team to grow and values diversity. Your employees will follow your lead.

Balance effort with reward
Invest in providing employees with adequate and concrete feedback and ask for feedback from employees in return. Research shows that employees who receive little or no feedback feel alone and underappreciated (Sirgy & Lee, 2018). Encouraging a culture of giving and receiving feedback also contributes to camaraderie among colleagues (Rashmi & Kataria, 2021a).

Company policy
Restrict emails after working hours, set boundaries for working hours, and set an example. If the company sends emails at all hours of the day and night or employees see that managers are working at the weekend, they will assume this is what is expected of them, too. While employers typically do a good job of highlighting work–life balance offerings to prospective new employees, the same cannot be said for communicating the importance of work–life balance to existing employees. Discuss the available options with employees regularly.

Increase vitality
Companies that invest in in-company physical and mental health programs can help employees cope with conflicting demands (Anand & Vohra, 2019). With respect to physical health, companies can nudge their employees towards healthier behaviors by replacing the cookie jar in the coffee room with a bowl of fruit, for example, or by making stairwells more attractive with art or music (and making the elevators slower) (Clear, 2021). To improve mental fitness companies can invest in psychological capital with mindset and resilience training (Eskreis-Winkler et al., 2014; Gander et al., 2016) (also see Chapter 23 in this volume). It is essential that these vitality programs are consistent

with company values, otherwise they are nothing more than window dressing and do nothing to improve work–life balance (Rashmi & Kataria, 2021b).

Workload Reduction

Workload depends on the interplay between working hours, caseload, and the amount of support received. Workload is both subjective (how does the employee perceive it?) and objective (number of working hours, cases, and amount of support). The perceived workload therefore depends on both individual and work-related factors. Over recent decades, workloads have generally increased substantially (Schaufeli et al., 2009). One of the best-researched interventions for improving work–life balance is reducing working hours with retained salary. Workload reduction positively influences sleep quality and sleep duration, with fewer somatic symptoms and lower perceived stress on workdays.

Workload varies between different professions. Occupations can be physically demanding, mentally demanding, or both. Whether and how workload reduction can be used to improve work–life balance depends on the type of occupation. In physically demanding professions, technological support may play an important role in workload reduction, while in mentally demanding professions a mentor support program or caseload reduction may be effective. Generalizable research on this topic is lacking (Schaufeli et al., 2009).

Promote (Gender) Equality and Diversity

The increase in women in the workforce has not been mirrored by an increase in male work in the domestic and family spheres. Informal care commitments, such as sharing roles and responsibilities with a spouse in a dual-earner family or providing care to elderly parents, tend to have a significant impact on women's career choices (Rincon & Martinez, 2020; Suto et al., 2022). Companies that invest in childcare and parental leave, possibly in combination with workload reduction, can positively affect their employees' work–life balance.

WHEN ARE EMPLOYER STRATEGIES TO IMPROVE WORK–LIFE BALANCE EFFECTIVE?

Employer strategies need to be consistent with company culture and values in order to have a lasting effect. Some organizations may have the required institutional support (such as policies and strategies) but still lack the required cultural support (such as a positive and enabling work climate) to encourage (gender) equality and diversity (Suto et al., 2022). Most research on equality focuses on working women, mothers, and dual-earner couples. Workers without children and single parents are overlooked in equality research. Research into how diversity and inclusion relate to work–life balance is also lacking.

CONCLUSION

The strategies and interventions discussed in this chapter can, when combined, create momentum for improving work–life balance (Burnett, 2016; Rashmi & Kataria, 2021b; Sirgy & Lee, 2018; Suto et al., 2022).

The practical, evidence-based advice for both employees and employers may help to improve work–life balance in our rapidly changing society. However, with regard to the long-term effectiveness of individual, workplace, and social strategies and interventions to improve work–life balance, much remains unknown, and further research is therefore needed. It seems likely that a mix of individual and collective strategies and interventions is generally needed to achieve a sustainable work–life balance.

REFERENCES

Alarcon, G. M. (2011). A meta-analysis of burnout with job demands, resources, and attitudes. *Journal of Vocational Behavior*, *79*(2), 549–562.

Albrecht, S. C., Kecklund, G., & Leineweber, C. (2020). The mediating effect of work–life interference on the relationship between work-time control and depressive and musculoskeletal symptoms. *Scandinavian Journal of Work, Environment and Health*, *46*(5), 469–479.

Anand, A., & Vohra, V. (2019). Alleviating employee work–family conflict: Role of organizations. *International Journal of Organizational Analysis*, *28*(2).

Aronsson, G., Theorell, T., Grape, T., Hammarström, A., Hogstedt, C., Marteinsdottir, I., Skoog, I., Träskman-Bendz, L., & Hall, C. (2017). A systematic review including meta-analysis of work environment and burnout symptoms. *BMC Public Health*, *17*.

Brand, S. L., Coon, J. T., Fleming, L., Carroll, L., Bethel, A., & Wyatt, K. (2017). Whole-system approaches to improving the health and wellbeing of healthcare workers: A systematic review. *Plos One*, *12*(12).

Brauner, C., Wohrmann, A. M., & Michel, A. (2020). Congruence is not everything: A response surface analysis on the role of fit between actual and preferred working time arrangements for work–life balance. *Chronobiology International*, *37*(9–10), 1287–1298.

Burnett, E. (2016). *Designing your life, build the perfect career, step by step*. Random House.

Clear, J. (2021). *Atomic habits: Tiny changes, remarkable results*. Random House.

Danzig, M. E. (1981). *Professional burnout in human service organizations*. Praeger Publishers.

Eskreis-Winkler, L., Shulman, E. P., & Beal, S. (2014). The grit effect: Predicting retention in the military, the workplace, school and marriage. *Frontiers in Psychology*, *5*.

Gander, F., Proyer, R. T., & Ruch, W. (2016). Positive psychology interventions addressing pleasure, engagement, meaning, positive relationships, and accomplishment increase well-being and ameliorate depressive symptoms: A randomized, placebo-controlled online study. *Frontiers in Psychology, 7.*

Gribben, L., & Semple, C. J. (2021). Factors contributing to burnout and work–life balance in adult oncology nursing: An integrative review. *European Journal of Oncology Nursing, 50,* 101887.

Launspach, T. (2022). *Crazy Busy: Keeping Sane in a Stressful World.* John Wiley & Sons.

Malik, A., Dhir, A., Kaur, P., & Aditya, J. (2021). Correlates of social media fatigue and academic performance decrement: A large cross-sectional study. *Information Technology & People, 34*(2), 557–580.

Maslach, C., & Leiter, M. P. (2008). Early predictors of job burnout and engagement. *Journal of Applied Psychology, 93*(3), 498–512.

OECD. (2019). *The future of work.* Secretary-General of the OECD.

Quirk, R., Rodin, H., & Linzer, M. (2021). Targeting causes of burnout in residency: An innovative approach used at Hennepin Healthcare. *Academic Medicine, 96*(5), 690–694.

Rashmi, K., & Kataria, A. (2021a). The mediating role of work–life balance on the relationship between job resources and job satisfaction: Perspectives from Indian nursing professionals. *International Journal of Organizational Analysis.*

Rashmi, K., & Kataria, A. (2021b). Work–life balance: A systematic literature review and bibliometric analysis. *International Journal of Sociology and Social Policy.*

Rincon, G. B., & Martinez, Y. M. (2020). Work/family life by 2040: Between a gig economy and traditional roles. *Futures, 119.*

Schaufeli, W. B., Leiter, M. P., & Maslach, C. (2009). Burnout: 35 years of research and practice. *Career Development International, 14*(2–3), 204–220.

Sirgy, M. J., & Lee, D. J. (2018). Work–life balance: An integrative review. *Applied Research in Quality of Life, 13*(1), 229–254.

Suto, M., Balogun, O. O., Dhungel, B., Kato, T., & Takehara, K. (2022). Effectiveness of workplace interventions for improving working conditions on the health and wellbeing of fathers or parents: A systematic review. *International Journal of Environmental Research and Public Health, 19*(8).

25. The Vocational Meaning and Fulfillment Survey: a new tool for fostering employees' work–life balance and career sustainability

Johanna Rantanen, Saija Mauno, Sanna Konsti, Sanna Markkula, and Gary Peterson

MEANINGFUL WORK, WORK–LIFE BALANCE, AND SUSTAINABLE CAREERS

In the field of work and organizational psychology, as well as career psychology, although meaningful work is regarded as a key determinant of work–life balance, studies of the relationship between the two have yielded mixed findings. Some scholars have conceptualized meaningful work as an *antecedent* of work–life balance and provided evidence for this (Bragger et al., 2019; Johnson & Jiang, 2017). In other studies, meaningful work has been conceptualized as a *mediator* – for example, between customer misbehavior (Loi et al., 2018), public service motivation (Zheng et al., 2020), decent work (Kashyap & Arora, 2022), and work influencing private life. Recently, Mostafa (2021) argued that meaningful work can also act as a *moderator* that suppresses the harmful effect of work–life conflict and helps to mitigate job exhaustion. Together, these studies seem to support the view that meaningful work and work–life balance are positively associated, and may together foster career sustainability.

To go beyond these currently existing research findings and produce a new understanding of this relationship, we approach these phenomena from the perspective of the process model of sustainable careers. According to De Vos et al. (2020, p. 1), "Careers form a complex mosaic of objective experiences and subjective evaluations, resulting in an enormous diversity in terms of how careers can take shape and a major variety of individual reflections regarding whether one's career is sustainable or not." Career sustainability is important because it consists of: (1) *happiness*, such as life satisfaction and career success; (2) *health*, both mental and physical; and (3) *productivity*, for example in the form of job performance and employability. Therefore, employees' happiness, health, and productivity are considered key indicators of a sustainable career, as they contribute to both employees' and organizations' shared goal of not just surviving but also flourishing in today's fast-paced employment market, society, and global economy.

Meaningful work positioned in the core of the process model of sustainable careers (De Vos et al., 2020) can be defined in various ways. Here, we rely on a definition from Allan et al. (2019, p. 502), according to whom meaningful work is "the global judgement that one's work accomplishes significant, valuable, or worthwhile goals that are congruent with one's existential values." There are also many definitions of *work–life balance*, and we see this as a construct that constitutes *both* specific dimensions and an overall work–life fit experience simultaneously. Accordingly, dimensions which, when combined, give a particular form to an individual's work–life balance experience are: (1) *work–non-work conflict*, defined as incompatible and bidirectional role demands and pressures between these life domains; (2) *work–non-work enrichment*, defined as bidirectional, beneficial effects, and shared resources between these life domains; and (3) *work–non-work balance*, defined as an overall positive evaluation of one's satisfaction, performance, and adequate involvement in all life domains (Jones et al., 2006; Kinnunen et al., 2023). Note that here we have substituted the term "family," as used by Jones et al. (2006) and Kinnunen et al. (2023), with the term "non-work," to cover all possible relationships, activities, and responsibilities that workers have outside of work, irrespective of their family status.

In this chapter, we aim to combine the perspectives of work and organizational psychology by focusing on concepts of meaningful work (Allan et al., 2019; Peterson et al., 2017) and career psychology and on models of sustainable careers (De Vos et al., 2020) and career decision making (Sampson et al., 2004) in order to advance our understanding of how we can support employees' balance and functioning across life domains and the life course.

THE RESEARCH AIM AND QUESTIONS

Previous research shows that both meaningful work (Allan et al., 2019) and work–life balance in their various forms (e.g., overall appraisal, conflict, and enrichment perspectives; Jones et al., 2006; Kinnunen et al., 2023) are positively related to many sustainable career indicators (e.g., high life satisfaction, low job exhaustion, and high work commitment). However, although an employee's sense of their work being *both* meaningful and compatible with their personal values and private life needs is perceived as highly relevant from the perspective of sustainable careers (De Vos et al., 2020), the relationship between meaningful work and work–life balance has remained understudied. Only a few studies have focused on this relationship (see our short overview above) and even fewer have examined meaningful work, work–life balance, and multiple sustainable career indicators simultaneously, which was our specific research aim when producing empirical findings for this chapter.

More specifically, based on previous research (Allan et al., 2019; De Vos et al., 2020; Peterson et al., 2017), we considered meaningful work – experienced when desired values, goals, and expectations in an employee´s current job are met – to be one of the key determinants for work–life balance and sustainable careers. To confirm this claim, we addressed two research questions. First, we investigated which kinds of sustainable career profiles, including the experience of work–life balance, could be identified in a sample of employees in various sectors. Second, and more importantly, we examined whether the profiles identified differed in terms of fit versus misfit across the dimensions of the Vocational Meaning and Fulfillment Survey (VMFS). Before we present our findings, the VMFS is briefly introduced in the following section.

THE VOCATIONAL MEANING AND FULFILLMENT SURVEY

To help employees make conscious and well-considered career decisions and enhance their work–life balance and career sustainability, Peterson et al. (2017) have developed a practical assessment tool to identify the potential underlying factors which lead employees to experience a lack of meaningfulness in their work. The VMFS is based on the cognitive information-processing theory used in career counselling (Sampson et al., 2004). According to this theory, individuals who have a clear picture of their own values, interests, skills, and employment preferences (i.e., self-knowledge) are more likely to engage in crafting in their job and other life domains (see Chapter 26 in this volume) and be better prepared to make decisions that can enhance their career sustainability.

Rantanen et al. (2022, 2023) have continued developing the VMFS, which currently enables employees, together with professionals, to explore fit versus misfit between their individual expectations (i.e., vocational meaning: "What aspects of work are especially important to me?") and the realization of those expectations (i.e., vocational fulfillment: "How well does my current employment meet my expectations of my work?") across seven dimensions. We present these seven dimensions of the VMFS in Figure 25.1, together with the graphical profile that can be generated for respondents at the levels of individual employee, work unit, and organization. Multidimensionality and inspection of the vocational meaning–fulfillment ratio are the two fundamental features of the VMFS instrument. This potentially also makes it a useful instrument for employees themselves, as well as for career counsellors, human resources professionals, and managers to decide where to focus energy, resources, and attempts to improve the situation, and more useful than one-dimensional measures of meaningful work. A full description of the VMFS dimensions and information about the psychometric properties of the VMFS can be obtained from the first author.

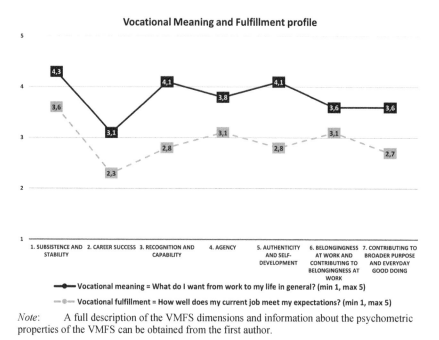

Vocational Meaning and Fulfillment profile

Note: A full description of the VMFS dimensions and information about the psychometric properties of the VMFS can be obtained from the first author.

Figure 25.1   An example of the VMFS profile based on the experiences of respondents with low career sustainability

RESULTS FOR CAREER SUSTAINABILITY AND VOCATIONAL MEANING–FULFILLMENT FIT

Our results are based on workers in various sectors ($n = 1\ 086$). The mean age of the participants was 44 years, 70 percent were women and 63 percent senior white-collar workers, and the data were collected in Finland in winter 2021 and spring 2022. Within this sample, we identified five internally homogenous subgroups when analyzing the simultaneous perception of work–life balance (five items; $\alpha = 0.70$), wellbeing (six items; $\alpha = 0.92$), burnout symptoms (12 items; $\alpha = 0.86$), job embeddedness (five items; $\alpha = 0.87$), and turnover intentions (two items; α = 0.69) (Lo-Mendell-Rubin adjusted likelihood ratio test *p*-values were 0.000, 0.028, 0.002, 0.022, and 0.609 for the two-, three-, four-, five-, and six-group solutions, respectively, and the method of analysis was latent profile analysis; Lubke & Muthén, 2005). These five subgroups represent various kinds of sustainable career profiles and differed as follows.

High career sustainability group (*n* = 355, 33 percent) showed the highest work–life balance, wellbeing, and job embeddedness combined with the lowest burnout symptoms and turnover intentions, while *low* (*n* = 167, 15 percent) and *extremely low* (*n* = 4, 0.4 percent) *career sustainability groups* showed the exact opposite profile. Both the *fair* (*n* = 325, 30 percent) and *contradictory* (*n* = 235, 22 percent) *career sustainability groups* were located between the high and low career sustainability groups in terms of experiencing moderate work–life balance, wellbeing, and burnout symptoms. The difference between the fair and contradictory groups was that the former reported rather high job embeddedness and lower turnover intentions, while the opposite was true for the latter group.

In answering our second research question, we found that the career sustainability groups presented above varied significantly on the meaning–fulfillment fit versus misfit ratios across the seven dimensions of VMFS (the method of analysis was multivariate analysis of covariance, $F(28) = 13.44$, $p < .001$, and included covariates were age, gender, and occupational status; extremely low career sustainability group was excluded from the analysis due to its very small size). As is clear from Figure 25.1, on each VMFS dimension the mean score for vocational meaning can be subtracted from the mean score for vocational fulfillment to obtain the vocational meaning–fulfillment fit versus misfit ratio. Near-zero values indicate fit, whereas below-zero values describe misfit in this meaning–fulfillment ratio of VMFS dimensions.

Overall, the largest difference was observed between high and low career sustainability groups, with the former showing good fit and the latter a substantial misfit on every VMFS dimension, as illustrated in Figure 25.1. Accordingly, the VMFS dimension misfit ratios ranged from −0.66 to −1.31 for the low career sustainability group. The fair career sustainability group in turn showed a moderate misfit (ratio range from −0.17 to −0.52) while the contradictory career sustainability group showed a relatively strong misfit (ratio range from −0.46 to −1.05) across the VMFS dimensions. Furthermore, the contradictory career sustainability group was very close to the low career sustainability group in its strong misfit on four of the seven VMFS dimensions (i.e., career success, agency, sense of belonging and contributing to it at work, and contributing to a broader purpose and doing good for others).

Finally, when the largest differences between all four career sustainability groups were considered simultaneously across the VMFS dimensions, "recognition and capability" and "authenticity and self-development" showed the highest significance. In other words, at the level of the whole sample, these two VMFS dimensions perhaps serve as the best precursors for sustainable career experiences including good work–life balance when these issues are considered from the perspective of different mechanisms and sources for meaningful work.

CONCLUSIONS AND IMPLICATIONS FOR RESEARCH AND PRACTICE

We observed very clear differences in vocational meaning–fulfillment fit versus misfit between the high, fair, contradictory, and low career sustainability groups across the seven VMFS dimensions. Overall, the low career sustainability group exhibited the highest misfit across all the dimensions (see Figure 25.1) in comparison to the other groups. Nevertheless, of these four groups, perhaps the most intriguing was the contradictory career sustainability group, since despite their moderate experiences of work–life balance and wellbeing and not particularly high incidence of burnout symptoms, the employees in this group expressed relatively low commitment to both their current work organization and their vocational field. Our further investigation revealed that the reason for this may lie in the fact that the employees in this group experienced as high a vocational meaning–fulfillment misfit in four out of seven VMFS dimensions as participants in the most disadvantageous low career sustainability group. The participants in both of these groups, in their current jobs, therefore longed for more career success, support for their agency, a stronger sense of community, and more possibilities to contribute to both doing good for others as well as building a better society and world through one's work.

Overall, these results support the validity and usefulness of the VMFS as a comprehensive tool for screening employees' experiences of meaningful work and identifying the areas – either at the group or individual levels – that merit attention when aiming to improve career sustainability in terms of a better work–life balance, general and work-related wellbeing, and organizational commitment. Based on the present study, two dimensions of the VMFS are particularly useful for differentiating employees in favorable versus adverse career sustainability situations: recognition and capability, and authenticity and self-development. This means, firstly, that employees appear to derive a sense of meaning from the extent to which they receive strong positive feedback and validation that their work and talents are being noticed, and also being perceived as contributing to the organization's mission (i.e., "I am a valued member of my team"). Secondly, the experience of personally meaningful work is also triggered by the extent to which employees feel they can pursue values and interests that are highly important to them through their work and that their work enables them to develop their personal capabilities and knowledge (i.e., "I am not stagnating in this job"). Future research using the VMFS could be directed toward investigating the extent to which know-ledge and understanding of the VMFS results affect *individual career decision making* both in terms of identifying ways to enhance meaning in current employment or whether to seek new employment opportunities, as well as *organizational decision making* regarding interventions to provide a more meaningful work environment for employees.

REFERENCES

Allan, B. A., Batz-Barbarich, C., Sterling, H. M., & Tay, L. (2019). Outcomes of meaningful work: A meta-analysis. *Journal of Management Studies*, *56*(3), 500–528.

Bragger, J. D., Reeves, S., Toich, M. J., Kutcher, E., Lawlor, A., Knudsen, Q. E., & Simonet, D. (2019). Meaningfulness as a predictor of work–family balance, enrichment, and conflict. *Applied Research in Quality of Life*, *16*(3), 1043–1071.

De Vos, A., Van der Heijden, B. I. J. M., & Akkermans, J. (2020). Sustainable careers: Towards a conceptual model. *Journal of Vocational Behavior*, *117*, 103196.

Johnson, M. J., & Jiang, L. (2017). Reaping the benefits of meaningful work: The mediating versus moderating role of work engagement. *Stress and Health*, *33*(3), 288–297.

Jones, F., Burke, R. J., & Westman, M. (2006). *Work–life balance: A psychological perspective*. New York: Psychology Press.

Kashyap, V., & Arora, R. (2022). Decent work and work–family enrichment: Role of meaning at work and work engagement. *International Journal of Productivity and Performance Management*, *71*(1), 316–336.

Kinnunen, U., Rantanen, J., Mauno, S., & Peeters, M. (2023). Work–family interaction. In M. Peeters, T. Taris, & J. de Jonge (Eds), *An introduction to contemporary work psychology*. Wiley-Blackwell.

Loi, R., Xu, A. J., Chow, C. W. C., & Kwok, J. M. L. (2018). Customer misbehavior and store managers' work-to-family enrichment: The moderated mediation effect of work meaningfulness and organizational affective commitment. *Human Resource Management*, *57*(5), 1039–1048.

Lubke, G. H., & Muthén, B. (2005). Investigating population heterogeneity with factor mixture models. *Psychological Methods*, *10*, 21–39.

Mostafa, A. M. S. (2021). The moderating role of self-sacrificing disposition and work meaningfulness on the relationship between work–family conflict and emotional exhaustion. *Journal of Happiness Studies*, *23*(4), 1579–1597.

Peterson, G., MacFarlane, J., & Osborn, D. (2017). The Vocational Meaning Survey (VMS): An exploration of importance in current work. *Career Planning and Adult Development Journal*, *33*, 49–59.

Rantanen, J., Martela, F., Auvinen, E., Hyvönen, K., & Feldt, T. (2022). Vocational Meaning Survey (VMS) kyselyn rakenne- ja sisällön validiteetti suomalaisen työelämä- ja uraohjauksen näkökulmasta [Construct and content validity of Vocational Meaning Survey (VMS) from the perspective of Finnish working life and career counselling]. *Pyskologia*, *5–6*, 391–407.

Rantanen, J., Konsti, S., Herttalampi, M., & Markkula, S. (2023). The MEANWELL Project: Developing meaningful work and a good work life together with organization. Conference proceedings paper presented at the 39th European Group for Organizational Studies Colloquium, Cagliari, July 6–8.

Sampson, J. P. Jr., Reardon, R. C., Peterson, G. W., & Lenz, J. G. (2004). *Career counseling and services: A cognitive information processing approach.* Belmont, CA: Brooks/Cole.

Zheng, Y., Wu, C., & Graham, L. (2020). Work-to-non-work spillover: The impact of public service motivation and meaningfulness on outcomes in work and personal life domains. *Public Management Review, 22*(4), 578–601.

26. Sustainable work through crafting

Anne Mäkikangas, Jessica de Bloom, Philipp Kerksieck, and Miika Kujanpää

INTRODUCTION

In today's knowledge and service economy and with the increasing trend towards multilocational work due to the COVID-19 pandemic, job redesign and self-management approaches (i.e. individuals actively shaping their own jobs) are increasingly important (Grant & Parker, 2009; Sjöblom et al., 2022). In this chapter, therefore, we focus on *crafting*, by which we mean individuals' proactive efforts to shape their own working conditions, the boundaries of their job, and also nonwork life domains to create healthy, motivating, and satisfying circumstances in which to live and work (de Bloom et al., 2020). The literature on crafting has its origins in *job crafting*, which refers to the proactive customization of working conditions that enables employees to adjust their work environment to suit their own preferences and abilities (Tims et al., 2012; Wrzesniewski & Dutton, 2001). However, since the theory and concept of crafting have recently evolved and broadened, our focus will be on these latest developments – namely, the integrative needs model of crafting (de Bloom et al., 2020) and on two new crafting constructs: *work–nonwork balance* and *off-job crafting*.

THE EARLIEST STAGES AND RECENT DEVELOPMENTS OF CRAFTING

While crafting may appear a very timely research theme, capturing the Zeitgeist of modern working life, the concept was actually introduced in the 1980s. In their paper on work design and person–job fit, Kulik, Oldham, and Hackman (1987) reported that employees occasionally redesigned their jobs on their own initiative in order to achieve a better match between their skills, their needs, and their job. Surprisingly, it took several decades before the topic was taken up again and theoretically refined by Wrzesniewski and Dutton (2001). The latter authors distinguish three different crafting strategies that focus on, respectively, (re)shaping job tasks (is task crafting), relationships at work (is relational crafting), and ways of conceptualizing one's work (is cognitive crafting).

Quantitative research on job crafting gathered momentum after Dutch researchers applied the well-known job demands-resources theory (Bakker & Demerouti, 2017) to job crafting research. Specifically, Tims and Bakker (2010) proposed that job crafting is a bottom-up process whereby employees proactively align job demands and job resources with their own skills and preferences, with the aim of achieving a better person–job fit. The job demands-resources theory posits that job crafting involves increasing structural job resources (e.g. opportunities for personal development), increasing social job resources (e.g. asking for feedback), increasing challenging job demands (e.g. starting new projects), and decreasing hindering job demands (e.g. reducing cognitive or emotional demands) (Tims et al., 2012). Accordingly, the focus of crafting is on the real-life behaviors that workers apply in their jobs, but it provides limited information about people's motivations for engaging in specific crafting behaviors. Consequently, a new theoretical framework known as the integrative needs model of crafting has been developed (De Bloom et al., 2020). The model proposes that crafting is grounded in and defined by the individual's psychological needs, which underlie specific crafting behaviors. This integrative model enables researchers to widen the focus of crafting to life domains outside work, including the crafting of work–nonwork boundaries and off-job crafting, as demonstrated in this chapter.

The integrative needs-based model defines crafting as "substantial behavior-al and cognitive changes [that] individuals deliberately apply to their roles to satisfy their psychological needs" (de Bloom et al., 2020, p. 1426). Drawing on the two-process model of needs (Sheldon, 2011), needs discrepancy and needs satisfaction are seen, respectively, as drivers and rewards of crafting behaviors. A needs discrepancy is what gives rise to any crafting episode (before crafting efforts are initiated), whereas the experiential reward of needs satisfaction is located in the concluding phase of a successful crafting episode (after crafting efforts). Actual crafting efforts are categorized into avoidance-focused (crafting aimed at avoiding or reducing the negative aspects of work or nonwork roles) and approach-focused (crafting aimed at approaching or adding desirable aspects of work or nonwork identities). According to the integrative needs-based model (de Bloom et al., 2020), crafting efforts which target unfulfilled needs are expected to be the most effective. For instance, if an employee is motivated to satisfy a specific psychological need (e.g. she perceives a discrepancy between her actual and ideal levels of relatedness) but directs her behaviors in a manner that is incompatible with satisfying that need (e.g. she engages in crafting centered around autonomy), she will not achieve optimal functioning. The model also enables an examination of the temporal unfolding and interactions of motives, crafting efforts, and optimal functioning over time. For instance, crafting is seen as a continuous process and a person's past experience of successful crafting reduces the need for future crafting efforts because needs satisfaction has already been achieved. Moreover, past successful crafting behaviors are assumed to be positively related to future crafting efforts; however, if crafting repeatedly fails and thus fails to fulfill needs, people may reduce or abandon crafting efforts (de Bloom et al., 2020).

As described above, previous theorizing on crafting has usually focused on the work domain. However, life domains are increasingly inseparable and an exclusive focus on work would neglect other important aspects of a person's life. After all, workers have many identities besides their work roles. Actions and experiences in these roles can significantly affect people's experience at work and vice versa. Importantly, crafting efforts may occur within the domain of each (role) identity that an individual has. While certain needs are more relevant within certain life domains (e.g. mastery in the domain of work), the needs-based crafting model assumes that needs are relevant in all life domains and that inadequate need satisfaction in one domain can be balanced by crafting in another life domain. To illustrate, if a person has a job with few opportunities to interact with others, they may choose to engage in hobbies which provide ample opportunities for social interaction.

Digitalization, flexible work arrangements, and the COVID-19 pandemic have led to the increased intermingling of work and nonwork life domains for many employees (Allen et al., 2021), thereby also increasing the need for crafting efforts to balance work with other relevant life domains, and also the need to craft off-job time. Next, therefore, we will address the novel and highly relevant crafting concepts that capture the work–nonwork balance and off-job crafting.

WORK–NONWORK BALANCE AND OFF-JOB CRAFTING

The concept of work–nonwork balance crafting (WNBC) refers to "the unofficial techniques and activities individuals use to shape their own work–nonwork balance under consideration of their boundary preferences and their favored combination of work and nonwork roles" (Kerksieck et al., 2022, p. 4). WNBC aligns well with the integrative needs model of crafting, which shows that crafting efforts can also take place at the interfaces of an employee's life domains and role identities (de Bloom et al., 2020). This could include proactively separating or integrating life domains and the respective identities and roles, for instance.

WNBC is built on the pioneering qualitative study by Sturges (2012) and proposes three crafting strategies. Physical crafting includes time management, selection, and alternating between work locations, such as leaving work early to attend to personal chores, or leaving home early to attend to work. Relational crafting refers to managing the quality of relationships during working hours and in one's personal life, such as going out for a drink with colleagues after work to strengthen social relationships. Finally, cognitive/emotional crafting refers to framing and redefining the work–nonwork balance in personal terms, prioritizing work or nonwork at the expense of some other life domain, by compromising an ideal work–nonwork balance in return for long-term and short-term benefits. Work–nonwork balance also involves crafting relevant life-domain boundaries to successfully integrate and balance multiple essential life roles across work and nonwork. Although WNBC strategies are the same as those presented in job-crafting literature, for example, the new context gives rise to novel crafting behaviors.

A series of longitudinal studies of WNBC indicates beneficial consequences across life domains (Kerksieck et al., 2022). In the work–life domain, WNBC is positively associated with higher job performance, job satisfaction, and work engagement. In the nonwork life domain, WNBC relates positively to family role performance, life satisfaction, and subjective vitality. Importantly, it has also been shown to facilitate work–nonwork balance (Wayne et al., 2021), as expected on the basis of its theorization.

Beyond crafting in the work domain and at the boundaries between life domains, employees can also seek to proactively shape their nonwork life domains (e.g. crafting leisure, homecare and childcare, or voluntary work). According to the integrative needs model of crafting (de Bloom et al., 2020), employees engage in off-job crafting to reduce perceived need discrepancies (e.g. a mismatch between the actual and ideal level of an individual's relaxation). In turn, crafting efforts are expected to bring about needs satisfaction and optimal functioning in the off-job domain, with positive spillover effects on well-being in the work domain as well. In other words, off-job crafting can enrich employees' lives whether they are working or not working (de Bloom et al., 2020). Importantly, needs satisfaction is conducive to optimal and balanced functioning across life domains. Therefore, addressing a needs imbalance (i.e. a perceived need discrepancy) through off-job crafting will likely also improve perceptions of work–nonwork balance (Biron et al., 2023). Off-job crafting can thus be a proactive strategy for employees to optimize their off-job lives in order to achieve a better match between their needs and interests on the one hand and off-job activities and experiences on the other hand. This match, in turn, contributes positively to work–nonwork balance.

Empirical studies support the idea that crafting in one's off-job time is conducive to optimal functioning in both the off-job and work domains. In a seminal qualitative study, Berg et al. (2010) interviewed 31 employees in various occupations. Their work revealed that employees engage in crafting efforts during their leisure time, both to create meaningful experiences and to achieve a sense of a balanced life through their hobbies and other leisure activities. Quantitatively, weekly leisure crafting is positively related to weekly satisfaction of the needs for autonomy and relatedness (but not for competence) (Petrou & Bakker, 2016). More recently, a longitudinal study among Chinese employees showed that online leisure crafting during the COVID-19 outbreak contributed positively to the experience of thriving at home and career-related self-management (Chen, 2020). Similarly, examining off-job crafting using a needs-based perspective (Kujanpää et al., 2022), Brauchli et al. (2023) found that the quintile of employees that engaged the most in off-job crafting displayed higher job and home resources and life and job satisfaction during the COVID-19 pandemic than the quintile that engaged in the least off-job crafting. Taken together, the findings from these and other studies suggest that off-job crafting may be a viable and potentially efficient way of gaining new resources, satisfying psychological needs, enriching off-job and work life, and achieving a better work–nonwork balance (see also de Bloom et al., 2020).

IMPLICATIONS AND FUTURE RESEARCH OF CRAFTING

This chapter demonstrates that although job crafting has been a popular topic in recent work–life research, there remains scope for new research perspectives. In order to fully understand the phenomenon of crafting, as noted in the integrative needs model of crafting (de Bloom et al., 2020), scholars must consider the specific need for crafting behavior. Furthermore, crafting behavior in life domains other than work – i.e. WNBC and off-job crafting – merits more attention because a large and ever-growing proportion of work is multilocational, knowledge-intensive, and highly autonomous in nature. Employees' skills in proactively managing both their work and other life domains are therefore crucial. This chapter also highlights that crafting behavior is strongly associated with several outcomes that help support a sustainable working life, such as employees' job-related attitudes, well-being and performance, satisfying the interface between work and other life domains, and increased contentment within each of these domains.

Due to the beneficial effects of crafting, interventions are encouraged. Crafting is initiated by employees, offering them a strategy by which to create a healthy and sustainable work–life balance, and more motivating and satisfying working conditions. Given the increasingly interwoven nature of workers' various life domains, organizational interventions that encourage crafting in multiple life domains would seem to be a promising tool in promoting well-being and optimal functioning. In particular, interventions are needed that can help employees focus on improving their work–nonwork balance by identifying and addressing perceived need discrepancies related to both work and nonwork domains. Organizational practices such as flexible working arrangements and supportive work–family policies are also vital to facilitating job autonomy, which is known to facilitate crafting behavior (Rudolph et al., 2017). Individual-level crafting at work and outside work may complement organizational interventions aimed at reconciling work and nonwork domains, thereby making them more effective.

It may be useful for future research to focus on the relevance of antecedents to engaging in crafting as outlined here. For example, allowing for various individual, team, and organizational preconditions for job crafting (see Mäkikangas et al., 2017) may also reveal their relevance to broader crafting behavior. This focus will also help us to understand how WNBC-related crafting efforts are beneficial in proactively adapting to work/nonwork situations with meager resources. For example, a reduction in WNBC has been observed with increasing job demands, which has been counterbalanced by supervisor support and job autonomy (Haar et al., 2019), both of which may also be relevant for engaging in off-job and WNBC crafting. Moreover, little is known about the motivational process around initiating these new forms of crafting. Studying the antecedents of crafting will shed more light on the possible drivers of crafting behaviors, such as avoidance or approach motives (de Bloom et al., 2020). Collaborative crafting in various life domains and its consequences – both benefits and possible adverse implications – also merit attention in future research (see Mäkikangas et al., 2017). Future studies could also look more closely at the effects of job crafting at the interfaces between life domains and crafting in off-job time for work–nonwork balance in different cultures. Hopefully this chapter will encourage researchers to consider the ideas of the integrative needs model of crafting (de Bloom et al., 2020) and to utilize novel crafting constructs to steer future research on crafting.

REFERENCES

Allen, T. D., Merlo, K., Lawrence, R. C., Slutsky, J., & Gray, C. E. (2021). Boundary management and work–nonwork balance while working from home. *Applied Psychology: An International Review, 70,* 60–84.

Bakker, A., & Demerouti, E. (2017). Job demands-resources theory: Taking stock and looking forward. *Journal of Occupational Health Psychology, 22,* 273–285.

Berg, J. M., Grant, A. M., & Johnson, V. (2010). When callings are calling: Crafting work and leisure in pursuit of unanswered occupational callings. *Organization Science, 21,* 973–994.

Biron, M., Casper, W. J., & Raghuram, S. (2023). Crafting telework: A process model of need satisfaction to foster telework outcomes. *Personnel Review, 52,* 671–686.

Brauchli, R., Kerksieck, P., Tušl, M., & Bauer, G. F. (2023). Staying healthy during COVID-19 crisis: Well-being and salutogenic crafting among German and Swiss working population. *Health Promotion International*, *38*, 1–13.

Chen, I. S. (2020). Turning home boredom during the outbreak of COVID-19 into thriving at home and career self-management: The role of online leisure crafting. *International Journal of Contemporary Hospitality Management*, *32*, 3645–3663.

De Bloom, J., Vaziri, H., Tay, L., & Kujanpää, M. (2020). An identity-based integrative needs model of crafting: Crafting within and across life domains. *Journal of Applied Psychology*, *105*, 1423–1446.

Grant, A. M., & Parker, S. K. (2009). Redesigning work design theories: The rise of relational and proactive perspectives. *Academy of Management Annals*, *3*, 317–375.

Haar, J. M., Sune, A., Russo, M., & Ollier-Malaterre, A. (2019). A cross-national study on the antecedents of work–life balance from the fit and balance perspective. *Social Indicators Research*, *142*, 261–282.

Kerksieck, P., Brauchli, R., de Bloom, J., Shimazu, A., Kujanpää, M., Lanz, M., & Bauer, G. F. (2022). Crafting work–nonwork balance involving life domain boundaries: Development and validation of a novel scale across five countries. *Frontiers in Psychology*, *13*, 892120.

Kujanpää, M., Syrek, C., Tay, L., Kinnunen, U., Mäkikangas, A., Shimazu, A., Wiese, C. W., Brauchli, R., Bauer, G. F., Kerksieck, P., Toyama, H., & de Bloom, J. (2022). Needs-based off-job crafting across different life domains and contexts: Testing a novel conceptual and measurement approach. *Frontiers in Psychology*, *13*, 959296.

Kulik, C. T., Oldham, G. R., & Hackman, J. R. (1987). Work design as an approach to person–environment fit. *Journal of Vocational Behavior*, *31*, 278–296.

Mäkikangas, A., Bakker, A. B., & Schaufeli, W. (2017). Antecedents of daily team job crafting. *European Journal of Work and Organizational Psychology*, *26*, 421–433.

Petrou, P., & Bakker, A. B. (2016). Crafting one's leisure time in response to high job strain. *Human Relations*, *69*, 507–529.

Rudolph, C. W., Katz, I. M., Lavigne, K. N., & Zacher, H. (2017). Job crafting: A meta-analysis of relationships with individual differences, job characteristics, and work outcomes. *Journal of Vocational Behavior*, *102*, 112–138.

Sheldon, K. M. (2011). Integrating behavioral-motive and experiential-requirement perspectives on psychological needs: A two process model. *Psychological Review*, *118*, 552–569.

Sjöblom, K., Juutinen, S., & Mäkikangas, A. (2022). The importance of self-leadership strategies and psychological safety for well-being in the context of enforced remote work. *Challenges*, *13*, 14.

Sturges, J. (2012). Crafting a balance between work and home. *Human Relations*, *65*, 1539–1559.

Tims, M., & Bakker, A. B. (2010). Job crafting: Towards a new model of individual job redesign. *South African Journal of Industrial Psychology*, *36*, 1–9.

Tims, M., Bakker, A. B., & Derks, D. (2012). Development and validation of the job crafting scale. *Journal of Vocational Behavior*, *80*, 173–186.

Wayne, J. H., Vaziri, H., & Casper, W. J. (2021). Work–nonwork balance: Development and validation of a global and multidimensional measure. *Journal of Vocational Behavior*, *127*, 103565.

Wrzesniewski, A., & Dutton, J. E. (2001). Crafting a job: Revisioning employees as active crafters of their work. *Academy of Management Review*, *26*, 179–201.

27. Resetting time and priorities: communicative sensemaking and implications of homeworking

Michael Coker, Sarah Riforgiate, Emily Godager, and Inyoung Shin

INTRODUCTION

In the United States (US), time is generally perceived as monochronic – a fixed and finite asset (Lee & Flores, 2019). Indeed, certain common phrases underscore how time is conceived, such as 'time is money' and 'spending time'. Thirty years of work–life research indicates how time allocated to paid work eclipses private time (Galinsky et al., 2005; Schulte, 2014). 'Work' comes first in 'work–life', with 'life' used as shorthand for 'everything else in life' (Kirby, 2017, p. 1). Again, this emphasizes work as a way of 'investing' one's time. The COVID-19 pandemic disrupted US work–life balance by forcing many employees to adopt homeworking and, consequently, negotiate their interpretation of time and work in relation to longstanding societal discourses.

This chapter uses a communication lens, drawing on Weick's (1995) sensemaking theory to analyze qualitative data from 602 US workers who transitioned from working on location to homeworking during the COVID-19 pandemic. The chapter identifies the discourses that have resulted from this transition to understand the implications of renegotiating time and enduring ideologies in response to worldwide disruption. To do this, we will consider the following research questions:

RQ1   How did US workers experience time during homeworking?
RQ2   In what ways were normative concepts of time challenged and reap propriated when homeworking?

THEORY

The dominant US discourses about work provide a context within which to understand the communication shifts regarding work and private life that occurred during the COVID-19 pandemic stay-at-home orders. In the US, work has historically been privileged over private life (Kirby, 2017). Even in cases where there are physical boundaries to separate the work and private spheres, work frequently permeates into people's private lives, whereas the boundaries around work resist interference from life (Pal et al., 2020). Policies on remote and flexible working designed to enhance work–life balance have, ironically, often resulted in employees working more hours to communicate their dedication and productivity (Kelly et al., 2010). Individuals perpetuate the notion of 'work now, life later' (Blithe & Wolfe, 2017, p. 1) through productivity-focused communication, which contributes to ideal worker norms, including working long hours, accepting additional responsibilities, sacrificing personal time, and perpetually deferring the ideal self (Pink & Godager, 2022; Ruder & Riforgiate, 2019).

US workers also encounter and adopt managerialist discourses, defined as everyday talk that serves to 'manage' or organize behaviors to be rational (un-emotional) and predictable to increase efficiency (Denker & Dougherty, 2013). Managerialist discourses emerged in US organizations in response to criticism of 'greedy' capitalism, providing ways for communication to organize work and increase profits (Deetz, 1992). US discourses emphasizing 'the growing centrality of work' guide individual and societal notions that privilege time spent working over private life (Tracy & Trethewey, 2005, p. 169), permeating even home interactions when individuals self-discipline in order to create efficiencies in private relationships (Denker & Dougherty, 2013). We underscore the importance of focusing on discourses that have historically organized time in pursuit of work over life, particularly during times of significant change or crisis.

The rapid shift to homeworking early in the COVID-19 pandemic was unprecedented and led US workers to begin noticing and questioning work–life time allocations to make sense of emerging possibilities (Gunasekara et al., 2022). Weick's (1995) sensemaking theory explains that individuals communicatively grapple with their identities during times of significant change – such as the COVID-19 pandemic – in order to create meaning and reduce uncertainty about an emerging reality. Through communication, individuals discuss and reconcile perceived gaps between who they have been and who they are becoming (Weick, 1995).

As US workers engaged in 'business as usual' before the COVID-19 pandemic, they perpetuated cultural scripts about time relative to work and life (Kirby, 2017). However, as sensemaking theory suggests, the disruption caused by the COVID-19 pandemic likely triggered equivocality and uncertainty about organizational and personal roles, necessitating communication to reduce uncertainty. When individuals encounter unfamiliar terrain, they draw on past experiences to make sense of uncertainty and reduce equivocality (Weick, 1995).

Uncertainty can prompt individuals to reimagine and retain interpretations for future use, redrafting their understanding of the change and their unfolding realities. Employees who transitioned to homeworking likely used communication to interpret how things were, their current and emerging experiences, and how things might be in the future – particularly in terms of work–life time allocations. While some individuals likely used communication to normalize the ways they experienced time during homeworking and perpetuated ideal worker norms, others may have reimagined work–life time allocations by reframing their understanding of the ideal worker and work–life balance. Considering these possibilities, this chapter explores how US workers experienced time during homeworking and how they challenged or reappraised conceptualizations of work.

METHOD

Qualitative data were gathered between April 29, 2020 and May 15, 2020 in order to capture the experiences of US workers who transitioned from working on location to homeworking during the US stay-at-home order (White House, 2020). Open-ended survey question responses were collected through Amazon MTurk and authors' personal networks (multiple start snowball sample) to gather a national convenience sample. The authors disseminated the recruitment message by email and social media, inviting contacts to share the message with eligible network connections. The questions were about communication with personal and professional contacts, the challenges and benefits of homeworking arrangements, and the challenges and benefits of personal pursuits during homeworking. Responses were collected from 602 participants, ranging from short phrases to multiple paragraphs for the seven open-ended survey questions, totaling 236 single-spaced typed pages of data for analysis.

The participants resided in 46 US states, were an average of 36.7 years old (SD = 11.21), and more than half were female (55.7 percent). Of the participants, 71.7 percent identified as white, 8.9 percent as Black or African American, and 18.5 percent as other races. Most participants reported completing at least four years of college education (78.3 percent), with 35.5 percent holding a master's, doctorate, or professional degree. Most participants were married or living with a partner (70 percent), and most indicated that their partner was employed (82 percent). Many participants reported living with at least one child under 18 in their household (39 percent). Household incomes ranged from less than $50,000 (28.8 percent) to greater than $110,000 (22.7 percent).

Participants worked in a variety of sectors; education was the most common, followed by technology and self-employment. Participants reported an average of 36.5 hours of homeworking per week ($SD = 14.69$) compared to working 41.6 hours per week at workplace locations before the COVID-19 pandemic ($SD = 5.81$). Finally, 53.7 percent of participants managed or supervised others.

Qualitative analysis began inductively, with the researchers individually reading responses from all 602 participants. The team discussed common words, phrases, and ideas that appeared in the data. The subject of time and the word itself occurred repeatedly in 407 of the 602 participant responses (67.6 percent). Therefore, the analysis focused on the 407 participant responses referencing time as a salient element that was celebrated, led to uncertainty, or necessitated (re)negotiation when transitioning to homeworking. After agreeing to use the 407 participant responses as data for this study, the team coded 10 percent of the data together, noting how participants articulated benefits and constraints regarding time to make sense of new homeworking arrangements. This resulted in an initial 157-item codebook (81 challenges and 76 benefits). After the initial coding meeting and reaching a code consensus, team members used the codebook to individually code portions of the remaining data. The team then collapsed the codes and analyzed how participants experienced time and communicatively engaged in work–life sensemaking, resulting in the following themes.

FINDINGS

We first inquired about how workers experienced time during homeworking. Results indicated that 43.7 percent ($n = 178$) of participants experienced time benefits during homeworking. Of those responses, 29.2 percent ($n = 52$) discussed work-related time efficiencies as a benefit of homeworking (e.g., uninterrupted work, flexible work time). Although work efficiencies were viewed as beneficial, few participants saw a benefit in having additional time to work ($n = 4$; 2.2 percent). Of the total benefit responses ($n = 178$), most participants noted life-related benefits, with 73.6 percent ($n = 131$) identifying spending time with family (e.g., spending time with kids, using time to reconnect with family) and 72.5 percent ($n = 129$) identifying more personal time (e.g., time for hobbies, reflection, and self-development). Participants' interpretations of work efficiencies perpetuated cultural scripts related to productivity (Kirby, 2017) and demonstrated that they drew on their past experiences with familiar discourses to understand their new experience (Weick, 1995). However, participants suggested that their work efficiencies were helpful in creating more time for life rather than more work time, which is a departure from historical US work–life discourses (see Kirby, 2017 for discussion).

Time was seldom discussed as a constraint during homeworking ($n = 24$; 5.9 percent), but time benefits were often juxtaposed with constraints. Although 32.2 percent ($n = 131$) of participants indicated they felt fortunate to spend more time with their families, many – particularly mothers – described feeling overwhelmed with competing demands on their time. One representative remark came from a 34-year-old female with four children, who reported that homeworking contributed to a 'lack of privacy, lack of alone time' making it 'hard to get everything done between homeschooling kids, working, keeping the house somewhat presentable'. This example and similar responses indicated that despite experiencing greater time flexibly while homeworking, participants experienced similar difficulties in managing multiple competing roles (e.g., homeschooling, homeworking, cleaning), causing them to experience and talk about time differently. Another 38-year-old female with one child noted feeling 'untethered and also trapped at the same time'. Participants drew on familiar heuristics to emphasize tensions between their work and life to interpret their perceptions of having more time with their families while simultaneously feeling overworked.

In view of the tensions that participants emphasized regarding time, we explored how participants communicatively (re)shaped their experiences of time and constructed new meanings, addressing our second research question: 'In what ways were normative conceptions of time challenged and reappropriated when homeworking?' Although some participants perpetuated corporate discourses and ideal worker norms that emphasize productivity (e.g., 'less distractions working from home and less interruptions from coworkers about non work-related topics'; 'I do a more effective job'), numerous qualitative references to time suggested a reprioritization of life as participants grappled with their emerging selves. A representative response from a 27-year-old married female (no children) explained:

> Slowing down has been the biggest benefit from the social distancing restrictions. My social calendar is empty, and it no longer feels like things are always 'go, go, go'. I have more time to dedicate to my hobbies and projects around the house. Being home with my partner and being able to spend more time has also been so appreciated ... I have also made an effort to enjoy the simple things in life. I notice the flowers blooming when I take walks, I smile when I see positive chalk messages on the sidewalks, and I think of how much fun the kids in my neighborhood are having.

This answer illustrates how this participant experienced time as slower and more expansive than before she transitioned to homeworking, which enabled her to manipulate her use of time differently and have 'room' (i.e., more time) to simply experience more. Although most participants drew on their past experiences to negotiate and understand their unfolding experience of home-working, many renegotiated their enactments of time (i.e., 'making an effort to enjoy the simple things in life') and interpretation of work–life balance (i.e., 'slowing down' and no longer feeling like it was always 'go, go, go'), providing new heuristics to retain for future use. As one 37-year-old female with two children explained, homeworking and slowing down was an opportunity for 'preventing my future self from being terribly overscheduled'.

Numerous participants shared how they refocused and reprioritized private life through experiencing time differently during homeworking. Responses included how participants felt 'more present' or 'peaceful', were 'enjoying the little things in life much more', had 'more time to devote to each other … and have more meaningful conversations', and valued being 'forced to relax and remember what matters – family and friends'. In terms of sense-making, participants used communication to reframe homeworking as not just productivity-driven, but an opportunity to reimagine and reevaluate their private lives.

Cultural shifts in the mid- to late-twentieth century normalized long working hours, promoted ideal worker norms and managerial discourses (Kirby, 2017), encouraged workers to sacrifice time at home for time at work (Costas & Grey, 2014), and defer their ideal selves (Blithe & Wolfe, 2017). The rapid shift to homeworking, by contrast, created an unstable environment and primed individuals' sensemaking to envision other possible realities. By communicating work–life experiences during homeworking, participants challenged and reimagined conceptualizations of time by reprioritizing life over work, retaking control of their lives, and leaning into fewer work obligations.

LOOKING FORWARD

The COVID-19 pandemic and experiences of homeworking provided opportunities for many US workers to challenge a status quo that privileged work and explore new time possibilities in private life. Our findings suggest that despite the work–life conflict created by work and life occupying the same physical space, homeworking arrangements allowed participants to engage in sensemaking to conceptualize time as overlapping rather than monochronic, and to renegotiate their work–life balance in new ways. Although the move to homeworking was initially temporary, the implications of renegotiating time extend beyond the COVID-19 pandemic.

The 'great resignation', a term that describes record job departures since the start of the pandemic (Bremen, 2022), is a marker of the far-reaching implications of sensemaking that came about through homeworking. Our participants wrote about 'slowing down', 'reinvesting in families', and the joys of 'flexible and less work time', emphasizing how mandatory homeworking policies enabled individuals to reduce the gap between their present and deferred selves; many participants experienced time as multi-faceted, rather than as a work–life dichotomy. The pandemic provided the impetus for workers to use sensemaking to acknowledge work–life imbalances and renegotiate time in ways that will shape future work–life experiences.

IMPLICATIONS FOR RESEARCH AND PRACTICE

As organizations and workers explore longer-term homeworking, work–life scholars will need to focus on the reconceptualization of longstanding organizational and ideal worker discourses. Workers have traditionally used and perpetuated managerial behaviors and discourses to promote the organizational bottom line (Deetz, 1992), but our data suggest that the pandemic enabled workers to renegotiate their overall understanding of work–life balance and reprioritize life over work in their communication. In other words, participants' sensemaking (Weick, 1995) to reduce their equivocality regarding an unfamiliar experience provided them with new heuristics to draw on in the future.

Researchers should also explore how individuals continue to shape emerging realities that deemphasize organizational and corporate control in pursuit of a 'life now' ideology (Pink & Godager, 2022), as well as how organizations might grapple with resuming control to reemphasize the 'centrality of work' (Tracy & Trethewey, 2005). To this end, practitioners should consider the benefits noted by participants regarding experiencing time and reprioritizing life while simultaneously navigating flexible working arrangements as an integral component of the organizational bottom line. Considering the tensions between work–life obligations articulated by our participants, future researchers and practitioners should also explore how homeworkers make sense of and navigate work–life arrangements when children attend school outside of the home, potentially alleviating the constraints associated with fulfilling multiple conflicting roles in the same physical space.

Finally, research should examine the shift towards homeworking and related discourses that shape ongoing socialization (i.e., processes involved in teaching and learning about work; see Lucas, 2011 for discussion) into work–life balance. Scholars can explore how children exposed to sensemaking discourses during pandemic homeworking might experience longstanding work–life norms differently. Alternatively, scholars and practitioners should consider the extent to which organizations, supervisors, and employees counteract, support, or alter sensemaking discourses that undermine the centrality of work (e.g., through flexible work policies; Kelly et al., 2010). As this chapter has demonstrated, practitioners have the ability to perpetuate histori-cal work–life norms by reinforcing ideal worker discourses or altering work policies and communication to create and celebrate new ideals established through homeworking. The findings presented in this chapter emphasize the importance of addressing work–life discourses before, during, and after the COVID-19 pandemic.

REFERENCES

Blithe, S. J., & Wolfe, A. W. (2017). Work–life management in legal prostitution: Stigma and lockdown in Nevada's brothels. *Human Relations*, *70*(6), 725–750.

Bremen, J. M. (2022, August 25). *2022 mid-year check in: Tracking changes on risk, COVID, the great resignation, hybrid work, ESG, and more*. Forbes. www.forbes .com/sites/johnbremen/2022/08/25/2022-mid-year-check-in-tracking-changes-on -risk-covid-the-great-resignation-hybrid-work-esg-and-more/?sh=16fda5397c5c [Accessed July 9 2022].

Costas, J., & Grey, C. (2014). The temporality of power and the power of temporality: Imaginary future selves in professional service firms. *Organization Studies*, *35*(6), 909–937.

Deetz, S. A. (1992). *Democracy in an age of corporate colonization: Developments in communication and the politics of everyday life*. SUNY Press.

Denker, K. J., & Dougherty, D. (2013). Corporate colonization of couples' work–life negotiations: Rationalization, emotion management and silencing conflict. *Journal of Family Communication*, *13*(3), 242–262.

Galinsky, E., Bond, J. T., Kim, S. S., Backon, L., Brownfield, E., & Sakai, K. (2005). *Overwork in America*. Families and Work Institute. http://familiesandwork.org/downloads/OverworkinAmerica.pdf [Accessed July 9 2022].

Gunasekara, A. N., Wheeler, M. A., & Bardoel, A. (2022). The impact of working from home during COVID-19 on time allocation across competing demands. *Sustainability*, *14*(15), 9126.

Kelly, E. L., Ammons, S. K., Chermack, K., & Moen, P. (2010). Gendered challenge, gendered response: Confronting the ideal worker norm in a white-collar organiza-tion. *Gender & Society*, *24*(3), 281–303.

Kirby, E. L. (2017). Work–life balance. In C. R. Scott & L. K. Lewis (Eds), *International encyclopedia of organizational communication*. Wiley-Blackwell.

Lee, S. K., & Flores, M. L. (2019). Immigrant workers' organizational temporality: Association with cultural time orientation, acculturation, and mobile technology use. *Management Communication Quarterly*, *33*(2), 189–218.

Lucas, K. (2011). Socializing messages in blue-collar families: Communicative pathways to social mobility and reproduction. *Western Journal of Communication*, *75*(1), 95–121.

Pal, I., Galinsky, E., & Kim, S. S. (2020). *2020 effective workplace index: Creating a workplace that works for employers and employees*. Families and Work Institute. www .familiesandwork .org/ research/ 2020/ 2020 -effective -workplace -index [Accessed July 9 2022].

Pink, K. J., & Godager, E. A. (2022). 'Avoiding beige cubicle hell': Emotions and work–life spillover among adventure workers. In J. Kahlow (Ed.), *Cases on organ-*

izational communication and understanding understudied groups (pp. 102–120). IGI Global.

Ruder, E. M., & Riforgiate, S. E. (2019). Organizational socialization of Millennial nonprofit workers. In M. Z. Ashlock & A. Atay (Eds), *Examining Millennials reshaping organizational cultures* (pp. 33–50). Lexington.

Schulte, B. (2014). *Overwhelmed: Work, love, and play when no one has the time.* Sarah Crichton Books.

Tracy, S. J., & Trethewey, A. (2005). Fracturing the real-self/fake-self dichotomy: Moving towards crystallized organizational identities. *Communication Theory*, *15*(2), 168–195.

Weick, K. E. (1995). *Sensemaking in organizations.* Sage.

White House. (2020, March 16). *The President's Coronavirus guidelines for America: 30 days to slow the spread.* www.whitehouse.gov/wp-content/uploads/2020/03/03 .16.20_coronavirus-guidance_8.5x11_315PM.pdf [Accessed July 9 2022].

Index